The American People and South Africa

Publics, Elites, and
Policymaking Processes

Edited by
Alfred O. Hero, Jr.
World Peace Foundation

John Barratt
South African Institute of
International Affairs

LexingtonBooks
D.C. Heath and Company
Lexington, Massachusetts
Toronto

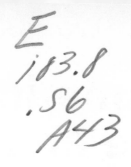

Library of Congress Cataloging in Publication Data

Main entry under title:

The American people and South Africa.

Continues: Conflict and compromise in South Africa/edited by Robert I. Rotberg, John Barratt.
Includes index.
Contents: Introduction/John Barratt—The American public and South Africa/Alfred O. Hero, Jr.—South Africa in the American media/Sanford J. Ungar—[etc.]
1. United States—Relations (general) with South Africa—Addresses, essays, lectures. 2. South Africa—Relations (general) with the United States—Addresses, essays, lectures. 3. South Africa—Foreign opinion, American. 4. Public opinion—United States. I. Hero, Alfred O. II. Barratt, John. III. World Peace Foundation.
E183.8.S6A43   327.73068   80–8632
ISBN 0–669–04320–6   AACR2

Copyright © 1981 by D.C. Heath and Company

Published simultaneously in Canada

Printed in the United States of America

International Standard Book Number: 0–669–04320–6

Library of Congress Catalog Card Number: 80–8632

Contents

Preface

Early in 1978 the South African Institute of International Affairs of Johannesburg and the World Peace Foundation of Boston initiated a joint program to study the broad issues of mutual concern in relations between the Republic of South Africa and the West. This program has included both research and exchanges among South Africans, North Americans, and Western Europeans. The Royal Institute of International Affairs (Chatham House) in London has cooperated in the program, with primary responsibility for British and other European participation.

The American People and South Africa is the second book to result from this joint program. The first, *Conflict and Compromise in South Africa,* edited by Robert I. Rotberg and John Barratt, was a product of the first phase of the program. It included chapters written by various authors—American, British, and South African—who participated in a private three-day meeting at Rustenburg, South Africa, in mid-1978 to discuss political alternatives for South Africa and implications for the West. The book provided an analysis, from different political viewpoints, of the possibilities of compromise and conciliation within South Africa to limit conflict and to enable black South Africans to participate effectively in their government. It also examined ways in which Western Europe and the United States might influence constructively the processes of meaningful change in South Africa.

The deliberations that led to the first book were followed by a second round of discussions at Jan Smuts House in Johannesburg in November 1979, in which Americans, Canadians, Western Europeans, and South Africans, representing various political viewpoints and professional interests, focused on pertinent economic and political issues in the dynamics of contemporary South Africa. These deliberations in turn were followed by a series of off-the-record meetings in the United States in May and June 1980 of fourteen leading South Africans, black and white, and their American counterparts, representing major sectors of opinion in the business, media, church, academic, and governmental fields, as well as in the black community and other groups with special interest in South Africa. These meetings were held in Boston, New York, Atlanta, and Washington, D.C. Their primary purpose was to enable the South Africans to obtain a clearer understanding of American attitudes and policies toward South Africa.

In December 1980, a similar group of South Africans met with a wide range of British participants at a three-day conference at Chatham House in London, organized jointly by the Royal Institute of International Affairs and the South African Institute. The director of the World Peace Foundation also participated in these discussions, which were concerned with the political and economic outlook for South Africa in the light of current developments in that country and its southern African neighbors, as well as with the role of the West.

This second book to be published in the ongoing program of research and discussion evolved primarily from the meetings in the United States in May and June 1980 and from some of the preliminary papers prepared as the bases for discussion at those meetings. The authors of the original papers benefited from insights gained during the exchanges of views between the South Africans and the leaders of the various American groups, and these insights have been incorporated into their papers, which appear as chapters in this book. Subsequently several chapters were invited from other participants in that interesting series of meetings. The coeditors are most grateful to all of the authors for their contributions and also for their general willingness to give constructive consideration to suggestions for revision of their respective drafts, which were made by the coeditors and other participants in the meetings.

This book is a sequel to the first. It deals with the American side of South Africa's relationship with the West, discussed in the concluding chapters of *Conflict and Compromise in South Africa*. This book is the first systematic attempt to examine the evolution of American public attitudes over time, analyze the thought and action among influential interest groups, and analyze the dynamic interplay of these groups with governmental policy-making and decision making and actions by corporations, churches, universities, and other private institutions pertinent to South Africa within a broad context of U.S. worldwide interests and relations.

The chapters were solicited to represent diverse viewpoints, groups, and institutions in the United States. The respective authors express, of course, their own perspectives and views rather than those of the editors. Moreover both of the cosponsoring institutions, which the editors respectively represent, are independent educational bodies, established to promote the type of thought-provoking analysis and balanced discussion reflected in this book. They are precluded by their respective constitutions from themselves taking partisan or other particular positions on issues of public policy.

The South African Institute of International Affairs, financed by its corporate and individual members, was founded in 1934 to promote on a fully independent basis a wider and more informed understanding of international issues, through its research, discussions, and publications. The World Peace Foundation was founded in 1910 by Edwin Ginn, founder of the educational publisher, Ginn and Company, and endowed in 1914 to carry out purposes comparable to those of its South African collaborator in the current program that has produced this book. The foundation also publishes the authoritative quarterly *International Organization*.

The editors wish to thank their two governing boards for their active support of the joint enterprise from which this book and its predecessor developed. Special thanks are also due to the corporate members of the South African Institute, who have given their encouragement and financial support. The editors are especially indebted to their respective staffs and to a number of readers of earlier drafts of parts of this book, who provided constructive criticisms and helpful insights.

1

Introduction

John Barratt

Americans interested or involved in virtually any aspect of the network of relations of their federal government and corporations, churches, and other private institutions with South Africa are increasingly aware of their highly controversial and divisive character in the United States. Although conflicting domestic views and contending efforts to influence public policy and private action typify much of American foreign relations, the affective intensity and contentiousness of those with South Africa have grown since the early 1960s to compare with the Arab-Israeli issue and perhaps one or two others in emotional sensitivity and volatility. American public policy and private action in regard to South Africa can be understood only within this dynamic domestic milieu.

To South Africans it may seem that another publication on Western attitudes, particularly those of the United States, is unnecessary and that more attention should be paid instead to South Africa's relations with and perceptions of the countries on its own continent. But as important as the need is for serious work on the latter question, these two dimensions of South Africa's external relations are interrelated. Relations with the West will remain of vital importance, especially in the economic field. And within the West, relations with the United States together with Britain are by far the most important to South Africa.

Although much has been written on United States–South African relations by scholars and other able analysts, predominantly Americans rather than South Africans, over the past decade or two, attention has largely focused on intergovernmental relations and the substance of policies of the respective governments. Little attention has been paid to pertinent components of the respective societies and their differing perceptions of the relationship, or to their varying degrees of influence on public attitudes and official policies. South Africans and Americans need to learn more of the wider dynamics of the two societies with respect to one another, especially at a time of significant political change in both, if there is to be clearer understanding of their relationships.

South Africans and Americans also need to appreciate that each have differing perceptions of their international environment. For instance, South Africans often overlook the fact that Americans see their relations with South Africa in the context of wider global concerns and that the world

1

does not appear the same from Washington as it does from Pretoria. In particular, there are differing perceptions of Africa itself, and white South Africans do not easily understand why Americans appear to use more lenient standards in judging black Africa than those used for South Africa.

Americans, for their part, need to understand this problem of white South African perceptions—or misperceptions—of Africa and of the consequent ambivalent attitude toward the rest of their own continent. It is often said that if South Africa could improve relations with its neighbors and the rest of black Africa, its relations with the West would also improve. This may be true because it would take the main foreign-policy pressure—of having to choose between black and white Africa—off Western governments, and it would also lessen the problems of multinational corporations. South African policymakers are aware of the importance of relations with Africa as a factor of relations with the West. But both sides need to understand that an improvement of relations is easier said than done, as the historical record demonstrates.

It is true that white South African political leaders—since before the National party came to power in 1948—have frequently referred to South Africa's "role in Africa." General Smuts had visions of pan-African cooperation; Foreign Minister Eric Louw spoke in 1957 of this role as a "vocation" and said that South Africa "must in all respects play its full part as an African power"; Prime Minister B.J. Vorster in his "outward policy" of the late 1960s sought, with only limited success, to develop dialogue and diplomatic links with other African states; Vorster also, in the early 1970s, emphasized cooperation in the southern African subcontinent; and the present prime minister has made the concept of a "constellation of states" in the region a major element of his policies.[1]

In recent times, since Vorster's outward policy, even more emphasis has been placed on the need for whites to accept that they belong in and are part of Africa rather than an extension of the West. Whereas, for instance, Foreign Minister Louw envisaged South Africa as a permanent link between the West and Africa, Foreign Minister "Pik" Botha has rejected the idea of automatic association with the West and has spoken instead of "neutrality."[2] However, while all this stress on Africa and more recently on the need for a change in white attitudes is no doubt motivated in part by a genuine desire to counter the tendency, inherited from colonialism, to look away from Africa toward Europe and the United States, it is clearly also a product of South Africa's international political isolation, including the deterioration of its relations with the West.

If the need to identify with Africa is to be fulfilled, then more is required than statements stressing an obvious geographic fact and the formation of regional structures for a constellation that because of political realities has to be confined to states created within South Africa's own borders.

The deeper problem that must be overcome is not to change white attitudes to the *rest* of Africa but to arrive at an accommodation with black Africans *within* South Africa. Without such internal accommodation, acceptance by and identification with the rest of Africa will not be possible. Relations even with regional neighbors will remain strained at best in circumstances full of potential for actual conflict, in spite of the existence of economic and functional interdependence within the region. The creation of a truly regional "power bloc" (former Prime Minister Vorster's term) or "constellation" that would be able to act independently of the West and defend its own interests against the encroachment of communism or any other outside force will not become a reality simply by stating it as a policy goal. It must be obvious to South African policymakers that as long as there is no political settlement in Namibia and within South Africa itself, the trend will continue to be away from effective regional cooperation. Under these circumstances, South Africa's options for alliances in Africa or elsewhere, which would give substance to the stated aspirations for some form of nonalignment, will become more limited.

One cannot avoid the impression that the recent emphasis on a regional grouping, acting independently in the world, and possibly even threatening the use of its mineral resources as a bargaining counter, is largely a reaction to perceived hostile Western attitudes. In reality there is still an overriding concern about relations with the West rather than with the rest of Africa.

It is not surprising that South Africans should have this priority concern about relations with the United States, Britain, and continental Western Europe. Apart from South Africa'a colonial history and the settlement in the country of a substantial population of European origin, with continuing language and cultural ties to the West, economic links with the industrialized West are vitally important and are constantly growing. There is in fact increasing economic interdependence between South Africa and its major trading partners. Trade with other African states has been growing significantly, but overall economic and financial considerations raise relations with the West (and also Japan) onto a much higher plane of importance, and this position will not change.[3]

The South African governmental system is derived from Western experience and values, at least insofar as it applies to whites. This may change the future in the process of political transformation, when the black majority comes to participate effectively in the exercise of political power, but the present debate about constitutional reform, including discussion of confederal or federal models, still draws mainly on experience in Western countries with ethnic problems. (One has heard very little discussion as to whether the experience of Nigeria, for instance, may be relevant.)

With the whites in political control, this constant looking toward the West may be ascribed in large measure to racial factors. But it is probably true to say that South Africa's black population, at least in the urban areas, has had more contact with the West and a greater absorption of Western values than has the population of any other African country. South Africa's relatively advanced state of industrialization, in which blacks are increasingly involved, is an influential factor in this regard. Even in the black liberation struggle there has been a significant drawing on the experience of American blacks, which has contributed to the philosophy of black consciousness, in contrast to the struggle in Zimbabwe and other southern African states where the prime target has been colonialism rather than racism, with African nationalism therefore more clearly predominant.

Thus South Africans of all ethnic origins have come to terms with their country's special position as both African and Western. There will have to be identification with Africa, both with the problems of development, which South Africa shares, and with the opportunities. But close links with the industrialized West, as well as influence from the West, are also unavoidable if the country is to prosper economically and politically in the future.

The question of links with the West has always been South Africa's basic foreign-policy interest, and the building of bridges in Africa has often been seen as a means of improving relations with the West rather than as an end in itself. The first prize would be a formal link in the defense field, signifying full acceptance as part of a Western alliance. To this end, over the years there has been the continual stressing of South Africa's strategic importance in the East-West conflict. Western governments, led by the United States, have not only turned a deaf ear to South African arguments in this regard but have even imposed embargoes on the sale of military hardware to South Africa and have broken off all cooperation in the defense field. Although this has not seriously harmed South Africa's own defense capability—and has in fact caused the development of a considerable domestic weapons industry—it has, together with the critical rhetoric from Western capitals, contributed to a visible anti-Western, particularly anti-American, mood among whites in recent years. For instance, in the general elections in the second half of 1977, the governing National Party fought a very successful campaign largely on an anti-American (or more specifically anti-Carter) plank. In late 1980 defiant statements by Foreign Minister Botha and other ministers in effect challenged the West to impose economic sanctions on South Africa, sanctions that the foreign minister actually described as "inevitable" after he had visited several European capitals to discuss the Namibian issue.[4]

This love-hate relationship with the West, however, is also reflected in the keen watching for signs of improvement in Western official attitudes. Thus the May 1979 victory of the British Conservative Party, under Margaret Thatcher, was welcomed, while Ronald Reagan's defeat of President Jimmy Carter in November 1980 and some of the senior appointments to his new administration created a mood of near euphoria in South African government-supporting circles, in anticipation of a significant shift in American foreign policy. This more optimistic mood regarding relations with the West is based on the assumption that those now in charge of policy-making in Washington have a geopolitical world view more in tune with that of the South African government. However, in nurturing these hopes for a substantive change in the American approach to South Africa, little attention has been paid to other factors in the American body politic, which serve to support continuity in basic attitudes and to prevent dramatic substantive changes in approach to an issue such as that of South Africa. The following chapters attempt to analyze some of the significant factors influencing public attitudes, official policies, and behavior of private enterprise and other nongovernmental institutions toward South Africa.

Although the political future is by no means settled, the major countries of the West have opportunities for considerable influence, and they are under pressure to use their influence to shape the direction of change in South Africa. The sources of this potential influence include economic links, the desire of South Africans to be accepted in the West, and their need for security in the face of perceived threats. The West does in fact protect South Africa, for instance, in the U.N. Security Council, against the imposition of sanctions, and the threat that this protection may be removed if the costs to the West become too great is deeply resented by the South African government. But at the same time it is a significant form of pressure, as has been demonstrated in the negotiations on Namibia.

In spite of this apparent potential for influence, there clearly are limits to what the West can effectively do in respect of a political settlement within South Africa. Apart from the fact that there is resistance within South Africa to what is seen as interference in domestic affairs, these limits are imposed by a variety of factors within individual Western societies. There is a high degree of skepticism, for instance, among South African blacks, as to whether the West will ever do much more than issue moral condemnations, and disillusionment with the West increasingly is expressed by black opponents of the South African government, as well as by whites (though for different reasons). But both sides must appreciate that any government is concerned with protecting and advancing its own country's interests, as it perceives those interests, and it is not motivated by altruism in its policies toward other countries (in spite of what may be said officially). Moreover, the determination of policies is influenced by a complex network of domestic pressures, as well as by foreign-policy considerations. No policy is simply made by a government in a vacuum, on a cool moral and rational basis, and this is particularly true of countries like the United States and the United Kingdom where public opinion and the media have a considerable influence on governmental decisions.

If there is to be a more informed understanding of the U.S. relationship with South Africa, it is essential that the various elements involved within American society should be analyzed and the extent of their respective influences assessed. As a contribution toward filling that need for both South Africans and concerned Americans, the following chapters first examine the views and roles of relevant institutions and segments of American society: trends in general public opinion, in major demographic groups, and among the small minority alert to and influential in foreign affairs; American printed and electronic media; corporations and business; black leaders; the churches; and universities and colleges. These analyses provide bases for consideration of linkages of these extragovernmental groups with the U.S. executive and Congress and their impacts on the making of policy toward South Africa. Subsequent chapters constitute overviews of potential significance and implications of these observations for the future as the Reagan Republican administration, a Senate with a Republican majority, and a more conservative House of Representatives takes office—for the American body politic and particularly the influential groups and policymaking processes considered earlier, for developments within South Africa itself, and for American international interests and policies generally.

Notes

1. For a summary of the development of these ideas on African and regional cooperation see Deon Geldenhuys and Denis Venter, "A Constellation of States: Regional Co-operation in Southern Africa," in *International Affairs Bulletin* (Johannesburg: South African Institute of International Affairs) 3 (December 1979), p. 43 following.

2. Address in Zurich, March 7, 1979, extract produced in *Southern Africa Record* (December 1980).

3. According to a report of the South African Department of Customs and Excise, quoted in the *Rand Daily Mail* (Johannesburg), December 31, 1980, exports to the rest of Africa during the January–November period of 1980 exceeded R1,000 million for the first time, while imports rose to a record R264.4 million for the same period.

4. *Rand Daily Mail* (Johannesburg), November 18, 1980.

2 The American Public and South Africa

Alfred O. Hero, Jr.

Most Americans do not ascribe much priority to issues of foreign policy. Many diverse opinion surveys of representative national samples since the mid-1930s and a variety of studies in depth of smaller samples since World War II confirm this fact. Among most of the public, views on international issues have little effect on their choices among presidential or congressional candidates and their evaluations of elected federal officials once in office. Nor are world affairs often what they choose to read in newspapers, magazines, or other print media, what programs they select on television and radio, or what they discuss with their families, friends, coworkers, and others. Exceptions have been limited to matters of war versus peace, military conscription, and the very few other issues that demand personal sacrifices or otherwise impinge directly and obviously on their individual daily, or at least short-run, interests and lives. Such domestic questions as inflation, unemployment, taxation, redistribution of wealth, social welfare, crime, and the like are typically perceived by the majority as more important.

Mass Opinion on South Africa[1]

South Africa (and for that matter Africa generally), except in periods of traumatic crises or events—such as that immediately after independence of the Belgian Congo in 1960, the Sharpeville riots, Soweto in 1976, Rhodesia-Zimbabwe developments in 1979–1980—has been ascribed relatively low importance within foreign affairs by most of the nonblack public who express opinions on world affairs, including the minority whose interest in that general field is more than marginal or spasmodic. In early 1979, for instance, only 7 percent of American whites (but 33 percent of blacks) replied that among Europe, Asia, Africa, and Latin America they had "most interest" in Africa. In contrast 37 percent mentioned Europe, 33 percent Asia, and 6 percent Latin America.[2] Rather large minorities—a fifth to a third depending on the issue, the perceived general international atmosphere of the moment, whether South Africa had been mentioned in most newspapers and television news programs that reach mass audiences, how the survey question was worded, and perhaps other factors—told interviewers they had no opinion, did not know, or were not sure about most issues of U.S. policy toward South Africa.

Furthermore, the proportion of the public willing to express views to interviewers is undoubtedly a considerable overestimate of that which held clear-cut views of sufficient saliency to be meaningful before the question was posed to them. Widespread ignorance revealed in replies to questions designed to ascertain respondents' knowledge of basic facts important to forming a stable or otherwise meaningful opinion further documents this conclusion.

Certainly no more than a limited minority of Americans, concentrated among the better-educated in general and, especially, educated blacks, are particularly interested or hold well-defined views regarding South Africa. Except among this relatively interested minority of perhaps 10 to 15 percent of the U.S. public, opinions on particular U.S. policy alternatives are likely to be weakly held, amorphous, and subject to change depending on developments in South Africa, as well as in the broader international contexts confronting the United States.

This rather unstable nature of mass public opinion and the paucity of general information about South Africa are highlighted by the finding in 1979 that only 18 percent of the public had ever heard of apartheid. Even among blacks, 25 percent said they had a favorable impression of South Africa, doubtless based on positive reactions to the word *Africa* and ignorance about the exclusion of blacks from political participation and race relations generally in the Republic.[3] Moreover, opinion surveys and other indicators have noted serious discrepancies between public support of such abstract concepts as trade sanctions versus a willingness to endorse specific measures to put them into practical effect.

Nevertheless a general tone does prevail among majorities of those Americans who do offer views. Majority American concerns relate either directly or indirectly to race relations and especially to the behavior of the South African government in that area. Most expressed opinions range from disapproval to revulsion regarding apartheid as policy and practice, the perceived inequalities of nonwhites—especially blacks—in South African society, their lesser opportunities regarding education, economic, and social advancement, and particularly their exclusion from selecting their government and participating in basic decisions regarding their country, society, low literacy, low education, and such. Large majorities of those expressing opinions over the past twenty years of polling have opposed separate development, apartheid, segregation of areas and facilities by race, and particularly exclusion of even relatively educated nonwhites from the vote and political participation generally. These negative reactions have prevailed even when such concepts have been posed in neutral terms. Opposition to these policies and practices and to the white regime responsible for them has been much more widespread when these issues have been cast in more moral or ethical terms. Only 12 percent of the total adult public—mainly less-educated, lower and working class, particularly older deep southern whites—in late 1977 felt the "system of apartheid in South Africa is justified" against 63 percent who argued it "not justified." In 1976 62 percent favored black rule wherever in Africa blacks were a majority; only 15 percent were contrary minded.

Thus racial issues are accorded priority over all other considerations in the images and attitudes most Americans hold regarding South Africa. They are either the only issues noted or the first or most prominent issues mentioned in open-ended questions about South Africa. Considerations of strategic interests, raw materials, investments, trade, and possible influence by governments or ideologies hostile to the United States (such as communism) are relatively seldom raised except when specifically posed in the interview.

The general public in 1979 did not believe that South African whites are justified in their economic, racial, and political control by force (56 percent versus 23 percent), thought blacks are justified in using nonviolent efforts to improve their situation (49 percent versus 11 percent), and rejected the homelands and separate-development policies of the South African government (68 percent to 13 percent).

Large majorities of those venturing opinions in recent years have felt that even should the United States and the West generally do little or nothing, control of government by the largely Afrikans white minority ruling a black majority and the prevailing segregated racial system are unlikely to continue for long, given black majority control of the rest of Africa south of the Sahara and black attitudes and objectives within South Africa itself. A general concern among those expressing opinions has related to likely violence and disorder and negative implications of such changes both for Africa and for the United States.

A significant majority feels that the United States should endeavor to persuade Pretoria to change its racial policies and practices. The proportions of the U.S. public favoring actions by the United States and other Western nations to encourage change of South African racial policies and practices have depended on the types of action suggested. The 20 to 30 percent who have disapproved of most or all types of likely action have been primarily general isolationists who favor minimum U.S. involvement in most aspects of the world affairs or neoisolationists who emphasize strategic and defense issues and the use of military means in American foreign policy. They also have been disproportionately concentrated among the minority who venture no opinion on most international issues, are the least informed about such issues, primarily among the less educated and least likely to vote or be otherwise politically active. The remainder have been for the most part white Republicans and self-identified conservatives, especially in the Southeast.

Thus in 1979, even before South Africa was mentioned, 44 percent felt as a matter of general principle that the United States should try to persuade governments "which practice discrimination against racial and religious groups . . . to change those practices." At that time 59 percent felt that the United States should limit trade with countries "which do things that go against our sense of right and wrong."

In respect to South Africa in particular, 44 percent in late 1977 favored the "United States and other Western nations putting pressure on South Africa to give blacks there more freedom and participation in government," while only 26 percent were opposed. A year and a half later, 53 percent thought the "United States should do something to try to get the white South African government to change its racial policies"; 35 percent thought it should not. Of those who so thought, 70 percent of the U.S. public agreed "with a U.S. position that called on South Africa to eliminate racial discrimination" (16 percent disagreed), 78 percent agreed with a position that "called on South Africa to allow everybody in the country to vote in national elections" (11 percent disagreed), and 83 percent agreed with one that "called on South Africa to start talks between black and white leaders there on the future of their country" (8 percent disagreed).

In November 1977, 51 percent to 24 percent of the American public favored cutting off arms sales to South Africa; 46 to 28 percent getting American companies in that country to put pressure on the South African government; and 42 to 33 percent preventing new U.S. business investment there. A year and a half later, 52 to 24 percent would "cut off all shipments of military supplies and replacement parts," 48 to 26 percent would "persuade allies to join in boycott of military supplies and replacement parts," 46 to 28 percent would "get U.S. companies now in business in South Africa to put pressure on the government to change its racial policies," and 42 to 33 percent would prevent all new investment in South Africa.

Only minorities in the late 1970s favored more-stringent measures to effect change in South African racial policies than those of then-prevailing U.S. policy. So far majorities have been reluctant for the United States to become more directly involved through policies forceful enough to have a major effect toward change by the Pretoria government. The minorities that favored such escalated U.S. pressures in the context of 1977–1979 were concentrated among blacks and university-educated whites who considered themselves liberals, and among the latter, particularly younger whites. For example, only 28 percent in 1979 favored "cutting down trade with South Africa to pressure them to make changes" and 24 percent would end all trade with that country; 31 percent "putting restrictions on American business investment" to achieve this end; 21 percent "forcing U.S. businesses to close down operations there"; and 36 percent "the United States giving money and moral support to black organizations in South Africa that are trying to bring about peaceful change there.'' Only a very small minority of 7 percent, concentrated among blacks and a relative handful of left-liberal whites, favored "giving money and moral support to black organizations" that have given up peaceful change and are willing to use violence to change the system.

Similarly, in late 1977, only 7 percent favored (and 73 percent opposed) "encouraging blacks inside South Africa to engage in guerrilla warfare against the white government," about the same ratio advocating U.S. military action to bring about change in South Africa. In the spring of 1979 only 13 percent favored the United States sending military supplies to black African states for use against South Africa, 12 percent favored helping build up military pressures in Africa against South Africa, 4 percent favored urging South African blacks to revolt and engage in guerrilla warfare against the white government, and 7 percent favored starting a limited military action against South Africa.

Finally, only small minorities in 1979 would support either whites (9 percent) or blacks (2 percent) "if the level of violence in South Africa increased and many whites were being killed by blacks." Only 10 percent would have the United States help mediate the conflict, and a significant majority (59 percent) would not get involved. Even should "communists" supply black revolutionaries with weapons, only 18 percent would have the United States get "involved." Only 20 percent felt so even if Soviet, Cuban, or other troops of communist non-African governments intervened on the black side.

Thus the cast of majority U.S. opinion in the late 1970s and in 1980 was congruent with the public stance of the Carter administration regarding South Africa. Moreover, majorities of even those Americans who have felt the United States should mind its own business internationally and should take no action to encourage change in South Africa have regarded the racial policies of South Africa's government with disfavor. For most of the public, little informed about developments in the Republic, its negative symbolic connotations are especially important. Public reactions to a crisis in South Africa would depend on the tone of coverage on television and in other popular media and on interpretations and policy preferences argued by leaders in and out of government who carry prestige with their particular political, ethnic, or other social group or with the public generally.

Comparative Attitudes of Major American Groups

The widest divergencies from these national norms understandably prevail among blacks as contrasted with southern whites (white inhabitants of those states that seceded in 1861). Blacks are the demographic group most critical of the South African racial system and most in favor of escalating U.S. pressure on that government. On average southern whites are the American group most sympathetic to arguments of the Botha government. American whites who consider themselves both conservative and Republicans are also generally less unsympathetic than most other whites to the policies of Pretoria and less favorable to U.S. efforts to change them than are self-described liberals and Democrats.

Among all groups, liberal-minded criticism of apartheid, separate development, and related policies of the South African government and approval of actions by the U.S. government to encourage change are rather highly correlated with level of educational attainment, less so with level of affluence, social, and occupational status, Democratic rather than Republican partisan affiliation, preference, and voting, and youth rather than late-middle and older age.

Blacks

Given their disproportionate concentration in less economically and otherwise privileged segments of American society, it is not surprising that blacks generally accord even higher priority than whites to such domestic issues as jobs, social welfare, urban programs, and local race relations. Such domestic priorities among blacks greatly overshadow international problems, including South Africa and Africa in general.

Insofar as blacks are concerned with international affairs, however, they are much more likely than whites to emphasize Africa and to single out South Africa as a particularly important issue. Even the general black citizenry is much less likely than their white compatriots to hold negative stereotypes of South African blacks and much more sensitive to and critical of racial discrimination in that country. Only 7 percent of blacks generally, contrasted with 26 percent of whites, in late 1977 opposed the U.S. government's putting pressure on the South African government "to give blacks more freedom and participation in government." In early 1979 only 11 percent of blacks, contrasted with 30 percent of whites, felt that if blacks gained political control, the result would be "economic chaos," only 15 percent versus 40 percent that "whites will either be killed or driven out," and 9 percent versus 40 percent that South Africa would be "heavily influenced by communists." At that time 70 percent of blacks versus 55 percent of whites favored official U.S. "public statements condemning South Africa's racial policies," 52 percent versus 41 percent favored "cutting down trade," 53 percent versus 47 percent favored "restricting business investments," 77 percent versus 53 percent favored "supporting black organizations seeking peaceful change," and 21 percent versus 8 percent favored "supporting black organizations willing to use violence."

At a more subjective level, even little-educated, working-class black Americans react viscerally to what little they have heard of South Africa very much in terms of their own experience, or that of their parents among younger blacks, with racial segregation, discrimination, and inequality in the United States—particularly, but not exclusively, in the South. The few who have visited South Africa see the similarities of that racial system and the one prevailing particularly in the American South until relatively recently. Virtually without exception they perceive the frustrations of and psychological impacts on black South Africans as déjà vu from their own experiences and feelings and those of other American blacks a generation or less ago. The attitudes of South African whites who resist change seem also much like those of American segregationists. The relative success of change toward racial equality at home inclines them to feel that Afrikaner fears of consequences of progress toward equality are exaggerated, as those of southern whites proved to be.

These differences in priorities and opinions regarding South Africa between blacks and whites in the general population are particularly striking in light of the sharply lower education and occupational status of blacks. Although the numbers of blacks in national survey samples have been insufficient to permit statistically reliable comparisons between blacks and whites of similar levels of education and occupation, other evidence indicates that differences between university-educated, middle-class and upper-middle-class, generally more politically aware and active blacks and their white counterparts are considerably wider than the above data might suggest. Thus in 1980, among readers of the influential magazine *Black Enterprise*—96 percent of whom had some university education, 44 percent had postgraduate or professional training, and half had annual family incomes over $24,500—77 percent felt U.S. firms should pull out of South Africa and 85 percent that black Americans should participate more in the liberation struggle there.[4] Two years earlier, 84 percent of blacks included in *Who's Who among Black Americans*—three-quarters of whom held graduate or professional degrees—favored an independent Namibia with black majority rule and 85 percent black majority rule in South Africa itself.[5]

Ideological and Partisan Differences

Americans who consider themselves liberals are significantly more critical of the racial policies of South Africa and more supportive of U.S. action to change them than are conservatives. For example, 60 percent of liberals contrasted with 42 percent of conservatives in late 1977 favored the United States putting pressure in this regard on Pretoria; 72 percent versus 60 percent considered apartheid unjust. In early 1979, 61 percent of liberals versus

48 percent of conservatives would cut off all military supplies and replacement parts, 59 percent versus 45 percent would attempt to persuade allies to join in a boycott along these lines, 62 percent versus 40 percent would get U.S. companies to put pressure on the South African government, 51 percent versus 38 percent would prevent all new U.S. investment, 26 percent versus 19 percent would force all U.S. businesses to close their operations there, 28 percent versus 19 percent would end all trade, 16 percent versus 11 percent would send military supplies to neighboring black states for use against South Africa, 15 percent versus 10 percent would build up African military pressure, 6 percent versus 3 percent would urge internal guerrilla warfare, and 10 percent versus 5 percent would start limited military action.

These ideological differences are undoubtedly considerably wider among more politically active, on the whole better educated minorities, as suggested by findings of studies of American elites. Among most of the general U.S. public, self-identification as liberal or conservative is more closely associated with views on domestic economics and welfare than with international attitudes. Americans in favor of more governmental intervention in the economy, more progressive taxation, and expanded transfer of wealth and services from the affluent to the less privileged tend to think of themselves as liberals, while those who oppose such policies—largely the more affluent business, managerial, and professional classes—are likely to regard themselves as conservatives. International liberalism, on the other hand, is concentrated among the university educated who tend to be more affluent and therefore often more conservative on domestic economic and welfare issues.[6]

Thus linkages between liberal views on domestic economic issues and criticism of South African policies are quite loose to nonexistent, but liberal thinking on U.S. domestic race relations with similar thinking on South African race relations is quite highly correlated. Emphasis on U.S. relations with Africa and with less developed countries generally, on multilateral rather than unilateral international action, and on dealing with Africa and third world countries primarily in terms of their indigenous problems more than in strategic terms closely associated with U.S.-Soviet relations is associated with criticisms of South African racial policies and support for U.S. action to change them.

Partisan differences are of similar orders of magnitude to those between Americans who view themselves as liberals versus conservatives. Because conservatives are more likely to consider themselves Republicans and to vote for Republican presidential candidates, liberals as Democrats and to vote for Democratic candidates, it is not surprising that Democrats are the more critical of and activist against South African racial policies. Independents are between the two main partisan groups, as might be assumed. Differences in views on South Africa typically are larger between adults who regard themselves as Democrats as contrasted with Republicans than between those who voted for Carter as contrasted with Ford in 1976, explained by the attenuation of partisan differences by the independents whose votes decide most presidential elections.

The concentration of the vast majority of blacks among Democrats and Carter voters on the one hand and the generally more conservative views on South Africa of southern white Democrats as compared with white Democrats elsewhere in the country distorts these overall partisan differences. When only whites are compared, southern whites are considerably less critical of South African governmental racial policies and practices and less supportive of U.S. efforts to change them than are northern Democrats. Self-declared southern white Republicans are usually too few in typical national survey samples to permit statistically significant comparisons with northern white Republicans, but the differences that do appear are usually toward less-conservative thinking on South Africa among nonsouthern Republicans.

Regional Differences

The Northeast tends to be the most critical of South African policies and the most favorable to U.S. actions, the Midwest and West less so, and the Southeast the least so—whether or not blacks are included in regional comparisons. Blacks among regional samples are too few for statistically significant interregional comparisons. Based on data gathered from surveys and extensive interviewing of southerners eighteen to twenty years ago, I concluded at that time that southern blacks were more conservative (or politically realistic, depending on one's point of view) on most international issues, including South Africa shortly after Sharpeville, than were their northern counterparts.[7] My hypothesis is that southern black attitudes have since evolved toward consensus with those of nonsouthern blacks but that the former as a group still remain somewhat more conservative than the latter.

Southern whites in individual national surveys have been too few to permit statistically valid comparisons among them. It seems, however, reasonably safe to assume that their thinking on South Africa is associated with the same demographic and social considerations as in the country generally—particularly level of education, partisan affiliation, whether they think of themselves as more liberal or more conservative than most of their peers, and age. White attitudes are very probably rather closely linked with attitudes about race relations locally, attitudes that have evolved markedly away from those supportive of racial segregation, resistance to change, and racial inequality generally of two decades ago. Moreover, the more conservative racial thinking in the white South, certainly on local race relations, and very probably on South Africa too, is concentrated in the traditional black belt (a term derived from soil rather than human skin color, though the two have been associated statistically with one another) of plantation traditions, away from the border states, the Atlantic and Gulf coasts, and with some notable exceptions, the Mississippi River banks. Even in the South of black concentration and slavery and later segregationist traditions, the more racially intransigent views tend to be among those in late middle age and older and among the lower social orders. And even among white southern racial conservatives, those who would actively support white South Africans against black demands for change at home and from beyond its borders are few.

Attitudes toward South Africa among southern whites have since likely evolved toward those of whites outside the South, as they have with regard to black-white relations in the United States. On most of the issues, differences between the South and the rest of the country among whites have been of the order of 4 to 17 percentage points, undoubtedly significant politically overall as well as statistically but doubtless less than a generation ago. Thus although 39 percent of white southerners opposed the United States' putting pressure on the South African government toward more black freedom and political participation in late 1977, contrasted with only 23 percent of non-southern whites, only a slightly larger, but still very small, minority of southern than northern whites would have the United States intervene on either side in case of armed revolt, guerrilla action, or the like.

Southern whites typically react to South Africa much in terms of their own experience with desegregation of the South since the mid-1950s. Whether they are among the white majority who opposed racial change or the liberal minority who favored it, most now agree that not only was change toward equality inevitable but on the whole more successful and much less horrendous than they had earlier assumed. While most southerners of either race with clear views on South Africa understand that realities of numbers, cultural differences, and attitudes in South Africa render such change there both more difficult and less predictable as to eventual consequences, their southern racial experience typically provides an important framework for their views on how South Africa might work toward a more racially egalitarian system.

Age, Sex, and Religion

Americans less than forty years old on the average are more opposed to racial policies of the South African government and more supportive of action by the United States to change them than are those fifty-five years and older. However, differences among the age groups on most of this range of questions are smaller than those related to race, level of education, political ideology, and partisan preferences. Much of the difference between older and younger Americans may be more due to the higher average level of education of the latter than to age itself. Unfortunately samples are typically too small to compare age groups while education is held constant.

Women as a group tend to be more idealistic about most aspects of world affairs, including South Africa, than are men. Thus they are somewhat more critical of the current racial situation in South Africa and more supportive of the United States' applying economic and other nonmilitary pressures than are men. But women are no more, and typically less, likely to advocate arming black guerrillas in South Africa or across borders, or military action by neighboring states or by the United States itself.

Differences between Catholics and Protestants at the mass level are minimal to nonexistent. However, the fact that the vast majority of blacks consider themselves Protestants (70 to 80 percent, depending on the wording of the question) rather than Catholics (6 to 10 percent) augments the statistical level of liberal thinking on South Africa much more among the former than the latter. These statistical effects are countervailed by the Protestant affiliations of an almost as large proportion of southern whites (90 percent or more outside southern parts of the states of Louisiana, Mississippi, Alabama, and Florida, and a handful of Southern metropolitan centers that have received many migrants from the urban Northeast and Midwest since World War II).

When whites only were compared in a survey in late 1977, Catholics were somewhat more likely than Protestants to feel that apartheid and separate development are not justified (65 percent to 58 percent), to favor pressure on the South African government by the United States (50 percent to 39 percent), to favor ending all trade (25 percent to 21 percent), to favor persuading allies to join in a boycott of military supplies and parts (51 percent to 45 percent), to favor getting U.S. companies to apply pressure on the Pretoria government (53 percent to 40 percent), to favor sending military supplies to black African neighbor states (12 percent to 8 percent), and to favor building up military pressure in South Africa (12 percent to 8 percent). On some other issues relating to South Africa, however, differences between white Catholics and Protestants were insignificant.

These differences probably would be somewhat greater if only non-southern whites were compared. Twenty years ago, however, southern white Catholics were also less conservative in their international views than were southern white Protestants on African and other issues, a comparison that probably still prevails.[8] Among Protestants, more conservative foreign-policy attitudes have also been associated more with evangelical, fundamentalist, and orthodox or conservative Calvinist theological orientations than with the more liberal theology prevailing among Episcopalians (Anglicans), Presbyterians, Methodists, and other member denominations of the National Council of Churches, a phenomenon also linked with the concentration of more conservative theological preferences in the former Confederacy.[9]

These attitude differences between Catholics and Protestant whites regarding South Africa are also related to the facts that Catholics are more inclined to consider themselves liberals and Democrats rather than conservatives and Republicans, to vote for Democratic rather than Republican candidates for the presidency and Congress, and to be urban rather than rural or small-town inhabitants.

However, the cause-versus-effect relationships between religion and international thinking, on South Africa as on most other issues, are indirect, amorphous, and probably complex. Although religious leaders of nonfundamentalist denominations, particularly the systematically theologically trained, have been among the most critical U.S. elites of the racial system of South Africa and the enforcement of it by its government and among the more articulate supporters of greater pressure by the U.S. government and American corporations on that government, frequency of church attendance of rank-and-file members in either Catholic or Protestant churches has had virtually no bearing on the opinions of their respective members on South African (or most other international) issues. Those who attend weekly Catholic mass or services in Protestant churches whose leadership actively argues for such strong measures as divestment and embargo of trade are no more likely to agree with the substance of the utterances of their leaders in Washington, New York, the Vatican, or elsewhere than are those who attend only once a month or less. The same situation has prevailed in respect to views on race relations in the United States as well. Involvement of most Americans in religious institutions apparently has had little influence on their views in such fields regardless of the public stances of national and international leaders of their denominations or of ecumenical institutions.[10]

Observations on Jewish attitudes must be tentative since Jews have been too few in most national surveys for statistically significant conclusions. However, a survey near the end of 1977 that included sixty Jews tends to confirm hypothetical interpretations derived from others based on smaller Jewish samples. Jews, more than Protestants and somewhat more than Catholics have long regarded themselves as liberals rather than conservatives and Democrats rather than Republicans and have voted for Democratic rather than Republican candidates. Such has been the case even when all other factors have been held constant: affluent urban, nonsouthern Jews compared with only equally affluent, urban, nonsouthern white Catholics and Protestants, and so forth. Jews have long harbored less conservative views on race relations in the United States—widely publicized frictions between Jewish merchants and black clients and in other Jewish-black relationships notwithstanding. Twenty years ago southern Jews also held more pro-black majority views on Africa as well, including South Africa, than did their white Christian neighbors.[11]

But American Jewish emotional and other ties with Israel—from diverse indicators still more intensive than those of American blacks with black Africans—coupled with the increasing international isolation of Israel and its growing linkages with South Africa, have apparently significantly attenuated American Jews' opposition to the racial policies of that country and their support for U.S. action in that regard. Perhaps American Jewish concerns for their South African coreligionists have been significant as well, although most South African Jews have supported the largely English-speaking opposition to the National party government. On most of the South African issues examined in the 1977 survey, Jewish respondents did not differ consistently from white Protestants. Israeli-South African cooperation, or even interdependence, had not made them less critical of the racial situation there than their white Christian countrymen, but it apparently had countervailed their normal tendency to be more critical of racial inequality and discrimination.

Foreign-Policy Influentials

Linkages of public opinion as indicated by national surveys with either the making of public policy by the federal executive and Congress or action by corporate enterprises and other private institutions have been loose, amorphous, indirect, and difficult to trace. Public opinion, or more likely federal politicians' and senior civil servants' usually imperfect perceptions of it, typically has been only one of a number of limiting factors affecting policy choices. For many officials in the executive branch, effective public opinion on foreign affairs has meant congressmen's behavior rather than voters' opinions.[12] These generalizations probably also apply to policy toward South Africa in particular.

Thus the interpretations and policy preferences of articulate elites who influence mass public opinion and, particularly, policymaking pertinent to South Africa in both the federal government and the private sector, are crucial.

Two studies in 1979 provide useful insights into the knowledgeable and influential group of American elites—those interested and active in international affairs, some of them in the federal government, but most leaders in private life in universities, law and consulting firms, trade unions, and the professional and corporate communities generally. Many of them move in and out of government from time to time, engage in national debates about foreign policy, and communicate their views through media, organizations, and informal personal contacts to both policymakers and wider publics. One study was a systematic survey of perceptions and policy preferences toward both Africa in general and South Africa in particular of members of the Council on Foreign Relations and its affiliated committees across the country.[13] The second provided over eighty in-depth interviews focused primarily on South Africa of a cross-section of such elites in the federal executive and Congress, public-policy organizations, churches, labor unions, corporations, major law firms, black groups, and universities.[14] The conclusions of these two independent studies largely supplement and reinforce one another.

The more nationally influential and internationally sophisticated members of the Council itself were more critical of the racial policies applied in South Africa and argued for more liberal policy preferences for the United States than did the members of its thirty-six local committees, whose influence tends to be more limited to their regions and communities and their respective senators and members of the House of Representatives. Both, however, were markedly more critical of the South African status quo than was the general public.[15] Their opposition to Pretoria's racial policies was even more marked than that of the university-educated, urban middle- and upper-class minority generally, of which this elite formed a particularly influential part. For example, 83 percent of the Council members and 67 percent of those of the committees, contrasted with 46 percent of the general public, would have the "United States and other Western nations pressure South Africa to give blacks there greater freedom and political participation." Seventy percent and 57 percent, respectively, contrasted with 46 percent of the general public, would "get U.S. companies in South Africa to put pressure on the South African government."

This sophisticated elite was more cautious and more pragmatic than even university-educated Americans generally in advocating specific measures the U.S. government should take beyond those it had already taken in early 1979 to press change on the South African government. Only 29 percent of Council members and 18 percent of members of affiliated Committees would "sharply cut back economic ties and end overt political support for the South African government, but work to keep open good channels of communications." No more than slightly over 1 percent of either would "sever virtually all contacts with the South African government and end all economic and political support."

On virtually all proposed policies more stringent than those prevailing in early 1979, these elites were more hesitant or opposed than the general public. For instance, only 16 percent of Council and 10 percent of Committee members would "prevent all new business investment," while 42 percent of the public would do so. Only 2 percent of both of the former compared with 24 percent of the public would "end all U.S. trade." Only 8 percent and 6 percent of Council and affiliated Committee members, respectively, versus 13 percent of the public, would "send military supplies to nearby black nations." Five and 3 percent, respectively, of these elites versus 12 percent of the public would "help build up military pressures in Africa on South Africa." Only approximately 1 percent of both elites contrasted with 4 percent of the public would "urge blacks inside South Africa to engage in guerrilla warfare;" less than 0.5 percent of both elite groups versus 7 percent of the general public would "start a limited military action against South Africa." Nor were more than a handful of either of these elites—2 and 3 percent, respectively—willing for the United States to intervene militarily even in case of active involvement by the Soviet Union or its surrogates.

This survey of elites and the extended interviews of over eighty (some were in both samples) found that differences among them were related to most of the same considerations as those among the general public. Thus Committee members in the South were on the whole more conservative about South Africa and pressures the United States should exert than those elsewhere, particularly in the Northeast. Republicans harbored more conservative, less interventionist views on South Africa than did Democrats; whites than blacks; business persons than lawyers and academic specialists on Africa; and older than younger elites. The attitudes of most were much influenced by their attitudes and experiences relative to black-white relations in the United States.

The in-depth interviews with the smaller elite sample found that although there were some anxiety about the security of sea lanes around the Cape of Good Hope, the supply of strategic minerals, and other strategic, economic, and political issues, these were relatively lesser considerations among even relative conservatives compared with South Africa's symbolic importance as the citadel of racism. Even those familiar with the complexity of South Africa's racial problems and sympathetic to the plight of its whites agreed that fundamental change from apartheid is both inevitable and desirable, albeit difficult, and that the United States should encourage such change.

The general impression was of an increasingly frustrated, politicized, and radicalized black African population, though a number of respondents hoped that the combination of growing needs for black participation at higher levels of expertise, management, and financial reward in an expanding modern economy, attendant improvement in black education, and hopefully growing flexibility of the government to accept change would avoid a major civil war along racial lines. There was a majority support, but with significant dissent, for the United States' promoting conducive economic progress through investment and trade in nonmilitary and nonpolice equipment. Most were fearful that the National Party government would not accept sufficient change in time, resulting in widespread violence. The predominant view was that the Afrikaner elite is ruthless, clever, and determined to control government virtually regardless of economic sacrifices and political unrest.

The foreign-policy community generally perceived the importance of South African racial implications for racial politics in the United States. As suggested by surveys of mass and upper-middle-class black opinion, blacks among the foreign-policy elite were particularly sensitive to South Africa in terms of their own experience with and sensitivities to racism in the United States. Their goal was not to deal with South Africa so as to minimize U.S. racial tension but to deal with it as an abhorrently racist system and as a test of U.S. white commitment to racial equality both at home and abroad. Black foreign-policy elites also anticipated growing U.S. black involvement and more politically effective demand for U.S. action toward what they expect to be an increasingly turbulent South Africa.

White elites as well feared divisive effects on American society of escalating racial tension and, particularly, violence in South Africa. Racial violence would not only sharpen policy conflicts between whites and blacks in this country but seriously engage other conflicting interests and emotions, such as between Jews with links to South African Jews, labor unions involved with black South African unions, religious organizations in rapport with South African church leaders, corporations with significant investments and trade, and more conservative groups emphasizing strategic and economic factors. Policy outcomes for the United States would be unpredictable and perhaps dysfunctional. But while elites of both races feared the effects of violence in South Africa on U.S. domestic cohesion and international interests, only a small minority of whites would take the much stronger measures advocated by a considerable number of their black counterparts.

Regardless of their race, occupation, politics, and policy preferences for the United States, most of this foreign-policy elite felt frustrated with their general impressions that the United States could at best exert but marginal influence on the course of events in South Africa. A majority seemed to feel, often grudgingly, that the United States should pursue a policy of staged disengagement should the South African government fail to respond realistically to a least the demands of the remaining black moderates in that country.

Notes

1. Except where otherwise indicated, this section is derived from results of a nationwide survey in February–March 1979 sponsored by the

Carnegie Endowment for International Peace and reported in greater detail in James E. Baker, J. Daniel O'Flaherty, and John de St. Jorre, *Full Report: Public Opinion Poll on American Attitudes toward South Africa* (New York: Carnegie Endowment for International Peace, 1979); a Harris Poll of late 1977; and Deborah Durfee Barron and John Immerwahr, "The Public Views South Africa: Pathways through Gathering Storm," *Public Opinion* (January–February 1979): 54–59.

    2. Baker, O'Flaherty, and St. Jorre, *Full Report,* p. 5.

    3. From material provided by J. Daniel O'Flaherty from the 1979 survey for the Carnegie Endowment for International Peace.

    4. *Black Enterprise* (August 1980): 49, 102.

    5. "First Biennial National Opinion Survey," *Who's Who among Black Americans* (Northbrook, Ill.: Educational Communications, Inc., 1978). This survey of black elites noted only minor regional, occupational, age, and sex differences. Black leaders in the South did not differ significantly from those in other parts of the United States.

    6. See, for example, Alfred O. Hero, Jr., "Liberalism-Conservatism Revisited; Foreign vs. Domestic Federal Policies, 1937–1967," *Public Opinion Quarterly* 31 (Fall 1969): 399–408.

    7. Alfred O. Hero, Jr., *The Southerner and World Affairs* (Baton Rouge, La.: Louisiana State University Press, 1965), pp. 509, 520.

    8. Ibid., pp. 451–473.

    9. Alfred O. Hero, Jr., *American Religious Groups View Foreign Policy* (Durham, N.C.: Duke University Press, 1973), pp. 173–178.

    10. For analysis of this phenomenon across a spectrum of American foreign-policy issues, see ibid., pp. 173–177, 213–232.

    11. Ibid., pp. 12, 21, 31, 39, 138, 143, 151, 192–193, 201–204.

    12. See, for example, Warren E. Miller and Donald T. Stokes, "Constituency Influence in Congress," *American Political Science Review* 57 (March 1963): 45–56, and Bernard C. Cohen, *The Public's Impact on Foreign Policy* (Boston, Mass.: Little, Brown, 1973).

    13. William J. Foltz, *Elite Opinion on United States Policy Toward Africa* (New York: Council on Foreign Relations, 1979).

    14. James E. Baker, John de St. Jorre, and J. Daniel O'Flaherty, "South Africa: The American Consensus," *Worldview* (October 1979): 12–15.

    15. The Foltz survey used a number of the same questions posed to a national sample in November 1977 by the Harris Poll.

3

South Africa in the American Media

Sanford J. Ungar

South Africans visiting the United States invariably are disappointed by the coverage their country receives in the American press. They consider it inadequate, hard to find (often tucked back in an obscure corner of the newspaper), and, when it is there at all, shallow and lacking in nuance. They can often be heard to mutter that they will have to go home, or at least to Europe, in order to gain perspective on what has happened in their absence. The situation is frustrating and, for some, frightening, because it seems to indicate that American policy and public opinion toward South Africa and its neighbors will be formulated on the basis of inadequate information. It is also insulting because it is a proof of the fundamental asymmetry in relations between the United States and South Africa: The United States is, on the whole, far more important to South Africa than is South Africa to the United States, arguments about the Cape sea routes and strategic minerals notwithstanding. When Washington sneezes, Pretoria catches a cold, or at least worries about getting one. When Pretoria sneezes, Washington may or may not proffer a handkerchief, depending upon its mood and its preoccupation with other matters.

Limited but Growing Coverage

Although South Africa is getting far more coverage in the American media than it did ten or fifteen years ago, it is rarely singled out for special attention. It is treated much like any other area of the world that is regarded, by a consensus of the press, as being of lesser strategic importance to the United States. This is true, first of all, because South Africa is in Africa, and there is no strong, widely shared tradition of American interest in the continent. Africa often seems remote, mysterious, and difficult to understand to the average consumer of a daily newspaper or nightly broadcast, and, as a result, old, unattractive stereotypes go undisturbed and uncontradicted. As one observer recently put it:

The author expresses his appreciation to Helen Kitchen, then director of the U.S.-South African Leader Exchange Program, for permission to use material from the paper she prepared in May–June 1980 for the discussions of South Africans in the United States from which this book was in part derived.

25

In 1869, James Gordon Bennett of *The New York Herald* sent Henry Morton Stanley off to Africa with these cosmic instructions: "I want you to attend the opening of the Suez Canal and then proceed up the Nile. Send us detailed descriptions of everything likely to interest the American tourists. Then go to Jerusalem, Constantinople, the Crimea, the Caspian Sea, through Persia as far as India. After that you can start looking around for Livingstone. If he is dead, bring back every possible proof of his death."

More than a hundred years later, the American press is still engaged in a voyage of discovery in relation to Africa. In contrast to Britain and France, where journalists have made a prestigious lifetime career of becoming authorities on Africa, an American journalist is expected to approach Africa as a short-term assignment in the safari tradition. The reward for those who explore their domain conscientiously is promotion to an area of greater journalistic (and diplomatic) priority. This practice of sending talented and innovative generalists to Africa produces the kind of "zingers" that please editors but result in an incomplete mosaic and a lack of institutional memory.[1]

"Incomplete mosaic" is an overly polite term for the picture of Africa that has emerged in the American press. To judge from the African news provided to the typical American newspaper reader, the continent is one of ruthless dictators, otherwise unstable governments, starving masses, and open sewers. Most Americans are shocked, if not disbelieving, to learn that Nigeria is the second largest supplier of foreign crude oil to the United States or that there is vast agricultural and industrial potential in Africa.

Southern Africa has actually been an exception to the rule in recent years. Perhaps for the first time since the burst of attention that was focused on Africa in the late 1950s and early 1960s, when stories about former European colonies becoming independent had a certain appeal, events in southern Africa have been able to compete for space in the newspapers and time on the airwaves. The chaotic departure of the Portuguese from Mozambique and Angola (where the U.S. Central Intelligence Agency had been involved in clandestine operations), the extended crisis in Rhodesia (now Zimbabwe), and dramatic developments in South Africa such as the Soweto uprising of 1976 and the death of Steve Biko—have tended to increase the American attention span for African news, as well as the number of American journalists paying attention. While their attention was focused there, Americans rediscovered apartheid as a phenomenon that held a morbid fascination—something to compare negatively to the American experience in handling race relations, something to deplore.

But even with the recent increase in attention to the region, except for foreign-policy specialists and other people with a particular reason to be interested, probably very few Americans could name South Africa's prime minister, describe its system of government, or explain the swings in

American policy toward that country. Were it not for the unusually direct clue provided by South Africa's name, many undoubtedly would be unable to locate it on a map of the world. They are far more familiar with, and concerned about, details of the domestic governance and foreign policy of the Soviet Union, China, European nations, Israel, and more recently Iran and Afganistan, all of which seem closer to immediate U.S. concerns than does South Africa.

Whether the general American ignorance about South Africa is a cause or a result of the level of coverage is difficult to say (and, in any event, beyond the scope of this analysis), but many people at the management level of American journalism assume that their audience does not want to know very much about the subject—indeed that typical readers, listeners, and viewers feel they are getting more South African news than they want.

Nonetheless the number of American journalists reporting from South Africa has grown dramatically in the past few years. It is impossible to know exactly how many reporters are operating for American news organizations in most places overseas since many do not register officially or work only part time for foreign news outlets while holding other permanent jobs at home at the same time. But it is clear that for much of the 1960s and the early 1970s, there were very few American news representatives in South Africa. (Some had been expelled for writing things considered unfriendly, while others had been withdrawn because of a lack of news and a lack of access.) Today according to William Nicholson, Associated Press bureau chief in Johannesburg and president of the Foreign Press Association, there are about forty reporters, approximately half of them U.S. citizens. Most of the Americans (and a fair percentage of the others, it is probably safe to assume) do not speak or read Afrikaans, the first language of South Africa's ruling white elite, even though they spend most of their time explaining and interpreting that country to the rest of the world.

What kinds of information about South Africa—of what quality and in what quantity—are available to Americans? For the purpose of this discussion, it will be useful to look at several separate categories of media: the special-interest periodicals relied upon by foreign-policy professionals and others who follow world affairs closely; magazines of opinion; newspapers, both national and regional; wire services; television and radio; and then the black press, the business press, and the ideologically conservative press.

Special-Interest Periodicals

Two of the most important sources of information and analysis for Americans routinely interested in international affairs are the quarterly magazines *Foreign Affairs* and *Foreign Policy*. Both publish broad overviews and theoretical discussions of world problems but also attempt to remain topical and relevant to policy issues in the news. Since the mid–1970s, both have presented more frequent articles about Africa generally, and southern Africa in particular, some of which have tended to set the agenda of discussion in policymaking and scholarly cicles in the United States.

In the January 1978 issue of *Foreign Affairs,* for example, Clarence Clyde Ferguson, professor of international law at Harvard University, and William Cotter, then president of the African-American Institute, argued that substantive reform would not occur in South Africa without international pressure.[2] They called for an awareness by the American government that a full-scale uprising by South African blacks was possible, if not probable, and for an abandonment of any U.S. policy or pretense on nonintervention in South African affairs. Reviewing economic, diplomatic, and military options open to the United States as means of pressuring South Africa, they presented forty-one graduated steps that Washington could take in an effort to bring about change. (Letters to the editor in subsequent issues of *Foreign Affairs* reflected the unpopularity of the Ferguson-Cotter argument among some former American diplomats and international businessmen.)

The spring 1980 issue of *Foreign Policy* included three articles on the potential American role in bringing about peaceful change in South Africa, including one by staff members of the Investor Responsibility Research Center, calling on the federal government to use tax credits and monitor labor practices to influence American business to be a force for reform.[3] Another article in the same group, by Randall Robinson, director of Trans-Africa, which lobbies on behalf of a friendlier American foreign policy toward black-ruled African and Caribbean nations, contended that equal-employment opportunities sponsored by American business would never be enough to bring about profound change in South Africa and that only Western-sponsored mandatory economic sanctions will do the job.

Many other policy-oriented articles in these journals have attracted attention in recent years (more so than those in specialized publications, such as *Africa Report,* that are specifically aimed at Africanists). In 1979 *Foreign Affairs* published a harsh warning by Donald Woods, the exiled former South African newspaper editor, that South African whites risked history's worst racial war if they continued on their present course.[4] The quarterlies have also published articles pointing to South Africa as an issue that affects American relations with other countries in Africa, especially Nigeria.[5] If they do not necessarily provide up-to-date reports of events in South Africa, they do offer a reliable, running account of the policy debate read by most Americans seriously interested in that debate.

Other magazines that tend to serve the American intelligentsia and the influential minority interested in foreign affairs—*The Atlantic Monthly,*

Harpers, the *New Yorker, Commentary,* and the like—often feature articles about South Africa, both reportorial and philosophical. Not long ago, for example, *Commentary* published the impressions of South African writer Dan Jacobson after his first trip home in many years.[6] The *Atlantic Monthly* presented one reportage based on a visit to South Africa in the fall of 1978—calling attention to the level of tension about the future there and to the widespread hostility among white South Africans toward the Carter administration[7]—and then another in the spring of 1980. In the latter, David Halberstam described South Africa as "a country no longer at peace and not yet at war."[8] He detailed the yawning gap between the Afrikaner establishment and the majority blacks, whom he described as increasingly angry, desperate, and militant. By the time the white government in Pretoria is willing to negotiate about sharing power—perhaps in ten or twenty years—Halberstam predicted it will be too late. From the black point of view, "the time for negotiating will have passed";[9] each generation, or class, of guerrilla fighters will have become stronger and more effective than the last.

The December 22, 1980, edition of the *New Yorker* featured South Africa prominently in "Talk of the Town," the section in the front of the magazine where the editors present unsigned commentaries and vignettes on subjects they especially want to call to their readers' attention.[10] In this case, it was a penetrating interview with the Reverend Leon H. Sullivan, a black Philadelphian who, as a member of the board of directors of General Motors, formulated a set of fair employment practice guidelines (the so-called Sullivan principles) for American companies doing business in South Africa. Fresh from a visit to South Africa, Sullivan was describing his own shock at the conditions of blacks and the lack of progress there. He recounted a confrontation with American business representatives who had expected to be congratulated by Sullivan for their constructive efforts but instead was excoriated for not going far enough.

News Magazines

One or more of the intellectually oriented periodicals discussed in the previous section reach most of the more cosmopolitan, internationally interested and active minority among university-educated professionals, managers, corporate circles, federal executive officials, and members of Congress or their staffs. Their total circulations are probably no more than a million; their combined readership is only a minority of the university-educated and but 2 to 3 percent of the U.S. adult population. The three general news magazines—*Newsweek, Time,* and *U.S. News & World Report*—are read by much larger numbers—a fifth or a sixth of the country—albeit also primarily limited to the middle and upper-middle strata of university background.

A decade ago it was common for all articles about Africa to be consigned to the last, least desirable space in the international sections of these weekly news magazines; only news about Latin America was as likely to be pushed to the rear. Now, presumably in recognition of Africa's growing role in world affairs and as a reflection of increased American awareness and interest, that has changed. Events in southern Africa are often featured prominently and given thorough, if occasionally simplistic, explanation.

In their issues of June 30, 1980, on the occasion of disturbances marking the fourth anniversary of the Soweto uprising of 1976, both *Time* and *Newsweek* led their international sections with reports on South Africa. The *Time* account, the shorter of the two, told of the spread of violence to various urban centers and Coloured areas and put this blunt point on the events:

> The new outbreak came after increasing protest and turmoil in recent months. The government's promised reforms, ranging from a gradual phasing out of the hated passbook system to a plan for enabling blacks to buy their own homes, have either not materialized or largely failed. Organizers of the African National Congress, the outlawed black political movement, operate with increasing ease.[11]

"Shooting to Kill in South Africa" was the title of the report in *Newsweek,* a reference to the orders given to police for dealing with the demonstrators. Explaining the origins of the latest trouble in a school boycott by Coloured students, *Newsweek* said that "the new surge of unrest was a dose of particularly unpleasant medicine" for Prime Minister P.W. Botha. "He had been seeking to humanize the face of apartheid," the magazine explained, but the nationwide outbreaks "were clearly warning that black and Coloured South Africans wanted much more than he was ready to give."[12] In sidebar stories accompanying the reports, *Time* interviewed Gerrit Viljoen, head of the Afrikaner secret society, the *Broederbond,* who said that if the "fair and reasonable offers of accommodation" thus far tried by South African whites were to fail, they might have to "ensure their political survival by more authoritarian means,"[13] and *Newsweek* provided a profile on Joe Slovo, a white communist living in exile in Mozambique who was described as directing a force of some four thousand trained guerrillas.[14]

Nearly every month during 1980 some reports about South Africa, often replete with apocalyptic conclusions, appeared in the news magazines. "Botha's inability to deliver on his previous racial promises all but guaranteed South Africa's continuing isolation from the world community," declared *Newsweek* in February.[15] A month later, a *Newsweek* correspondent filed an analysis from Cape Town predicting that unless Afrikaners soon begin to think about meaningful compromise with blacks, "the turbulent history of Rhodesia will repeat in South Africa".[16]

In the same week's issue, *U.S. News & World Report,* a magazine with a more conservative tradition that has also begun paying greater attention to Africa, had two reports from South Africa. A brief item in the magazine's "Worldgram" section suggested that the heat was off Pretoria for a time because the West's preoccupation with the crises in Iran and Afganistan.[17] On the other hand, a longer story in the main body of the magazine spoke of "rumblings of race war in South Africa." *U.S. News & World Report* was even more direct in its predictions than *Time* and *Newsweek:* "In city and countryside, whites are bracing to meet the black challenge. As tensions rise, full-scale conflict seems inevitable."[18] The focus of the article was on South Africa's defense effort and its prospects for beating black guerrillas and taking action against neighboring countries that are giving them sanctuary. A month later, *U.S. News* again featured a major article about South Africa, this time looking at the question of American investment there. The message was, "American companies are spending millions to ease racial tensions and protect investments worth billions of dollars. It's far from clear whether the strategy will work."[19]

Magazines of Opinion

Another category of magazines with an audience more varied than those of the foreign-policy quarterlies but smaller than those of the monthlies and much smaller than those of the news weeklies, is the more ideological ones, exemplified by the *Nation* on the Left, the *New Republic* left of center, and *National Review* on the right.

The *Nation,* a weekly with a long tradition as a barometer of American liberal causes, may publish more frequent articles about South Africa than any other American magazine. One article, which appeared in August 1979, began by citing statements by Piet Koornhof, South Africa's minister of cooperation and development, during an appearance before the National Press Club in Washington, D.C. "We are entering a period of complete reformation," Koornhof had declared in a speech that became controversial both at home and abroad. "Apartheid, as you came to know it in the United States, is dying and dead. We are in a period of reform." But the author of the article, Aryeh Neier, former head of the American Civil Liberties Union, said that on a three-week visit to South Africa he found Koornhof's claim "not so much a lie as a deceptive half-truth." Apartheid was being replaced, Neier said, by "something more sinister: denationalization of all South Africa's blacks" through the homelands policy. Neier drew a comparison with Nazi Germany, which "denationalized its Jews in 1941 but, having passed the point of caring about international opinion, did not bother with subterfuges."[20]

In February 1980 the *Nation* published an article by Roger Wilkins detailing an excursion to the Transkei, the first of the "independent" homelands, in the midst of an extended visit to South Africa. Wilkins, like many other Americans who have written on the same subject, found the Transkei's independence a sham.[21] Other articles in the *Nation* during 1980 included a description of the "South Africa Lobby" and its attempt to win prominent friends and gain influence in the United States;[22] a report on the growth of the black guerrilla movement in South Africa, including a call for the application of full economic sanctions against the government by the international community;[23] and a discussion of "the illegal exploitation of Namibia" by South Africa, explaining how the Pretoria regime and multinational corporations had profited from the removal of uranium, diamonds, zinc, and copper from the territory South Africa had been ruling as Southwest Africa since taking it over from the Germans after World War I.[24] In general, the articles in the *Nation* have had a strong tone of hostility and outrage toward South Africa.

The tenor of writings about South Africa in the *New Republic* is not much different, except that some of the outrage is replaced by irony and humor. One 1980 report, "The Smut-Hounds of Pretoria," gave an amusing tour through *Jacobsen's Index of Objectionable Literature*, the complete list of publications and other items banned from importation into South Africa.[25] Another described "South Africa's war of words," detailing the euphemisms commonly used in official parlance to discuss South Africa's internal struggles and its difficulties with the rest of the world.[26] A third, in diary form, offered random observations on life in South Africa, mocking the country as "an immense, austral Dogpatch, run by a capricious bunch of Lester Maddoxes speaking Afrikaans." It also quoted a commander in the African National Congress as saying that whites would have every opportunity to remain in South Africa and enjoy full rights if blacks were to rule the country, and it called on Western governments to have courage to institute total sanctions in order to avert "the coming bloodbath."[27]

National Review, a conservative biweekly edited by William F. Buckley, Jr., is entirely different in its stance. It also pays frequent attention to South Africa but appears to be if not sympathetic with, at least understanding of, the problems of the white minority. One lengthy reportorial article published in April 1979 concentrated exclusively on the black township of Soweto outside of Johannesburg. "What I labor to establish," said the author, "is that Soweto, *the candid racism of the National Party aside,* is no worse than, indeed better than some, settlements on the fringes of major cities around the globe.'' Some of the other cities he had in mind were "Caracas, Santiago, and maybe Saint Louis.''[28] The author went on to trace Afrikaner nationalism and xenophobia, and he pointed out, as many Afrikaners do, that white Americans conquered their land by not dissimilar methods; racist laws in South Africa, he implied, were not only reasonable but also probably necessary. While Soweto leaves much to be desired, he acknowledged, it is nonetheless ''no mean achievement'':

> Alluding to the misery that exists in other lands—including, here and there, our own—is not by way of excusing what remains deplorable about the housing in Soweto; it is by way of keeping matters in perspective. Also, I think, it is fair to recall that most of these people would otherwise still be living in beehive, wattle-and-thatch huts, sans water, sanitation, medical attention, or educational and recreational facilities. In fact, the housing that is deplored in Soweto is the same kind that in India and Tanzania is singled out as a triumph of government planning.[29]

Another issue of *National Review* reprinted one of Buckley's columns attacking black American civil-rights leader Jesse Jackson for calling South Africa a ''terrorist dictatorship.''[30] An editorial in a third issue said that P.W. Botha, by instituting careful and meaningful reforms, had ''earned the benefit of a doubt from responsible critics'' and insisted that it is ''grotesquely inappropriate to demand market sanctions against South Africa, which will inevitably hit blacks first and hardest.''[31]

Daily Newspapers and Wire Services

To analyze the coverage of South Africa in U.S. daily newspapers is a far more complex task. The influence of several papers is national in scope; a somewhat larger number influence regional opinion, while the vast majority are read only in their respective communities and nearby environs. *The New York Times* is read by most of the foreign-policy-interested minority in and out of the federal government, including journalists who cover world affairs for other publications and radio and television. Although most of its daily circulation is among readers in the Northeast, the foreign-policy-alert minority across the continent follows its coverage, particularly in the Sunday edition.

The *Wall Street Journal,* regional editions of which are available on the day of publication virtually everywhere in the United States, is read by much of the corporate and business community and local community leaderships of moderate to conservative political persuasion. In areas where the local paper is weak on world affairs, the *Journal* is also a major source of international information and analysis for more liberal people interested in foreign policy. The international views advanced in the *Journal* tend to be more conservative than those in the *Times, The Washington Post,* and the *Christian Science Monitor,* for example.

The *Washington Post* is read not only by most members of Congress, their substantive staffs, and decision makers in the federal executive but also by thousands of private citizens who follow developments in the federal government. Its circulation beyond the national capital area is still limited, however. The *Christian Science Monitor,* of considerably smaller circulation than the others, is also read beyond Christian Scientists, primarily by a national audience interested in foreign affairs. It is sometimes the most worldly newspaper readily available in small towns.

The *Los Angeles Times,* the *Chicago Tribune,* and the *Atlanta Constitution/Journal* have a wide following beyond their metropolitan areas in the West, the Midwest, and the Southeast, respectively. A few others, such as the *Denver Post,* the *Baltimore Sun,* the *Nashville Tennesseean,* the *Boston Globe,* the *St. Louis Post-Dispatch,* the *St. Petersburg Times,* and the *Minneapolis Tribune* have a regional impact considerably broader than their metropolitan areas. Most of these papers devote attention to world affairs considerably beyond the extent and above the analytical quality of that of most American local dailies. Here several recent events and how they were treated in terms of quantity, prominence of treatment, and tone in major American newspapers need be considered.

For spot news, which may catch South African–based American correspondents unprepared or out of the country on other assignments, newspapers tend to use routine wire stories. In January 1980 after four people were killed during a black guerrilla raid on a bank in the Pretoria suburb of Silverton, *The New York Times* published a report from Reuters, noting that the incident had left South African whites "wondering whether black opposition to segregation is entering a new and violent phase."[32] The *Chicago Tribune* on the same occasion used an Associated Press dispatch, explaining that one of the demands of the gunmen who attacked the bank was the release of (ANC) leader, Nelson Mandela, from prison on Robben Island in Table Bay near Cape Town.[33]

But in June 1980, when the demonstrations occurred on the fourth anniversary of the 1976 Soweto uprising and South Africa seemed to be thrown into great distress, most newspapers' correspondents were on hand and filed major accounts. *The New York Times,* the *Washington Post,* the *Chicago Tribune,* and the *Los Angeles Times* all ran their stories on the front page, in some instances with major headlines. Caryle Murphy's report in the *Post* on June 18 conveyed a genuine aura of crisis across the nation, although much of the information she included came through the South African Press Association.[34] (These events marked the first time that the South African police tried to make it difficult for foreign correspondents to get near the scene of the disturbances and provide firsthand accounts.) The *Chicago Tribune,* like some other newspapers, went to great lengths to explain the significance of the fact that Coloureds as well as blacks, were now participating in violent protests.[35] The same was true in the *Christian Science Monitor,* whose South African correspondent, a man also employed by a South African newspaper, discussed the "tragic alienation" of the Coloureds from the whites.[36] Earlier the *Monitor,* more so than other mainstream American dailies, had traced the evolution of the coloured school boycott and explained in detail some of the grievances at issue.[37]

South Africa also captured a prominent place on the front page of most American newspapers in October 1979 when the U.S. government claimed, on the basis of data from a satellite, that the South Africans may have exploded a nuclear device in the atmosphere. The American suspicions, the South African denials and denunciations, and the comments at the United Nations and in European capitals received considerable attention and provided an opportunity for in-depth discussion of South Africa's nuclear energy program. There were also mentions, in the *Los Angeles Times,* among other places, of South African–Israeli cooperation on nuclear matters.[38] Similarly the news magazines discussed the mystery of the apparent blast near the southern tip of the African continent. The extensive coverage in *Newsweek* related the blast less to South African–American relations than to the worldwide picture in the area of nuclear proliferation; the same article contained a review of the nuclear programs of Pakistan, South Korea, Taiwan, Argentina, and Brazil.[39] *Time* also took up the issue of the explosion, saying one week that "South Africa's possible possession of the bomb was at least a distant menace to international security"[40] and the next that Pretoria's "haughty denials did little to quell international fears" on the subject.[41] But it was a complex subject, and in neither the daily newspapers nor the weekly news magazines could it survive the competition from other events. The American reading public never was told the conclusions of its government, or any other, about the mysterious blast.

It is also important to look at the editorials about South Africa in the major American newspapers. South Africa is a subject of growing preoccupation for editorialists, who have ranged widely over the country's policies. *The New York Times* in December 1979 called attention to the plight of 80,000 blacks in a rural area of South Africa who would be required to resettle against their will in an undesirable location because whites had long been promised the chance to acquire the land where the blacks were living. The situation, said the *Times,* demonstrates "the cruel costs" of white South Africans' dreams of an all-white nation.[42]

Reacting to an ANC bomb attack on three heavily guarded South African energy installations, the *Washington Post* editorialized in June 1980 that "time is short" for Pretoria to salvage a process of peaceful change—perhaps only "two or three years." One important step, it said, "would be the release of black political prisoners who have a claim to national leadership," including Mandela.[43] In October 1979, in the midst of the uproar over the possible nuclear explosion, the *Post* had opined that "the very thought that the ruling white minority in Pretoria would secretly equip itself with a nuclear bomb . . . is chilling."[44]

In two articles published on the editorial page of the *Wall Street Journal* in October 1979, George Melloan, deputy editor of that page, offered a relatively optimistic appraisal of the prospects for change in South Africa. The dream of "social harmony based on racial separation" has become a nightmare, he conceded, but added that "enlightened self-interest requires that (the ruling Nationalists) dismantle the most obnoxious features of the curious social structure they have built. And this, for better or for worse, they are setting out to do." Melloan also suggested that the movement of American companies into progressive social policy would help South Africa to solve its problems.[45]

The *Chicago Tribune* in June 1980 reacted to the riots across South Africa by editorializing that progress toward racial equality there had been too slow. "The Botha government deserves credit for pushing for reform against the opposition of powerful conservative forces in the ruling party," the *Tribune* said. "But its good intentions alone will not meet the legitimate grievances of people who are oppressed, often savagely, for no reason other than the color of their skins. White South Africa must make good its government's promise now—while it still can."[46]

The *Los Angeles Times* basically took the same line. Writing in the same period, it said, "The way for Botha and his government to counter (guerrilla attacks) is to come up with meaningful proposals to achieve political and economic gains for the nation's blacks."[47]

"What is needed now," said the *Christian Science Monitor* the same month, "is a continuation of moderating efforts by South Africans themselves to lift the burden of racial injustices from a land of such extraordinary achievement in many ways and of such extraordinary potential for all its people. . . . The basic challenge remains for enough South Africans to get into the spirit of addressing their mutual problems with the openness and cooperation that are demanded—to do for themselves what more and more of them see needs to be done."[48]

All of these citations from the news coverage and editorial comment about South Africa in major American newspapers should not lead to the automatic conclusion that newspapers across the country are equally concerned with the subject. Most editors and commentators based in small towns or in the center of the country view South Africa as a very remote subject. In their newspapers or columns, South Africa is likely to get less frequent mention and less prominent play. And if and when it does come up, it may be treated more sympathetically. As a representative of the Charleston, South Carolina, *News and Courier* recently told a discussion group composed of Americans and visiting South Africans, he was less inclined than some other American journalists to "lecture to South Africans about their own affairs" and tended to view a pro-Western, industrially healthy South Africa as important to U.S. strategic and economic interests. (A representative of the *Wall Street Journal* said he felt the same way.)

Much of the news that American citizens (or for that matter, any others) get from South Africa comes through the Western wire services, the most important of which are Associated Press (AP), United Press International (UPI), Reuters (British owned), and Agence France Presse (AFP). At one point, all of them (with the probable exception of Reuters) operated with skeleton staffs or possibly only part-time reporters in South Africa, and they were often responsible for covering much of the rest of the continent from there too. But there has been a recent growth in attention to South Africa. For example, AP now maintains a five-person bureau in Johannesburg. However mixed American journalists' feelings might be about their working conditions in South Africa, the AP foreign editor, Nate Polowetzky, pointed out in a recent interview, their access and capacity to function is greater in South Africa than in any other country on the continent. A content analysis of wire service coverage is virtually impossible to conduct, but on the whole it tends to stick to factual recitations and leave analysis to other correspondents on the scene. The existence of so much wire service competition in a spot like South Africa, however, may make some of the reporters dig more deeply and make their news leads stronger in order to try to have their copy appear in more newspapers than that of their competitors.

Electronic Media

Increasingly most Americans get a large percentage of their news and information from the broadcast media. In the case of commercial radio and television, this can cause certain problems for reliable, in-depth international coverage because there may be few people working in the news departments of the networks who have a strong background in foreign affairs and a paucity of research to back up wire-service copy. (There are important exceptions, of course, including the Sunday television interview programs and such documentary-style programs as "Sixty Minutes".)

The treatment of South Africa by the three commercial television networks can vary considerably, and it is difficult to track and codify every reference. But a computer check at ABC indicated that during the first eleven months of 1980, there had been 27 mentions of South Africa on the

"World News Tonight," that network's nightly prime-time news presentation. (This figure compares with 126 mentions of Europe during the same period and 7 mentions of Venezuela.) Inevitably many of these are not full-fledged stories but brief, shallow, and occasionally sensationalized glances. Transcripts indicate that even when "World News Tonight" prominently featured South Africa during the June 1980 disturbances, the correspondent on the scene had time for only a few cursory sentences to go with his videotape. Although the Coloured school boycott had been going on for some time, it was apparently not mentioned on ABC until June 2, when two people were killed by the police near Cape Town.

The record is somewhat different in public broadcasting. South Africa frequently comes up in discussions of foreign policy on the nightly "Mc-Neil-Lehrer Report," for example, and when it does it is likely to be discussed in some depth. A record of McNeil-Lehrer broadcasts since 1976 shows at least a dozen programs specifically concerned with southern Africa, including one on the "independence" of the Transkei, several on Namibia, and one interview with former South African prime minister John Vorster directed by satellite from South Africa. (Many of the others were about the evolving situation in Zimbabwe and inevitably contained references to South Africa.)

The records of National Public Radio (NPR) indicate that in the eighteen-month period from October 1978 through March 1980, there were eighty-six pieces about South Africa on the air, or an average of about five a month. Most of them would have been presented on NPR's nightly ninety-minute news magazine, "All Things Considered," or its two-hour morning program, "Morning Edition," and they typically consisted of a report from a part-time correspondent based in Johannesburg or an interview with a principal in or observer of breaking events. Their average length was four to five minutes. Since March 1980, the frequency of NPR reports on South Africa has increased.

The Black Press

Other parts of the media serving groups with a special interest in the subject have begun to focus more intensely on South Africa in recent years. The black press, for example, has come to regard southern Africa generally as an important issue, a kind of foreign-policy extension of the civil-rights struggle at home. Whether its constituency—with all of its more immediate economic and political concerns—has developed the same level of interest is hard to say, but increasingly African policy is seen as a potentially divisive topic in black-white relations in America.

The black press itself is stratified. *Black Enterprise* is aimed at professionals and other successful, well-educated blacks. Its April 1979 issue featured a group of articles about American policy in Africa, including a discussion of the role of then-U.N. ambassador Andrew Young in formulating that policy and a description of the evolving debate over South Africa in the U.S. black community.[49] "Clearly, South Africa is on the minds of black Americans," said *Black Enterprise*. "Today, the trend of thinking among black leaders is in favor of some form of economic sanction in the absence of substantial improvements in the life of South African blacks . . . . Most of the black American leadership agrees that the anti-apartheid movement has important implications for the domestic civil rights movement." It also compared the reform ideas of the Reverend Leon Sullivan with more militant strains of opinion.[50]

Other black-oriented magazines, such as the Johnson publications *Ebony* and *Jet,* which aim at somewhat less affluent, more typical middle-class audiences than does *Black Enterprise,* have also increased their attention to South Africa. Perhaps more significant, however, are the black weekly newspapers that circulate widely in major American cities as a supplement or even an alternative to the largely white-owned and -managed mainstream newspapers. The *Amsterdam News,* one of the largest black newspapers, published in New York City, does not offer as much African news as, say, the *Baltimore Afro-American,* but the events of June 1980 had headline coverage in the *Amsterdam News,* and the tone was decidedly hostile: "Determining the precise extent of this latest South African racial explosion is difficult because of press restrictions enforced by the Apartheid government."[51] A week later, the same newspaper complained in an editorial that the Carter administration had offered only a "limp-wrist response" to the excesses of the Botha government in handling the demonstrations—"a bit like trying to tame a man-eating tiger by spraying it with rose water." The situation in South Africa, it contended, was a greater threat to world peace than the hostage crisis in Iran, and it concluded, "If ever a situation justified American-led sanctions against a dictatorship, South Africa presents the most deserving target since Nazi Germany."[52]

A more thorough and subtle discussion of the demonstrations and other developments in South Africa at the time appeared in the *Baltimore Afro-American.* In several articles published in June 1980, the newspaper explained the significance of new militance by the Coloureds and spoke of the "new unity" that was emerging among opponents of the white minority government.[53] It also discussed the strategy and methods of the ANC.[54]

Raymond Boone, vice-president of the *Afro-American,* said in an interview that about 85 percent of the newspaper's foreign-news coverage is devoted to Africa, particularly the "liberation struggles" in the south. He said frankly that he regarded newspapers generally, and black newspapers in particular, as "political weapons" and that at the moment his weapon was aimed at "the white racist regime in South Africa." Boone noted, however, that financial problems were requiring the *Afro-American* to curtail its foreign-news coverage. By contrast, Simon Obi Anekwe, a reporter for the *Amsterdam News,* said that despite his own efforts to the contrary, his newspaper does not provide a great deal of coverage of Africa or the rest of the world. He said he had been told by management that Africa was not a high priority for the newspaper's readers and that they had a survey to back up their conclusions.

At least two black radio networks operate in the United States, the National Black Network and Sheridan Broadcasting (formerly the Mutual Black Radio Network). Jerry Lopes, news director for Sheridan, said in an interview that his network gives a great deal more coverage to South African affairs than do the major networks, including U.N. deliberations relating to South Africa. He noted that the National Black Network pays even more extensive attention but speculated that it might have reduced its market by overdoing African coverage and overlooking local issues.

Business Media

The business press has also discovered South Africa as an area of interest in recent years. *Business Week,* for example, publishes a wide range of material about South Africa, from descriptions of how the country's reserve bank helps manipulate the world price of gold to general political overviews, written from a business perspective.[55] A story in February 1980 noted that South African blacks were having to channel their political aspirations through labor organizations and observed that "American companies may be hardest hit" by the tensions that result.[56] In July the magazine discussed the prospect of U.S. legislation requiring compliance with codes like the Sullivan principles by American businesses operating in South Africa.[57] Pretoria's success in expanding its foreign trade was the subject of a commentary in *Business Week* in September 1980. Even Nigeria, the writer pointed out, "receives South African meat and other products through such devices as double invoicing and false certifications of origin. And much of the oil imported by South Africa originates in Nigeria's offshore wells."[58] But a month later *Business Week* was sounding as pessimistic about South Africa's future as were most other American publications. In a major report on U.S. investment there, it said that potential investors in South Africa had to balance "the appeal of high profits and fast growth" against "the hassle factor"—"a blend of South African constraints, polemics back home from antiapartheid spokesmen, and pressure from stockholding churches, universities, and other institutions on U.S. companies to divest themselves of their South African operations." Indeed, *Business Week* pointed out that American companies are now taking money out of South

Africa at almost the same rate they are putting it in, and it told how International Telephone & Telegraph Corporation was trying to reap political and financial benefits by selling its South African operations. The magazine quoted the general manager of Caterpillar for South Africa on the evolving investment climate: "We are secure here for five years. Up to 10 years it is a matter of caution. After that it is anybody's guess."[59]

The conclusions of other business magazines on the investment issue have frequently been favorable to South Africa. *Forbes* magazine, relying heavily on interviews with Zulu chief Gatsha Buthelezi, ran an article in November 1978 stating the case for American corporations to remain in South Africa.[60] A few months earlier, *Fortune* presented a major report stating "the case for doing business in South Africa." The author, Herman Nickel, who has considerable experience in South Africa, argued that because U.S. companies provide education to black workers and otherwise set a good example, they are "a needed force for peaceful change."[61]

Archconservative Publications

One other, somewhat aberrational element of the American media deserves mention for its comment on South Africa: the right-wing press. Such archconservative magazines as *Human Events* usually take the South African point of view in various controversies or defend that country against criticism from American and other Western sources. It generally does not have a great impact on policy or public opinion, however, because it tends to be preaching to an already converted readership. (To a lesser extent, the same can be said about the *Nation* and *National Review.*) Certain conservative columnists have also taken up the cudgel on behalf of white minority regimes in southern Africa whenever possible. Patrick Buchanan, for example, attacked both the Ford and Carter administrations for their involvement in efforts to bring black majority rule to Rhodesia; to him, as to other like-minded writers, the willingness of Ian Smith's regime there and the National Party Government in Pretoria to declare themselves "pro-Western" and "anti-communist" was enough to earn them American support.[62]

Occasionally an American publisher or editor will turn up as a vehement defender of South Africa. That was the case with John F. McGoff, president of Panax Corporation, which owned a chain of small-town Michigan weekly newspapers and eventually became co-owner of UPI Television News. For a time, particularly in the mid 1970s, McGoff and his Washington correspondent, Tom Ochiltree, harped on the theme of the need for improved relations between the United States and South Africa. On one occasion during the 1976 presidential campaign, McGoff pressed President Gerald Ford to say he was willing to meet with Smith and

Vorster.[63] Pro–South African testimony before the Senate Foreign Relations Committee was given inordinately strong coverage in Panax newspapers that were otherwise dealing primarily with such issues as bills before
the Michigan state legislature and local-government recall petitions.
McGoff himself even testified before the Senate Foreign Relations Subcommittee on Africa against any attempt to limit U.S. investment in South
Africa and then had Ochiltree write a news story about his testimony that
received headlines on the Panax editorial pages.[64]

During his testimony, McGoff acknowledged that he had business
interests in South Africa, but only later did it become public knowledge that
the South African Department of Information had given McGoff $10 mil-
lion to help him try to buy the *Washington Star.* As part of their extensive,
secret campaign to buy influence in the United States, the South Africans
also funded other business deals by McGoff and were owners of a yacht that
he claimed as his own (the sinking of it at sea was chronicled by Ochiltree in
a long article in the Panax newspapers).[65]

Another important defender of South Africa on the Right is a self-
appointed watchdog organization based in Washington, Accuracy in
Media. AIM has complained that major American newspapers give too
much attention to human-rights stories from South Africa (75 percent of all
The New York Times coverage of South Africa in 1978 was related to
human rights, according to the organization) and not enough to the human-
rights abuses in such countries as Cambodia, Vietnam, or Uganda under Idi
Amin. AIM also contends that the same problem exists in television
coverage of South Africa. According to Bernard Yoh, director of communications for the organization, AIM has no affinity for apartheid; "It's not
that the South African whites are so good," he said, "it's just that they are
not so bad either."

AIM publishes a semimonthly newsletter, the *AIM Report,* in which
Reed Irvine, chairman of AIM, takes the media to task. The organization
also sponsors Irvine's weekly syndicated column, purchases advertisements,
writes letters to the editor to "correct errors" in the press, and files com-
plaints with the Federal Communications Commission under the fairness
doctrine. AIM sells various categories of Annual Memberships, for tax-
deductable contributions ranging from $15 to $100.

An Overview

What conclusions are to be drawn from this survey of the coverage of South
Africa in the American media? It is safe to say that most American news
organizations have and convey a negative perception of South Africa. Their
view is shared by much of the American intelligentsia and is reflected in
most of the high-level policy discussion that takes place in specialized jour-

nals. There is an abhorrence of apartheid, a distrust and mockery of the homelands policy and other South African attempts to put a euphemistic face on its social order, and an impatience for the time when South Africa will finally begin to move in the direction of one-man, one-vote. But while this basic establishment view rejects the South African government's handling of the country's racial situation, it also tends to reject violent solutions. The mainstream press holds a persistent—perhaps naive—view that peaceful change is still possible in South Africa and that it is the role of the United States to help promote it.

To be sure, this press consensus is being whittled away by both the black press and the right-wing media. For different but equally strong reasons, both of those dissenting points of view may take on new credence and influence in the next several years, especially because of political developments within the United States.

The question remains, Can Americans who want a reliable and accurate picture of events in South Africa, with the necessary background and perspective, get that from the American press? Probably, but they almost certainly will have to work at putting together such a picture from various sources. They probably would have to consult more than one newspaper and a number of magazines and pay fairly close attention to public television and radio. One thing is certain: it is far easier to learn about South Africa from the American media than to learn about any other country or issues in sub-Saharan Africa.

Future coverage of South Africa will reflect the various dilemmas in the American attitude toward South Africa and the rest of Africa. Foremost among them is the issue of whether Africa should be regarded by the United States primarily as a vast piece of geopolitical turf, complete with precious resources, to be fought over by East and West; as a unique continent with diverse cultures, enormous human resources, and acute basic needs; or as some combination of the two. The press will be considering this issue, both implicitly and explicitly, and it will also be wrestling with the conflict between the basic affinity that so many Americans seem to feel toward the land and people of South Africa, on the one hand, and the contempt that has developed for its governing racial philosophy, on the other. The American press will continue to feel a strong kinship for the South African opposition press, especially the English-language press, and will take many of its cues from that source.

Notes

1. W.A.J. Payne, "Through a Glass Darkly: The Media and Africa," in Helen Kitchen, ed., *Africa: From Mystery to Maze* (Lexington, Mass.: Lexington Books, D.C. Heath and Company, 1976), pp. 219–247.

2. Clarence Clyde Ferguson and William Cotter, "South Africa: What Is to Be Done?" *Foreign Affairs* (January 1978): 253–274.

3. Robert I. Rotberg, "South Africa under Botha: How Deep a Change?" pp. 126–142; Desaix Myers III and David M. Liff, "South Africa under Botha: The Press of Business," pp. 143–163; and Randall Robinson, "South Africa under Botha: Investments in Tokenism," pp. 164–167; all in *Foreign Policy* (Spring 1980).

4. Donald Woods, "South Africa's Face to the World," *Foreign Affairs* (April 1978): 521–528.

5. See, for example, Sanford J. Ungar, "Dateline West Africa: Great Expectations," *Foreign Policy* (Fall 1978): 184–194.

6. Dan Jacobson, "Among the South Africans," *Commentary* (June 16, 1978): 32–48.

7. Sanford J. Ungar, "South Africa: The Siege Mentality," *Atlantic Monthly* (September 1978): 6–16.

8. David Halberstam, "The Fire to Come in South Africa," *Atlantic Monthly* (May 1980):87.

9. Ibid, p. 95.

10. "The Talk of the Town," *New Yorker* (December 22, 1980): 25–26.

11. "South Africa: Nights of Rage and Gunfire," *Time* (June 30, 1980): 30–31.

12. "Shooting to Kill in South Africa," *Newsweek* (June 30, 1980): 26–28.

13. "Looking to a Precarious Future," *Time* (June 30, 1980): 31.

14. "Public Enemy No. 1," *Newsweek* (June 30, 1980): 28.

15. "South Africa: Botha Backs Down on Racial Reform," *Newsweek* (February 18, 1980): 58.

16. Susan Fraker, "Will South Africa Learn?" *Newsweek* (March 17, 1980): 49.

17. "Worldgram," *U.S. News & World Report* (March 17, 1980): 41–42.

18. Robin Knight, "Rumblings of Race War in South Africa," *U.S. News & World Report* (March 17, 1980): 43–44.

19. Robin Knight, "Crucial Stakes for U.S. Firms in South Africa," *U.S. News & World Report* (April 28, 1980): 43, 46.

20. Aryeh Neier, "Selling Apartheid," *Nation* (August 11–18, 1979): 104–106.

21. Roger Wilkins, "Dependent Independence: The Talk of the Transkei," *Nation* (February 16, 1980): 167–170.

22. Karen Rothmyer, "Americans for Sale: The South African Lobby," *Nation* (April 19, 1980): 455–458.

23. James North, "Blues for Mr. Botha: Black Power on the Move in South Africa," *Nation* (August 30–September 6, 1980): 178–182.

24. A.W. Singham, "Uranium Colony: The Illegal Exploitation of Namibia," *Nation* (October 18, 1980): 371–373.

25. Paul Fussell, "The Smut-Hounds of Pretoria," *New Republic* (February 23, 1980): 20–23.

26. James North, "South Africa's War of Words: The Euphemizers," *New Republic* (October 4, 1980): 20–22.

27. James North, "Johannesburg Diarist," *New Republic* (July 19, 1980): 39.

28. F.R. Buckley, "Soweto Visited: Another Country," *National Review* (April 13, 1979): 482–486.

29. Ibid., p. 486.

30. William F. Buckley, Jr., "On the Right," (August 31, 1979): 1113.

31. "Botha's Courage," *National Review* (November 9, 1979): 1409–1410.

32. "Raid by Blacks at Pretoria Bank Leaves Whites Worried but Firm," *The New York Times* (January 28, 1980) [Reuters].

33. "Four Killed as Raid Ends Siege by Black Gunmen in South Africa," *Chicago Tribune* (January 26, 1980) [AP].

34. Caryle Murphy, "Racial Grievances Erupt into Fatal Riots in South Africa," *Washington Post* (June 18, 1980).

35. Ray Moseley, "Death Toll Reaches 36 in New South African Riot," *Chicago Tribune* (June 19, 1980).

36. Humphrey Tyler, "South African Riots Reflect 'Tragic Alienation,'" *Christian Science Monitor* (June 19, 1980).

37. See Gary Thatcher, "South Africa Cracks Down on Growing School Boycott," April 25, 1980, and "Stay-Away Spreads in South Africa," May 1, 1980, *Christian Science Monitor.*

38. Jack Foisie, "Nuclear Projects Peaceful, South Africans Insist," *Los Angeles Times* (October 27, 1979).

39. "A Flash of Light," *Newsweek* (November 5, 1979): 64–65.

40. "South Africa: Nuclear Clue," *Time* (November 5, 1979): 58.

41. "South Africa: Superbolt?" *Time* (November 12, 1979): 62.

42. "Chief Ramokgopa's Appeal," *The New York Times* (December 13, 1979).

43. "Bombs in South Africa," *Washington Post* (June 5, 1980).

44. "Nuclear Whodunit," *Washington Post* (October 27, 1979).

45. George Melloan, "South Africa's Great Reappraisal," and "The Pressures on Apartheid," *Wall Street Journal* (October 18, 29, 1979).

46. "South Africa's Slow Progress," *Chicago Tribune* (June 27, 1980).

47. "South Africa: 'Adapt or Die,'" *Los Angeles Times* (June 6, 1980).

48. "Four Years since Soweto," *Christian Science Monitor* (June 16, 1980).

49. Henry Jackson, "A Policy with No Plan," *Black Enterprise* (April 1979): 30–34.

50. Emile Milne, "From Selma to Soweto," *Black Enterprise* (April 1979): 46–47.

51. "'Shoot to Kill' in Capetown," *New York Amsterdam News* (June 21, 1980).

52. "South Africa and Jimmy Carter," *New York Amsterdam News* (June 28, 1980).

53. "War Heats up in South Africa," and "New Unity Grows out of South African Killings," Bennet Akpa, *Baltimore Afro-American* (June 10, 28, 1980).

54. "Guerrillas Turn Deadly in South Africa," *Baltimore Afro-American* (June 10, 1980).

55. "South Africa: Stalling on Sales to Prop Gold's Price," *Business Week* (January 28, 1980): 55.

56. "Blacks Grab for Political Action," *Business Week* (February 25, 1980): 164–165.

57. "South Africa: Pushing U.S. Business to Liberalize Faster," *Business Week* (July 7, 1980): 32–33.

58. Jonathan Kapstein, "Rising Trade Makes It Difficult to Boycott South Africa," *Business Week* (September 22, 1980): 56–57.

59. "South Africa's Foot-dragging Vexes U.S. Companies," *Business Week* (October 20, 1980): 56–58.

60. John Train, "South Africa: U.S., Don't Go Home," *Forbes* (November 27, 1978): 33–35.

61. Herman Nickel, "The Case for Doing Business in South Africa," *Fortune* (June 19, 1978): 60–74.

62. See, for example, a column distributed by *The New York Times Special Features* in September 1976 and published in *The Mellus Newspapers* in Michigan under the headline, "Carter Showing How to Boot President's Post."

63. Tom Ochiltree, "Ford Attempts to Strengthen U.S.-South African Ties," *The Mellus Newspapers* (June 23, 1976): 9–A.

64. Tom Ochiltree, "McGoff Warns about Investment Ban in South Africa," *The Mellus Newspapers* (October 6, 1976): 8–A.

65. Tom Ochiltree, "Panax President's Ship Sinks in Stormy Atlantic," *The Southgate Sentinel* (Lincoln Park, Michigan, November 17, 1976): 1.

4

United States-South African Economic Relations: Major Issues in the United States

Philip L. Christenson

The issue of American economic links with South Africa has been part of a wide-ranging debate on the desirability of any form of contact with the Republic for at least two decades. The level of interest in the issue has varied, with interest strongest immediately after major and widely publicized incidents such as Sharpeville in 1960, Durban in 1973, Soweto in 1976, and the widespread repression of black leaders in 1977 following the death in custody of Steve Biko. While public interest waxes and wanes according to the number of articles in the U.S. press, a number of groups maintain a rather steady interest.

The most widely publicized of these groups are those associated with the mainline churches. The National Council of Churches sponsors an organization, the Interfaith Center for Corporate Responsibility (ICCR), that seeks out institutional investors such as churches, religious orders, foundations, and pension funds to support shareholder resolutions at corporations' annual shareholder meetings that ask the corporation management to adopt various positions on South African links. ICCR and its affiliated groups have adopted positions on a wide range of corporate issues, such as the sale of infant formula in third world countries, the manufacture of arms for U.S. defense forces, nuclear power, and a number of other non-South African issues. Although nuclear-power issues have received growing support at annual meetings, South African issues remain the most widespread and receive the greatest level of support by shareholders.

Shareholders in American corporations have a right to raise issues before the corporation's annual meeting. To limit frivolous resolutions, the U.S. Securities and Exchange Commission prescribes rules for these resolutions. Any shareholder can raise an issue once, but it must receive an initial 3 percent of the shares voted to be raised at the subsequent meeting. At that meeting it must receive 6 percent of the shares voted, and at the third meeting it must receive 10 percent in order to be submitted to a vote at subsequent meetings. A vote large enough to allow the issue to be raised again is considered a victory.

Shareholder resolutions before a corporation's annual meeting are filed in advance and are sent to all shareholders, who may vote their stock by proxy, come to the annual meeting to cast a vote in person, or (in the absence of a proxy or an in-person vote) allow management to cast their votes. Statistics on the number of shareholders who actually cast their votes by proxy and on how they vote on South African issues are not available, although the number of votes received in support of the South Africa–related resolutions suggests that the majority of individual shareholders support management positions on South Africa.

During the annual meeting season in 1980, for example, the largest percentage of shares voted in favor of a South Africa-related shareholder resolution was 11.27 percent who voted in favor of a resolution at Dresser Industries asking management to sign the Sullivan principles. The next most successful resolutions received 10.5 and 7.4 percent, both at California banks asking them to cease loans to South Africa. The level of support for these resolutions is believed to represent the decision of California's Governor Jerry Brown that California state-controlled shareholdings be voted in favor of such a resolution.

Church groups associated with ICCR are not the only ones pressuring management to withdraw from South Africa. Universities, foundations, pension funds, and other institutional investors have also adopted such positions. A number of universities have established committees to advise the boards of trustees on investment decisions. Some have adopted positions of not investing in companies with South African operations, and others have supported companies' compliance with the Sullivan principles.

It is easy to overestimate the extent of the effectiveness of pressures on managements from church, universities, and other investors. The largest church in the United States, the Catholic Church, is not a member of the National Council of Churches and the U.S. Conference of Catholic Bishops does not participate in the ICCR. Although individual religious orders associated with the Catholic church participate in the ICCR shareholder resolutions, the Catholic Church as such has taken no official position publicly on South Africa, reportedly because of pressure from the Vatican and the Catholic Church in South Africa. Therefore the actions of religious orders cannot be taken to represent the general attitude of Catholics on this issue. The most rapidly growing churches in America, the evangelicals, for the most part have not adopted public positions on South Africa, while those in the forefront of the anti-investment movement—mainly those of more liberal theological orientation such as the United Methodist, Episcopal, United Church of Christ, and United Presbyterian churches—have experienced losses in membership over the past two decades. Many press reports do not distinguish among the various churches with similar names or heritage. It is important to avoid the assumption that the American Baptist Church position reflects the position of all Baptists because the much larger

Southern Baptist Convention, with six times the membership, has not taken a position on South Africa. Besides the Southern Baptists, the largest Protestant church in the United States, other larger churches of relatively conservative theology, such as the Lutheran Church Missouri Synod, have not adopted positions on South Africa. More important, the congregational nature of many Protestant churches means that positions adopted by the national church elites may not necessarily reflect the investment decisions of the various congregation treasurers.

Similarly the divestment decisions of a few colleges and universities may not necessarily reflect the views of a majority of the three thousand universities, colleges, and other institutions of higher education in the United States. Many of these institutions have considered the issue of South Africa with extreme care and have decided upon a policy of conditional investment in corporations with investments in South Africa. (See Stevens and Lubetkin following.)

As a pressure on corporate management, divestment policies are particularly difficult to judge. The widely publicized decisions of various institutions to divest themselves of their South Africa-affiliated stock are only part of the story. A fuller story is that the institution sells and someone else buys the shares. It is impossible to judge the real attitude of American investors or church members from such transactions. The transactions may be of little importance to the company because there is little evidence to suggest the corporate managements are particularly concerned with the identity of the shareholders. It would seem, furthermore, that any corporate preference would be for investors who are less concerned with corporate policies on South Africa and other controversial public issues.

Aside from the negligible financial impact of the anti-investment shareholder resolutions, the movement has changed the environment in which corporations operate in South Africa. It has tended to strengthen the position of those managers in South Africa who wish to increase budget allocations for improvements in working conditions for black employees and has forced senior management to examine corporations' involvement in South Africa. This has raised the level of consciousness of management of the need to become positively involved in activities seeking progressive change in South Africa. On the other hand, some corporations have decided not to become involved with South Africa because of the disproportionate amount of senior management time that is devoted in other companies to controversy over a relatively small market.

Companies have made every effort to respond to the critics and have made changes in their South African operations in order to offer credible responses to the critics. The shareholder movement probably has resulted in an increased level of wages for the very lowest paid African workers in American companies. Business executives, like anyone else, are concerned with their standing within their communities and wish to maintain the respect of their peers. To be portrayed as exploiters of the black South Africans, to be accosted at the office and at home, and to have doubts raised among their employees as to the morality of their activities in South Africa are matters of deep concern to corporate executives. Employee sensitivities, especially those of black employees, are a pressure not fully appreciated in the debate. It is also not fully appreciated that many corporate managers have a personal commitment to doing what is right in South Africa, a commitment that is reflected in corporate policies.

U.S. Direct Investment

The most widely publicized U.S. economic link with South Africa is the level of U.S. direct investment, defined as all investment in which U.S. investors have an effective voice in the management of the overseas operation. In practice, the U.S. Department of Commerce considers an investment to be direct if the U.S. investor holds 10 percent or more of the outstanding shares of the overseas affiliate and has the right to nominate one or more directors. Other countries apply different criteria. The South African Reserve Bank, for instance, considers a 25 percent shareholding to be direct investment.

The U.S. definition of direct investment's book value is the corporate equity plus the net value of intracorporate loans. The inclusion of net intracorporate loans can make an overseas investment negative. In 1976, for instance, three countries in Africa were listed by the Department of Commerce in restricted-circulation documents as having a negative U.S. direct investment. Loans from the subsidiary to the parent companies exceeded the parent companies' direct investment.

In the mineral extractive industries, the U.S. investors frequently hold minority shareholdings and are major customers of the affiliate. Sales by the subsidiary or affiliate to the parent company on credit, a common practice, reduce the official book value of the U.S. investment. Because of the reduction in book value due to intracorporate loans from the affiliate to the parent company, it is economically valid to use the official statistics to determine corporate profitability in a given country.

Despite frequent claims by persons with a broad range of attitudes toward foreign investment in South Africa that investment there is highly profitable to overseas investors, U.S. direct investment in South Africa as a percentage of total overseas investment by U.S. firms has remained remarkably stable at 1.1 to 1.2 percent since 1950. The fact that it has remained at this level has important implications for both South Africans and Americans. South Africans should consider why they have been unable to attract U.S. investment at a rate greater than the average for all countries despite the numerous tax and other financial consessions they offer, and Americans should reconsider the widespread assumptions about the profitability of U.S. investment in South Africa and assumptions about the attractiveness of cheap labor.

Because of the nationalization of U.S. investments in many countries, especially in Cuba where 6 to 7 percent of U.S. direct investment was located in 1950, it would have been expected that U.S. investment in South Africa would have increased as a percentage of total investment had South Africa maintained its competitiveness with other market economies. Table 4-1 suggests that U.S. investment has not been particularly attracted to South Africa in spite of its cheap labor.

The countries listed in the table were chosen somewhat at random, although those that chose to reduce foreign investment through nationalization or local ownership requirements (which would eliminate the nations belonging to the Organization of Petroleum Exporting Countries and many in Africa) were omitted. Because statistics are not divulged where there are fewer than a certain number of U.S. investors, the only nation in Africa that is not an OPEC member for which statistics are available is Liberia. Because the bulk of U.S. investment in Liberia consists of the equity value of U.S. ownership in Liberian-registered but U.S.-owned ships, the overall

Table 4-1
Book Value of U.S. Direct Investment, Selected Years
(in millions of dollars)

	1950	1958	1968	1978
World	11,788	27,255	64,983	168,081
Canada	3,579	9,338	43,500	37,280
Mexico	415	745	1,466	3,712
Panama	58	268	919	2,385
Brazil	644	795	1,484	7,170
Belgium and Luxembourg	69	208	981	4,739
France	217	546	1,904	6,772
Italy	63	280	1,275	3,571
Spain	31	48	582	2,097
Denmark	32	49	204	857
Philippines	149	341	673	1,003
Australia	201	655	2,652	6,368
Japan	19	181	1,050	4,963
South Africa	140	321	696	1,994

value of U.S. investment by official statistics is not a valid reflection of the Liberian investment climate.

Table 4-1 shows that the preferred locale of U.S. investment has been in the countries with relatively high wage rates, possibly because the level of wages reflects in broad terms the size of the local consumer market and often a desired level of political stability.

U.S. companies investing in South Africa have done so in order to serve the local market. South Africa's geographic isolation from the major manufacturing centers of the north creates inherent advantages to the local manufacture or assembly of many items. These advantages are reinforced by relatively high tariff and nontariff barriers to imported goods in many sectors. According to a survey conducted by the U.S. Department of Commerce in 1976, $5,196 million (89 percent) of the $5.9 billion in goods sold by American companies that year were sold locally. Only 1 percent of the sales were exported to the United States. The relatively high cost of local manufacture (except in industries in which South Africa's mineral and energy resources are important cost advantages) suggests that export markets will remain closed for some time to come. Thus the major impediment to increased U.S. investment in South Africa is the limited size of the domestic market. This obstacle can be removed only through a substantial increase in the purchasing power of the nonwhite population because the white market for many goods is almost saturated.

The cheap-labor explanation for U.S. investment in South Africa frequently assumes that labor costs are an important element in corporate investment decisions and an essential element in corporate profitability. The high-wage-area preferences of U.S. investors and South Africa's continuing inability to develop export markets in the labor-intensive product fields (such as apparel and textiles) create doubts about the validity of this explanation.

Role of U.S. Companies in the South African Economy

Because of the highly political nature of the argument about investment in South Africa and the political overtones that accompany each corporate announcement of an expansion of their operations in South Africa, there has been an overemphasis on the normal operations of foreign investors in South Africa. It is absurd but commonplace to attach political significance to announcements by companies of an expansion of their warehousing facilities or their retooling and renovation activities. Both sides tend thus to interpret the routine, day-to-day activities of companies in South Africa.

U.S. majority-owned corporations account for 3 percent of the annual capital spending in South Africa for replacements and new plants and equipment. In 1978 U.S. majority-owned firms spent $300 million of a $11.4 billion gross domestic investment in South Africa. About 85 percent of these expenditures are funded through depreciation and retained earnings and are not subject to the jurisdiction of the U.S. government. These figures show that the cutoff of new investment from the United States would reduce South Africa's gross domestic investment by less than 0.5 percent.

As companies improve their labor practices and as the recent balance-of-payments surpluses have made arguments that U.S. corporations are financing apartheid less tenable, the interest of the anti-investment groups has shifted to the corporate role in providing technology to South Africa. The argument is made that U.S. technology is being used to provide the government with the ability to enforce apartheid through the sale of computers, automobiles and trucks, and petroleum products. Although the argument is made about all investment, the companies in these fields are particular targets of this argument.

The argument has strong appeal to those persons not trained in the sciences or engineering fields who continue to believe that the United States has the world's most advanced technology and that other countries are incapable of duplicating or substituting for U.S. technology. There is no field in which an American firm operates in South Africa without other foreign and increasingly local competitors. IBM and the other American computer companies know that South Africa is the largest overseas market for the British computer company, ICL, and they know that ICL would be pleased to pick up whatever market share the American companies abandoned to it. The recent reentry of Siemens, the German computer firm, into the South African market suggests that ICL is not alone in its desire to increase sales in the market. Ford and General Motors are aware that the number of motor vehicle manufacturers in South Africa is excessive and that their own departure from the market would have little significant impact on the South African economy. U.S. oil companies know that 50 percent of the South African market is controlled by non-U.S. companies.

The technology of many industries is becoming increasingly widespread in South Africa. The motor vehicle and petroleum industries have been established in South Africa for over fifty years, and it is reasonable to assume that the basic technology of their operations is fully understood by the South Africans who manage them. Although there are undoubtedly some long-term consequences of a cutoff of the West's technology, it is unreasonable to assume that such a change would have a significant impact on the economy in the short term, especially if the provisions included in the 1978 Patent Act allowing South Africa to violate the patent rights of overseas patent holders who refuse to make their technology available to South Africa are employed on a large scale. It is important to remember in this regard that the reason technology is patented is because it can be duplicated.

The experience of other countries at South Africa's level of development, such as Mexico and Brazil, is worthy of close examination before judgment can be reached on the loss of overseas technology. A July 1979 World Bank study on international technology transfer suggested that indiscriminate imports of technology from developed nations inhibits the development of local technology partly because the foreign technology is associated with foreign trademarks that have a marketing advantage over locally developed technology. The bank also notes that technology recently developed in the advanced countries tends to be inappropriate for less-developed countries because it tends to be increasingly capital intensive. Technology imported from overseas also tends to be duplicative of technology existing within the country and is used to compete with local interests. If the bank's staff paper is correct, a cutoff of access to overseas technology could contain significant benefits to South African industry to mitigate many of the harmful effects.

The flow of investment capital into South Africa frequently is claimed to be supportive of apartheid. It is asserted that a cutoff of the flow of funds from the West would place the South African economy in jeopardy. This assertion is based on the widespread belief that South Africa has a chronic balance-of-trade deficit, a belief that seems to be due to peculiar and misleading trade statistics published until recently. These statistics, published by the South African Department of Trade, excluded exports by the South African Reserve Bank of gold and imports of petroleum and arms. Although the sale of gold by nonproducing countries is a sign of a balance-of-trade deficit, to treat gold sales by producer nations in this way is questionable. International Monetary Fund statistics include all imports and exports of whatever nature. These statistics show that during the period 1971–1978 South Africa had a balance-of-trade surplus of approximately $6.5 billion overall. South Africa's balance-of-payments deficit is due to the $8.9 billion in interest and dividends that it paid to overseas investors during the same period. One of the reasons why there is little likelihood of investment sanctions against South Africa is that it is understood that South Africa could easily counter such sanctions by restrictions on the remittance of earnings abroad, which would strengthen rather than weaken the South African balance-of-payments position.

A more worrisome possibility from the point of view of South African decision makers would be a gradual decision of private investors to delay or forgo investments in South Africa until the direction of government policy is clearer or until a democratic government encompassing all citizens within the 1961 boundaries of the Republic is achieved. In this event, there would be no government action against which South Africa's government could retaliate, and the flow of dividends and profits would have to be continued while the offsetting capital flow would be reduced.

There are signs, however, that the South African economy has reached a level of maturity at which some weeding out of foreign investors will normally occur. The relatively small market is fragmented among an excessive number of competitors, most with important overseas links. There are also signs that the trend in South Africa is toward greater local management control over industrial enterprises operating within the country. The recent sale of the domestic appliance divisions of the U.S. General Electric and the U.K. General Electric Company (nonrelated firms) to local interests, the growth of Anglo American's Sigma Motors subsidiary through acquisition of the plants and operations of departing overseas investors, the recent acquisition of 20 percent of the Total petroleum (a French company) operation by Rembrandt interests, and so forth suggest that this trend is well underway. South African financial mining houses have the resources to acquire much of the overseas investment in their country. Anglo American and De Beers have even purchased 25 percent of the U.K.-based Consolidated Gold Fields Ltd., which gives them important interests in several other countries. De Beers is reported to have cash and liquid assets of $1.5 billion, equal to 75 percent of the book value of all U.S. direct investment in the country.

It is ironic that disinvestment pressures by reinforcing this trend may tend to strengthen the economic and commercial strength of South African controlled firms.

U.S. Indirect Investment

Indirect investment is defined as that investment in which the U.S. investor does not have an effective voice in the management of the foreign firm. It consists primarily of bank loans to overseas organizations and small shareholdings in overseas firms held by Americans. The ownership of shares in South African mining houses and individual mines is widespread in the United States. De Beers, for instance, is the largest firm in terms of sales on the over-the-counter market, with about 70,000 shares traded daily. East Driefontein and other individual mines shares are also actively traded in the United States. A study by the Johannesburg stock brokerage house of Davis, Borkum, Kare placed the market value of U.S. shareholdings in 1978 at $2.3 billion, approximately 25 percent of the South African mining industry shares. Although American shareholdings are equal to that of the U.K. shareholders, only a few Americans have been appointed to the boards of directors of the South African mining houses, while U.K. citizens are well represented. This phenomenon may reflect a much greater dispersion of shareholdings among American investors as compared to the British.

Because individual shareholders are difficult to identify, little public attention has been focused on the potential issue of American shareholdings in South African-controlled corporations, despite the magnitude and potential influence of this form of investment.

Bank loans, the other form of indirect investment, were placed at $2.2 billion at the end of 1976 according to a report prepared by the Congressional Research Service. It is believed that since then the level of bank loans has decreased significantly, in part a reflection of the substantial balance-of-payments surpluses achieved by South Africa since then. Under pressure from anti-investment groups, some banks have adopted positions of not lending to the South African government or its parastatal agencies and corporations, while others have decided not to lend except for export financing for regular customers. The payments surpluses in recent years in South Africa have diminished the importance of the bank loan issue, although it could reemerge.

U.S. Trade with South Africa

U.S. exports to South Africa in 1979 have reached $1.4 billion, up 30 percent from the 1978 level. It is commonly believed that this level of exports supports 50,000 jobs, or approximately 0.05 percent of the 97.2 million jobs in the U.S. economy. Although this is a miniscule percentage of total U.S. employment, 50,000 additional unemployed workers would be a matter of some concern to U.S. policymakers. Because of the income-maintenance provisions built into the U.S. economic system, the loss of 50,000 jobs would result in an additional cost to the government from various welfare programs, such as unemployment benefits, food stamps, and medical care expenditures, and loss of tax revenue of approximately $1 billion. Congressional members whose constituents have been adversely affected by policy decisions on South Africa have attempted, at times successfully, to intervene on their behalf and are expected to continue these interventions.

Because of rhetoric emanating from the Carter administration in 1977, some analysts attempted to link a declining U.S. market share in South Africa during 1978 to the Carter administration's political stance. Historic trends, repeated in 1978 and 1979, indicate that U.S. trade with South Africa lags six to nine months behind the overall trend of South African imports because of the higher proportion of capital equipment and components for capital equipment included in U.S. exports to South Africa in comparison to exports from other major trading partners. Demand for such items occurs at a different point in the business cycle than does the demand for consumer goods and their components.

U.S. imports from South Africa doubled during the period 1977–1979, almost entirely because of price increases in the precious metals and gem diamonds imported from South Africa. The 1979 imports of $2.7 billion included $522 million in numismatic coins (Krugerrands), $708 million in gem diamonds, and $551 million in platinum group metals. These three items accounted for 67 percent of total U.S. imports from the Republic.

The Mineral Debate

In 1980 two contradictory reports were issued by the Congress on the role of sub-Saharan Africa and South Africa in the field of raw materials. The Senate subcommittee on Africa issued a report generally downplaying the importance of South African mineral exports, claiming that alternatives were easily available, while the House subcommittee on mines and mining issued a report describing the region as the "Persian Gulf" of minerals.

U.S. import data underestimate the level of trade between the two countries because of an important triangular trade. South African diamonds are cut in the United Kingdom, Belgium, and Israel; platinum is refined in the United Kingdom; and chrome and manganese ores are processed in Japan and France prior to export to the United States as ferroalloys. Import data list imports as originating in the country where they were last processed.

The trade in luxury items such as gold and diamonds may be of little importance to policymakers, but South Africa's exports of certain strategic or industrial minerals are a matter of some concern. U.S. officials estimate that South Africa is the ultimate origin of 55 percent of the ferromanganese, an essential element in the manufacture of steel, consumed in the United States. Because 26 percent of all jobs in manufacturing industries include the transformation of steel, concern for adequate and assured supplies of manganese and ferromanganese exists in many quarters. Similarly chromite and ferrochrome are essential to the manufacture of many products whose availability is essential to modern industrial life. One report by the National Research Council of the National Academy of Sciences concluded that the United States was more vulnerable to a long-term cutoff of chrome than of any other mineral commodity, including petroleum. Platinum plays an important role in the catalytic converter installed on American cars to meet the requirements of the Clean Air Act of 1974 and in the petroleum-refining process that produces the unleaded gasoline cars so equipped require.

It is frequently argued that South Africa is the only source of supply other than the Soviet Union for these critical commodities. South African analysts frequently provide charts of the combined Soviet and South African reserves of these materials to point out the importance of their country. In fact, the Soviet Union is not an alternative supplier of these materials because it lacks the installed capacity to replace South Africa in many of these materials and, more importantly, it has proven itself to be a highly unreliable supplier of commodities to the West. Because of the secrecy surrounding the Soviet economy, few businesspersons would be prepared to rely upon the Soviet Union as a supplier of essential raw materials because information that is vital for corporate planning is unavailable. The Soviet activities in world markets are often capricious, as shown in their withdrawal from markets for lengthy periods without explanation. Western estimates of Soviet reserves of many commodities are unreliable.

There are signs of a growing concern in the West about South Africa's political future. This concern is neither rhetorical nor ideological and has nothing to do with political pressures in the United Nations or the third world. Instead it is reflected in recent decisions of the major European powers (the United Kingdom, West Germany, and France) to develop and maintain mineral stockpiles of commodities imported from South Africa and a limited number of other countries. Events in Iran, where political instability has prevented the production of petroleum for export, has made the need for these stockpiles more compelling.

The United States has maintained strategic stockpiles of minerals as part of an overall program for future long-term military contests. The willingness of the American government to draw upon these stockpiles in the event of political disruptions in South Africa is a matter of some debate. During the loss of some cobalt supplies due to disruptions in Zaire's Shaba province in 1978, the United States did not make deliveries from its stockpiles.

Regardless of U.S. stockpile policies during a disruption, the remaining producers of minerals undoubtedly would demand substantially higher prices, perhaps resulting in the transfer of several billion dollars annually to overseas suppliers, thus exacerbating the United States' already critical balance-of-trade difficulties. Physical shortages are also likely. The disruption of Iran's petroleum exports because of internal political upheavals caused substantial shortages and price increases despite the fact that petroleum was in excess supply during the period immediately preceding the departure of the shah and Iran produced only 10 percent of the world's petroleum. In minerals such as manganese, for which South Africa is the producer of 40 percent of the supply exported outside the Council for Mutual Economic Assistance (COMECON) nations, the cost to the United States and its major partners of a disruption in supply would be enormous.

The most optimistic projections of the time needed to develop alternative supply sources range from three to five years. A World Bank publication, *The Mining Industry and the Developing Countries,* suggests that about four years after exploration and feasibility studies is needed for mine development and plant construction for a modern large-scale mining project. In many cases, exploration and feasibility studies for alternatives to South African resources have not been conducted, adding greatly to the time needed to bring alternatives into production. Because of the time lags inherent in mining, the industry is noted for its financial planning based on long-term investment for long-term profits. Thus it can not be assumed that a medium-term (three to ten years) interruption in supplies from South Africa would be followed by large-scale investment in alternative supply sources by the private sector as the likelihood of profitable long-term operation of such sources in competition with many existing, known deposits of minerals in South Africa cannot be assured. Government financing thus would be required.

Another factor in mineral dependence is the need to construct processing facilities. Increasing environmental protection legislation and citizen opposition to smelters and other mineral-processing facilities in the United States have resulted in a lack of construction of new facilities for some time, and environmental regulations have forced some operations to close. This vacuum has enabled South Africa to develop an important ferroalloys industry over the past decade. Similar situations exist in many of the European nations. In combination with increasing energy costs that affect the economics of transportation of unprocessed materials, this trend has resulted in an increasing reliance by the West on South Africa as a mineral producer and as a processor of the minerals into a semifinished state.

The mineral-dependence argument has often been used to urge the United States to accept the status quo in South Africa. While U.S. need for South African minerals does place serious restrictions on U.S. policy options, it could be used to urge a deliberate and totally self-interested policy of reducing American dependence on (hence trade with) South Africa for raw materials in the absence of substantial and meaningful political reforms.

Importance of U.S. Trade to South Africa

U.S. imports from South Africa accounted for 4 percent of that country's gross domestic product (GDP) in 1978. With the standard multiplier of three, it can be postulated that a cutoff of U.S. imports, assuming alternative markets are not found, would reduce South Africa's GDP by 12 percent. Gold and gem diamonds, however, are easily marketed, and raw material imports could not be halted without considerable cost. Such a cutoff is therefore extremely improbable.

An argument that has gained considerable popularity in certain circles in South Africa contends that an import substitution boom would result from trade sanctions. Although plausible in economic theory, as a practical matter there are structural dependencies between South Africa and its Western trading partners that guarantee that any cutoff of trade would be expensive and damaging to both sides. The West needs South Africa for its minerals, and South Africa needs the West for its components and capital equipment for its industries.

Detailed studies by the Afrikaanse Handelsinstituut, the South African Federated Chamber of Industries, and the Steel and Engineering Federation of South Africa have estimated that 14 percent of imports could be substituted by local manufacturers immediately and that an additional 11 percent could be substituted by local manufactures in the medium term. Conversely 75 percent of South Africa's imports have no immediate- or medium-term local substitutes.

Manufacturing in South Africa is based on the assembly of locally manufactured components with imported components. If suddenly deprived of their imported components, South Africa's manufacturing industries would be unable to continue operations because the country has neither the trained personnel nor the installed manufacturing facilities to substitute for imported components on a massive scale. The example of the fourteen-year Rhodesian sanctions is frequently cited by boom theorists, but this ignores the fact that Rhodesia could rely upon South Africa to filter through essential imports. Even if the Zimbabwean government were willing to assist South Africa in evading sanctions, the volume of trade would be too great to be hidden in Zimbabwean trade with the West.

U.S. Government Policy on U.S.-South Africa Economic Links

The basic U.S. policy toward South Africa economic links was established in 1965 by President Lyndon B. Johnson. Under this policy, the United States neither discourages nor encourages U.S. private investment in South Africa. For balance-of-payments reasons, the United States encourages U.S. exports to South Africa. The official neutrality toward private investment is frequently cited by Department of State officials as a sign of our disapproval of the South African regime. The neutral policy, however, is the official one toward private investment in all countries at South Africa's level of development. What is unique is the scrupulous observance of the policy by the Departments of State and Commerce and the U.S. government personnel in South Africa.

In promoting U.S. exports to South Africa, the government seeks to avoid giving the appearance of closeness to the South African regime. Because so many commercial transactions are interpreted as political gestures in South Africa, this policy prevents the official American participation in trade fairs and official government-sponsored trade missions. Some state governments and private trade associations have sent trade missions to South Africa on occasion and have received quiet support from the U.S. embassy and consulates-general personnel.

The early rhetoric of the Carter administration led some observers to conclude that U.S. policy toward South African economic links had changed, but the underlying 1965 policy remained unchanged. As U.S. Ambassador William Edmondson pointed out in a speech soon after his arrival in Pretoria in 1978, the policy toward South Africa was a bureaucratic one and would not change easily with a change in administration.

The Carter administration became more cautious over time about creating expectations that U.S. actions should and could play a crucial role in the development of an acceptable political dispensation in South Africa. In contrast to earlier statements that emphasized a strong American role in political solutions to Zimbabwe, Namibia, and South Africa, U.S. Assistant Secretary Richard M. Moose stated before a House subcommittee on April 30, 1980, "We cannot afford to let our desire to help obscure other facts—that the South African economy is unusually self-sufficent; that the dependencies between western economies and South Africa's are mutual; and that no amount of political action from overseas can overshadow the solution to be worked out by South Africa's own people."

The recognition and public admission that economic links between the West and South Africa over the past two centuries have created mutual dependencies undoubtedly will be considered by some as a shift in policy, but it is not. The Carter administration opposed every congressional bill since 1977 that sought to impose economic sanctions against South Africa.

Congressional interest in South Africa seems to have diminished during 1979 and 1980, in part a reflection of a lowering of public interest. In 1978, at least twenty bills or resolutions were introduced calling for economic sanctions of one nature or another. None passed. A resolution condemning the circumstances surrounding the death in detention of Steve Biko passed the House despite certain opposition.

The bills introduced by various representatives and senators on South Africa are only a small number of the 20,000 bills introduced during each two-year Congress. None of the bills on South Africa has ever been reported out of the committee or committees to which they were referred. It is important that even bills introduced by reportedly powerful influences such as former Subcommittee on Africa chairman Charles Diggs or his successor, Steven Solarz, have never been reported out to the full committee of the House Foreign Affairs Committee.

The many pressing issues that Congress must decide virtually assure that bills on relatively minor issues for the United States, such as South Africa, do not reach the floor of either the House of Representatives or the

Senate. Foreign-policy issues in the Congress generally are included as amendments to legislation that must be passed. The famous Byrd amendment authorizing the importation of commodities considered strategic from Rhodesia if they were also imported from the Soviet Union was attached to a military-procurement bill that had to be passed. Similarly the only successful legislative initiative on South Africa in recent years was an amendment to the Export-Import Bank Authorization Bill in 1978, the so-called Evans amendment, which limited access to Export-Import Bank (Eximbank) facilities to borrowers in South Africa not associated with the South African government who were certified by the secretary of state to be making good progress in implementing a code of conduct that is essentially the Sullivan principles. Although the result of the amendment has been an effective cutoff of Eximbank credit guarantees and credit insurance programs with respect to South African borrowers, the amendment was offered as a compromise for a provision included in the bill as reported out of the House Banking Committee that prohibited Eximbank activities in South Africa. Proponents of completely eliminating Eximbank activities in South Africa did not have the support of a majority of the House and accepted the compromise. Later they used congressional harassment to intimidate the bureaucracy into inaction on the certification requirements by the secretary of state.

U.S. exports to South Africa increased 30 percent in 1979 over 1978 levels, suggesting that Eximbank loan guarantees and insurance programs are not a decisive factor in the level of trade with South Africa. The programs available to South Africa since 1964 when the United States prohibited Eximbank direct loans as a reprisal against the introduction of the homelands policy in Southwest Africa (Namibia) are relatively expensive. The effective interest rate, once Eximbank fees have been included, of loans under the insurance and guarantee programs is 2.5 points higher than prime, not a major inducement for a country able to borrow commercially at one and a half points over the London interbank offering rate (LIBOR) as South Africa has been able to do recently. Eximbank facilities are important or significant, however; long-term (over five years) loans and imports that normally are financed for such periods seem now to be financed from South African sources. The programs are also important to American banks, which are able to use Eximbank guaranteed loans as part of their reserve requirements (South Africans refer to this as "prescribed investments") and therefore are able to increase the level of their loans.

Foreign tax credits for taxes paid to the South African government frequently are attacked in some circles, and efforts have been made in the Congress to deny credits or deductions for taxes paid to the South African government. These efforts have been opposed by both Democratic and Republican administrations on the basis that the uniform treatment of foreign taxes is an important element in our Internal Revenue Code and these bills have been killed in committee. (Major trading partners and competitors such as the United Kingdom and France do not tax income earned overseas. Treaty obligations with South Africa require that a year's notice be given dating from January 1 in order to change tax treatment of income earned in each other's country. Thus on January 2, 1981, the earliest possible date of such a cutoff was January 1, 1983.)

As a practical matter, U.S. income taxes are levied only on income that is remitted to the United States. In the event of increased taxation (with effective tax rates that may reach 97 percent), companies are unlikely to remit the income to the United States and would retain them in South Africa. How an increase in the level of retained earnings by U.S. subsidiaries in South Africa would pressure the South African government has not been adequately explained.

Although the basic economic policy toward South Africa has not been revised since 1965, in 1977 an embargo on the sale of U.S.-origin goods and services to the South African police and military forces was imposed. The rationale for this decision was that this would enable the United States to remain in the forefront of the U.N. arms embargo that had been voluntarily observed by the United States but was made mandatory in 1977.

The United States was able to impose controls over the sale of any item of U.S. origin because the Export Control Act passed immediately after World War II allows the government to control the export of any item. These broad controls were established to prevent short supply conditions in the United States during the period of European reconstruction by preventing European purchases from interfering in the American economy. The United States is unique among the major Western industrial powers in claiming the power to control all exports.

The broad controls required by Export Administration Regulation (EAR) 175 have been a bureaucratic nightmare, and in retrospect the decision seems to have been made only because of the Carter administration's inexperience with bureaucratic relationships and responsibilities after less than a year in office. The Department of Commerce, which is charged with the responsibility of administering the export control legislation, was not consulted prior to the decision to prohibit these sales and was informed only after considerable delay.

Effective control over the sale of U.S.-origin goods and services to the South African police and military forces would require effective controls over the export of any U.S.-origin goods and services. The Congress is unwilling to provide staff and funds to the Department of Commerce to administer such a program. Moreover, such a program would decrease the international competitive position of the United States and prove harmful to the U.S. national interest in maintaining a reasonably competitive export industry. The lack of effective controls combines with the various South African regulations allowing military procurement by secret and compulsory orders to ensure that the embargo on sales to the police and military forces has little effect.

Conclusions

The debate about the present and potential U.S. role in the evolution of South Africa's society toward one that is more reflective of Western democratic traditions has been dominated by those who advocate economic sanctions as the primary policy tool. Yet serious economic sanctions against South Africa are unlikely and, with the exception of comprehensive trade sanctions that would interrupt South Africa's manufacturing processes, the adoption of such sanctions would have little impact on the South African economy since appropriate countermeasures could be taken. Trade sanctions themselves offer opportunities for South Africa to retaliate with serious consequences for Western economic prosperity.

Retaliation or countermeasures are not regarded as serious options available to the South African government. It is assumed that sanctions would be sufficiently severe as to force majority rule against strong white opposition, yet the South African economy would continue to produce the raw materials needed by Western economies. Proponents of sanctions seem to believe that the commitment to continued white rule is secondary to economic growth. South Africa's recent experiment with a recession resulted in white unemployment's reaching 0.7 percent, a level that seems unlikely to result in major political changes even if economic sanctions could result in creating a recession in South Africa.

If the argument about sanctions is unlikely to succeed in its objectives, then perhaps there is a need to explore a more positive role for the United States than merely one of continued threats about sanctions that will never be implemented. Support for such efforts as the Sullivan principles, the Urban Foundation, educational programs for black South Africans, and hundreds of other programs existing in South Africa for the benefit of blacks seems to have become the exclusive responsibility of a relatively limited number of firms with direct investments in the Republic. The clear interests of the noninvesting firms and indeed of all Americans in the peaceful and progressive change in South Africa toward a country within the democratic tradition of the West suggest that a broader base of support for these efforts should be developed, perhaps even with government assistance or incentives.

The admission that economic sanctions are unlikely should have little impact on South Africans' attempting to encourage domestic reform within the Republic because questions of economics have a decided second place in comparison with the political fact that 26 million South Africans of all races urgently need to come to terms with themselves on the basic issue of how they will interact and share the modern society into which they are increasingly drawn.

5

U.S. Domestic Controversy over American Business in South Africa

Desaix Myers III

A remarkably visible aspect of U.S.-South African relations over the last decade has been the public debate over the role and performance of American companies in South Africa. Thousands of students across the United States have demonstrated against investment in South Africa; representatives for church group, union, and public pension funds have questioned companies on their activities there, and some have divested stock or withdrawn funds from corporations and banks involved in that country. Chief executive officers at corporation annual meetings have faced more shareholder proposals on issues relating to operations in South Africa than on any other question. In 1980 alone, forty-five shareholder resolutions were proposed to thirty-seven corporations, questioning the companies on their employment practices, sales, loans, and investment in South Africa.

Participants on both sides of the debate over U.S. investment in South Africa share a common concern about the political situation in South Africa and the South African government's apartheid policies. They differ radically, however, in their perception of the role that American business plays there and how corporate ties to South Africa might be used best as a force for change.

Most U.S. companies have rejected suggestions that they withdraw from South Africa. To do so, they say, would only aggravate unemployment there and strengthen the resolve of whites to resist external pressure. They say that U.S. companies can set a positive example for other employers and act as a progressive force for change by remaining in South Africa and by liberalizing employment practices. They believe that by increasing economic opportunities for blacks, and thereby elevating their standard of living and security in the labor market, they contribute to a process that will facilitate the integration of blacks into society on all levels. And as evidence of their commitment to be progressive employers, more than 130 companies have endorsed a set of six equal-opportunity-employment principles drawn up under the aegis of Reverend Leon Sullivan, a Philadelphia minister and a member of General Motors's board of directors.

Critics of American companies in South Africa are not unified in their prescription for the role the companies should play. Some ask only that companies continuing to do business in South Africa follow equal-employment practices. Others argue that continued U.S. business activities in South Africa contribute capital and technical expertise that strengthen the economic system and make it less susceptible to international pressures for political change. They call the Sullivan principles cosmetic only and question the premise that economic growth benefits all South Africans, contending that the trickle-down may never reach blacks or that even if it does, it does not bring accompanying political or social rights. They argue that by ending expansion of operations or by withdrawing completely, U.S. companies can deal a severe psychological blow to the morale of the white regime in South Africa. The ensuing economic recession, coupled with political isolation in the world community, they say, would force the government to abandon apartheid and to work out a system for sharing power with the majority black population. They admit that sanctions would be most injurious to blacks but say that temporary hardships would be offset eventually by political freedom.

U.S. Business in South Africa

American business involvement in South Africa is not large by U.S. standards. About 350 of the best-known companies in the United States, including more than half of Fortune's top one hundred companies, have subsidiaries operating in South Africa, and six thousand more do business there through sales agents and distributors. But the value of direct U.S. investment at the end of 1979—$2.01 billion, up 2 percent from the previous year—represented only 1 percent of total U.S. direct investment abroad.[1] (In addition, Americans have indirect investment through shares held in South African companies, gold stocks, or bonds estimated at $3 billion.) And for most American companies, their investment in South Africa represents less than 1 percent of their total assets.

Within the South African context, however, U.S. subsidiaries play a more important role than these figures may imply. The prime minister's economic adviser, Simon Brand, has described foreign investment as the "engine of growth in South Africa, responsible in the past for one-third of the country's annual growth rate." U.S. direct investment provides 17.4 percent of the foreign direct investment and 4 percent of all private investment in South Africa.[2] Many of the subsidiaries are large by South African standards, employing more than 250 workers, and several, such as Mobil, Caltex, General Motors, and Ford if listed along with privately held South African firms, would rank among the top fifty companies on the Johannesburg stock exchange in terms of assets. American companies control about 40 percent of the petroleum market, 23 percent of automobile sales, and nearly two-thirds of the computer business.[3]

U.S. companies also provide a tangible link to the West that is reassuring to a white population in South Africa that often describes itself as beleaguered. As one South African government official said recently, "If not exactly the Good Housekeeping seal of approval, the presence of companies like Ford and GM is at least a sign of international support."

The U.S. business presence in South Africa encourages the flow of American technology and capital in licensing agreements and trade and bank loans. In June 1979 loans by U.S. banks, estimated at $1.7 billion, constituted 22 percent of all foreign loans to South Africa.[4] U.S. trade with South Africa in 1979 placed the United States at the top of South Africa's bilateral trading partners, with 19 percent of its total foreign trade.

Participants in the debate over U.S. business in South Africa—both those who advocate withdrawal and those who argue that business can act as a progressive force for change—tend to overstate the ability of American companies to produce major changes in South Africa's apartheid policies. In the heat of debate, it is easy to lose track of several basic facts:

American companies are not about to withdraw from South Africa voluntarily.

There are insufficient domestic or international sanctions that would force them to consider withdrawal seriously, and such sanctions are not likely to be imposed in the foreseeable future.

The willingness and ability of companies to act as a progressive force in South Africa have been limited in the past. The introduction of improved labor practices at companies today, while important to employees and their families, does not change the basic political opportunities available to blacks in South Africa.

Without a far more activist posture in South African politics, business in general, and U.S. business in South Africa in particular, is likely to affect change only on the margin.

The fact that change is limited to the political margin means that concern over the role of U.S. business in South Africa is unlikely to fade. The strength of the withdrawal campaign depends in large part on events in South Africa. Although the campaign is relatively quiet now, institutional stockholder concern about the role and performance of American companies in South Africa is stronger than ever before and could provide a constituency favoring stronger action in South Africa if events such as those in 1976 and 1977 recur or if the pace of change does not pick up.

Withdrawal

Despite continued calls for corporate withdrawal both from activist blacks within South Africa and from critics abroad, the likelihood that companies will withdraw in large numbers in the near future is slim. Business has been good in South Africa for most investors, and it appears to be getting better. Moreover, withdrawal could impose real economic and opportunity costs for companies.

U.S. companies have been attracted to South Africa because of its economic potential and the attractive rate of return on investment that could be earned there. Until 1975 the rate of return there for them was generally higher than it was in most other parts of the world. Return on investment in manufacturing, for example, averaged 16 percent a year in 1973 and 1974. Worldwide figures for rates of return on foreign investment for those years averaged about 13 percent. But between 1975 and 1979 many U.S. companies operating in South Africa felt the impact of what developed into the worst recession in that country in forty years. Nationwide, one in five machines stood idle. The automotive industry operated at 60 percent of capacity. Rates of return in manufacturing dropped to 8 percent in 1975. They rebounded to 11.7 percent in 1977 and 14.2 percent in 1978 but remained about equal to figures for return on investment worldwide.[5]

Despite general recession, the economic picture in South Africa has been bright for many companies. Computer companies experienced annual sales growth between 20 and 30 percent during the recession, and in 1979 computer sales grew more than 35 percent. Mineral prices continue high, and the mining boom promises to carry the rest of the economy along with it. South African real economic growth was 8 percent in 1980, and a turnaround is already visible in some sectors of importance to American investors such as motor vehicle manufacturers.

In addition to opportunity costs, companies deciding to withdraw face major costs in removing their assets. Because of South Africa's foreign-exchange regulations, repatriation of income gained from the sale of assets can be both difficult and costly. Unless the assets are bought by another foreign investor, proceeds from the sale must be invested in South African securities or government bonds for up to five years before they can be redeemed in dollars. Alternatively, a company leaving South Africa could exchange rands for dollars at a discounted rate that has varied between 20 and 40 percent over the last year. And there are no signs that the U.S.

government will impose sanctions that would force companies to accept such losses.

Sanctions

Resolutions calling for economic sanctions against South Africa raised repeatedly in the U.N. General Assembly have received little support from Western European countries or from the United States. The lack of enthusiasm on the part of Western policymakers may be attributed to concern about the potential costs of sanctions to the United States, its allies, or South Africa's neighboring black states; inadequate public support for the sacrifices sanctions might entail; and an inability to determine conclusively the potential effectiveness of sanctions, the connection between economic pressures, and the kind of political change that might take place in response to such measures. The dynamic growth in the value of South Africa's mining industry, particularly gold, adds to their caution, as does a rising concern about Soviet intentions worldwide and the belief held by some strategic analysts that South Africa's position at the tip of Africa give it particular geopolitical significance.

Also affecting the potential for sanctions is the lack of broad agreement on their limits, aims, and implementation. Although South Africa's major trading partners—in the European Economic Community, the United States, and Japan—may share a common concern about the government's policy of apartheid, they have different interests, pressures, and perspectives. Few countries besides the United States and the United Kingdom have experienced widespread public pressure on corporations doing business in South Africa. The exceptions are Sweden and Denmark, which have relatively little financial stake in South Africa and can afford to take strong stands such as one taken in Sweden to curtail further investment. West Germany, France, and Italy have seen little public agitation over corporate ties to South Africa; they call publicly for improved labor practices by their companies active there but have no strong compulsion to introduce effective enforcement measures. Relying on South Africa as an important supplier of strategic minerals and lacking the stockpiles that exist in the United States, few European countries are anxious to take steps against South Africa that might interrupt supply, and most are hesitant to jeopardize what has been a small but important export market.

For the United Kingdom the situation is particularly complex. The United Kingdom's relationship with South Africa is unique. Its lengthy historical relationship with that country has produced ties of kith and kin that greatly intensify the debate over Britain's role there. The depth of Britain's economic involvement encourages critics of apartheid to press for its use as a lever for change. In response, business representatives and government officials argue that it is exactly the importance of Britain's economic link with South Africa that makes the use of economic sanctions costly, if not impossible. According to the United Kingdom-South African Trade Association, British direct investment in South Africa is currently about $6.8 billion dollars, equal to about 10 percent of the U.K.'s total direct investment abroad. Its indirect investment is an additional $5.1 billion.[6]

For Great Britain, the consequences of a trade boycott against South Africa would be severe. According to a study done by Lawrence Franco for the Carnegie Endowment for International Peace, South Africa is the second largest external buyer of British metalworking machinery and motor vehicles. Where there are few product areas in which South Africa represents more than 1 percent of the U.S. export market, in nine sectors including organic and inorganic chemicals, agricultural machinery, electric power machinery, and telecommunications equipment, South Africa buys between 6 and 8 percent of Britain's total export and is Britain's largest purchaser.[7]

Imposition of sanctions could well affect neutral countries as well. A cutoff in supplies to South Africa or the development of a recession there would affect a number of other countries in the region that are heavily dependent on South Africa for trade: Botswana, Swaziland, Lesotho, Malawi, Zimbabwe, and, to a lesser extent, Mozambique and Zambia.

Because sanctions would carry considerably lower relative costs for the United States than for its allies, it is possible that the U.S. government could act unilaterally. In fact, it has already done so twice by placing stricter licensing controls on computer sales and by limiting sales to the military and police. But the goal of these measures was to ensure that American companies did not make certain types of sales and to send a message of discontent to the South African government; they were not designed to cut off the entire supply of these products to the South Africans. Any effort that seeks to tighten pressures on South Africa—by denying South Africa access to certain products or markets or by damaging the South African economy—requires significant collaboration between the United States and its allies and a greater willingness by all parties to risk some economic sacrifices.

As findings from public-opinion surveys demonstrate, even in the United States where the economic cost of pressure against South Africa is relatively small, there is little support for greater efforts. Although the public is likely to oppose a purely cynical policy of economic self-interest, it is willing to make economic sacrifices to force change in South Africa. And without clear perception of how the economic sacrifices accompanying greater pressures against South Africa would produce political change there, policymakers are hesitant to advocate a more activist role.

U.S. Policy

State Department officials have said that the U.S. government's policy is to encourage South Africans to work for "a society in which there could be full rights, justice and political participation for all of her people." The department during the Carter administration continued to follow the policy of the Nixon and Ford administrations, putting some pressures on the South African government but closing few doors. The policy was one of encouraging gradual change, not major confrontation. Investment in South Africa by U.S. corporations was neither encouraged nor discouraged. U.S. opposition to apartheid was made clear, and U.S. investors were urged to become forces for change by taking steps to help their nonwhite employees.

Implementation of this policy moved along two paths: stated support for the Sullivan principles for equal-employment opportunity as a voluntary corporate-sponsored effort to improve labor practices and an effort to ensure that, in the words of one official, "the United States should act in no way to increase the operational capacity of the South African military and police." Responding to the arrests and bannings in South Africa in October 1977, the Commerce Department issued regulations in February 1978 designed to curb sales of U.S. products and technology to the South African police and military. In 1976 the U.S. Commerce Department had taken steps to restrict sales of computers and computer technology to strategic or security-related agencies and departments of the South African government.

The Carter administration opposed more stringent controls on trade and investment, arguing that actions such as those suggested by proposed legislation that would tie investment to labor practices would be ineffective and run counter to U.S. policy on foreign investment worldwide. Despite administration opposition in 1978, Congress passed a bill prohibiting the Export-Import Bank (Eximbank) from extending credit for any export that would contribute to the maintenance of apartheid by the South African government. In addition, the bank was prohibited from extending credit for any other export to the government of South Africa unless the president determined that it had made significant progress toward the elimination of apartheid and transmitted this finding to Congress in writing. It was prohibited from extending credit for exports to other purchasers in South Africa unless the secretary of state certified that the purchaser had endorsed and was adopting employment principles similar to those contained in the

Sullivan code. The impact of the amendment to the Export-Import Bank Act has been the effective curtailment of Eximbank facilities in South Africa.

Labor Practices

By early 1980, more than 130 American companies active in South Africa had endorsed an equal-employment-opportunity code drawn up by the Reverend Leon Sullivan. The Sullivan principles pledge signatory firms to desegregate their work facilities; to pay equal wages for equal work regardless of race; to improve training and promotion opportunities for black staff; to provide assistance to black workers in such areas as housing, education, and health; and to acknowledge the right of black workers to join or establish trade unions if they choose. According to Sullivan, the principles are a "voluntary effort among companies to end racial discrimination in their operations . . . and to take a stand against apartheid."

The Sullivan principles and the fair-employment-practice codes subsequently developed by the European Economic Community (EEC), the Canadian government, and South African businessmen have undoubtedly affected corporate performance in South Africa. Until recently signs designating separate facilities were rife throughout the work place, eating areas were divided by kitchens or walls, and black clerks often found themselves boxed into a corner blocked from their white colleagues by strategically placed filing cabinets. Apartheid even reached down to the color of uniforms on the factory floor at some companies—black for Africans, blue for whites— separate time clocks, divided medical-aid stations, and even different types of crockery and utensils at lunch.

Since the promulgation of the Sullivan principles in 1977, a number of signatory companies have torn down walls, removed signs, and moved cabinets. Goodyear and Ford, among others, have committed millions of dollars to replace existing separate facilities with modern, desegregated lockers, restrooms, and eating areas. As late as November 1977, R.J. Ironside, director of personnel at General Motors in South Africa, commented that the company could not be desegregated because "tearing down the existing cafeterias and kitchens. . . simply couldn't be justified under existing and foreseeable business conditions in a depressed economy." A year later, under some pressure from its home office, General Motors pledged to spend $4.5 million on new locker and restroom facilities and on a new center of industrial training. Union Carbide, IBM, and Caterpillar Tractor have initiated housing loan programs that make it possible for black workers to buy or build their own homes.

In the less visible but potentially more important areas of training and job advancement, some companies have made limited but measurable progress. For the first time, Goodyear, Ford, Union Carbide, and General Motors are training African apprentices for artisan-level positions. Several companies that have moved Africans into positions formerly held by whites report increases in productivity. For example, Coca-Cola's South African managing director, Fred Meyer, states that African driver-salesmen have generally performed better than their white predecessors of ten years ago.

Blacks have also made gains in the area of worker representation. Ford and Kellogg recognized unregistered African trade unions in 1980, General Motors recognized a coloured union that has merged with a black union in 1981, Firestone is negotiating with a coloured and black union (June 1981), General Motors has begun to deduct union dues for some of its African employees, and Goodyear has accepted the credentials of a coloured union.

To many workers and to most business, developments stemming from the codes constitute real progress. One black union official told an American visitor to Port Elizabeth in 1979 that although many people consider desegregation of eating and toilet facilities largely cosmetic, "it is important because it institutes a process to change attitudes. Using the same facilities, the white guy will learn that the black guy is just the same—another human being—and the black foreman will learn to look the white foreman straight in the eye."

An accurate comparison of companies in South Africa is extremely difficult. The performances of individual companies differ both from company to company and industry to industry, affected by a myriad of factors, of which nationality is only one. The greatest outside pressures on companies in South Africa have come from the United States. The pressures are being brought on home offices by stockholders and other critics and, in turn, passed on to subsidiary managers in South Africa. The pressures in Western Europe and Japan, occasionally pushed by unions or by government, have been neither as severe nor as sustained, nor have they succeeded in enlisting the collective corporate response that pressures have brought about in the United States. The Sullivan principles reflect a collective corporate recognition of pressures and at the same time provide a framework for further pressures.

A major difference between American companies and their non-American counterparts has been their response to the codes of conduct. Where many European companies have tended to view the EEC code as an unwarranted intrusion by government into their activities in South Africa, the major American companies operating in South Africa, by and large and sometimes reluctantly, have agreed to endorse the Sullivan principles. There have been exceptions, of course, among companies on both sides of the Atlantic. A number of American companies have declined to endorse the principles, some offices have signed but done little or nothing to enforce them, and a few subsidiaries take the position that the principles are the home office's doing, not theirs. On the other hand, some European companies have moved ahead to recognize African unions and to develop training and/or housing programs.

Two areas in which American performance has differed from most non-American firms have been in desegregation of facilities and affirmative-action programs, both areas in which Americans have unique experience. A number of European and South African managers have argued that desegregation of facilities is a largely irrelevant distraction. Several have opposed affirmative action—slotting jobs for blacks, establishing quotas or goals, drawing up long-term black development plans—as a form of reverse discrimination.

But there is some evidence that the policies of American companies have begun to affect the thinking of local South African firms as well. For example, a spokesman for Barlow Rand, a South African conglomerate that employs more than 100,000 workers, told a foreign visitor in 1978 that the company would never have desegregated its eating and restroom facilities if American companies had not led the way.

Recent developments in government policy also reflect the impact of the codes. The Wiehahn commission, established to investigate labor legislation affecting nonwhite labor, wrote in 1979 that

> it would be naive to deny the fact or ignore the effect of international attempts to influence labor and other policies in South Africa. The presence of subsidiaries of multinational enterprises within a country's borders creates a conduit through which strong influences and pressure can be exerted on that country's policies and practices.[8]

With specific reference to desegregation, the commission wrote that because

> desegregation of facilities is one of the principles in the many labor codes subscribed to by the 300 plus multinational companies, . . . current practice is no longer in line with legislation, and the commission is of the opinion that the situation can only create an embarrassing situation for South Africa.[9]

The scope and significance of these changes should not be exaggerated, however. U.S. companies in South Africa employ only 60,000 to 70,000 black workers, representing less than 1 percent of the black work force. Even if all foreign companies were to adopt progressive practices, the number of workers affected would be limited. Efforts to improve wage, training, and promotion programs have by no means been universal, and the speed and interest with which foreign companies are trying to carry out equal-employment-opportunity codes vary considerably.

Many of the initial cosmetic steps taken by foreign firms have been relatively easy. The real problems will arise as companies move to close the wage gap, train and move blacks into white-collar and management positions, deal extensively with black unions, and end the current system of migratory labor and separation of families. Progress in these areas will require major changes in attitudes by all South Africans, changes that are counter to decades of historical conditioning.

A prime example of the problems associated with worker attitudes and the limits on progress can be seen in the strikes in 1979 at Ford's Cortina plant near Port Elizabeth. Reputed to be one of the most socially conscious American companies in South Africa, Ford was the first to recognize an African union and one of the first to train African apprentices. It began a major effort to desegregate all work facilities. In late 1979 Ford was hit by a series of wildcat strikes that began with a protest over what Africans interpreted as the forced resignation of an African community leader. When the company allowed the African strikers to return to work without penalty, white workers accused management of toadying to blacks and threatened to walk out. Africans staged a second walkout demanding the transfer of a white supervisor who had accused blacks of abusing the recently desegregated cafeteria facilities. The strikes were settled in January when Ford offered striking workers unconditional reinstatement with full seniority benefits. But the leader of the strikes, Thozamile Botha, was banned and eventually fled the country.

Changes in the work place have yet to touch the core of apartheid. Events in offices and on the factory floor have had very little impact on Pretoria's commitment to separate living areas, separate schools, and separate political rights for each racial group. Echoing the sentiments of most black activists, Lebamang Sebidi of the Soweto Committee of Ten, a body of community leaders, described changes that skirt the issue of black citizenship and political participation as simply "gilding the prison."

Business and Politics

More important to many people than the labor practices of American companies is the degree to which American companies, by their presence, are able to influence change in areas such as the racial zoning laws, education, labor mobility, rights of black businessmen, political representation, and discriminatory laws against sex and marriage across race lines.

The ability of business to effect change in these areas by exerting a form of lobby pressure on the South African government is largely untested, although it may be on the rise. Traditionally business has hesitated to involve itself in what have been viewed as political issues. Companies have long been willing to make presentations to government on business subjects, but traditional distrust between a business sector dominated by English speakers and a government run by Afrikaners has discouraged communication on political issues. And business had no real interest in affecting the political situation. As Afrikaner insurance leader A.D. Wassenaar has stated during the economic boom of the 1960s and the early 1970s, the government provided law, order, stability, and profits, and business had little to complain about. The few times business did make statements on political issues occurred when political events—Sharpeville, Soweto, the bannings of October 1977, and Steve Biko's death in detention—threatened to bring international isolation and declining economic growth. And when businessmen did speak out, they were not always well received. In response to Associated Chambers of Commerce suggestions in 1976, Prime Minister John Vorster counseled business to mind its own store.

The subsequent formation of the Urban Foundation, supported by Afrikaner, English, and black business, provided a new outlet for business activists and signaled a growing potential for business activism in areas largely relegated to government in the past. The successes of the Urban Foundation have not been without their limits, however. The foundation lobbied for two years for land tenure for Africans in urban areas. The ninety-nine-year lease was the result, a reflection of both the potential and the limits of business influence on political issues.

The role of business may be changing under the new prime minister. P.W. Botha's administration has demonstrated a greater interest in business support than have those of any of his predecessors. Botha considers business an important ally in his efforts to build a black middle class at home and to persuade critics abroad. He offers business greater access to policy-making through private consultation and through appointment to commissions. In November 1979, he held an unprecedented conference with 250 business leaders to solicit support for, and to entertain comments on, his plan for a "constellation of states" in southern Africa, which would cooperate particularly in trade, development, and other economic fields.

The prime minister's approach to business offers companies, including American companies with subsidiaries in South Africa, new opportunities to push for changes in the government's racial policies, but it also provides the danger that they will be, or be perceived as being, co-opted by the government. The *Financial Mail* commented after the conference, "Businessmen may have lost an opportunity to hasten a new dispensation for blacks— and South Africa as a whole—by failing to assert a tough, independent stance. For Botha can hardly be blamed if he interprets the uncritical attitude of South Africa's leading industrialists and financiers as an endorsement of his strategy." The *Financial Mail* went on to comment that "if the Carlton meeting is any indication of how organized business will deal with government in the future when hard bargains need to be struck, it is clear that the Prime Minister has managed to stack the odds in his favor.[10]

Outlook

Unless business in general and American companies in particular are seen to be taking a more active role in areas of political concern, the debate over U.S. business in South Africa is unlikely to fade away. In its April 21, 1980, issue, *Africa News* listed a number of developements in the economic campaign against investment in South Africa, including:

1. The University of Wisconsin's divestment over a two-year period of $9 million in stock in companies involved in South Africa.
2. A statement by Michigan State University trustees that they had divested their stock in companies with subsidiaries in South Africa and gained $1 million in the process.
3. A decision in March 1980 by the National Council of Churches, Union Theological Seminary, and the United Methodist church to withdraw $65 million from Citibank in New York in protest of the bank's lending to South Africa.
4. An announcement by the Federation of Protestant Welfare Agencies that it intends to divest its portfolio of South African related stock.
5. Passage of a bill introduced in the Nebraska State legislature by twenty-eight to zero prohibiting the investment of state trust funds in corporations with operations in South Africa.
6. An executive order by California's Governor Jerry Brown ordering the trustees of the state's public investment funds, valued at $20 billion, to vote against management on issues relating to investment in South Africa proposed at annual meetings.
7. A variety of bills introduced in Massachusetts, New York, and Illinois relating to investment in South Africa.
8. Union actions such as the AFL-CIO statement in fall 1979 calling for "total cessation of U.S. government support for economic transactions in South Africa," and a United Auto Workers' contract stating that the trustees of the Chrysler pension funds will refrain from investments in five companies per year identified by the union as having bad records in South Africa.

A 1979 survey of institutional investors conducted by the Investor Responsibility Research Center found a growing level of involvement and sophistication among investors around the country on issues relating to investment in South Africa. Of the 115 universities and colleges contacted,

51 have established procedures for voting at corporate annual meetings on shareholder resolutions relating to investment in South Africa. Thirty-five have policies providing for votes in favor of resolutions encouraging progressive labor practices in South Africa; 13 support resolutions calling for an end to bank loans to the South African government; 10 have policies that express support for each of three other issues (halts to strategic sales, nonexpansion, or corporate withdrawal); and 11 opted for selective divestment of their portfolios in 1979.

The growth of institutional activism on these issues was apparent in the 1980 proxy season. Not only were a large number of resolutions concerning activities in South Africa proposed to companies at annual meetings this year, but a number of universities are proposing resolutions for the first time, and more institutions are voting on the issues than ever before. The impact of their votes is reflected in the very high count against management at their annual meetings. A resolution requesting that Dresser Industries sign the Sullivan statement of equal-employment principles received 11 percent at the company's meeting in April, and a recent resolution asking Wells Fargo to bar new loans to the government of South Africa or state-owned corporations received more than 10 percent. Both votes represent greater support than any other resolution on South Africa has received in the past.

Although the college demonstrations against investment in South Africa that swept across campuses after the Soweto demonstrations have largely disappeared, concern over the role of American companies there remains strong. Because it has been largely institutionalized now in investment review committees, it no longer depends on the vagaries of campus activists. And events in South Africa, such as the 1980 boycott by colored students, the banning of Thozamile Botha, and of black union officials or government reaction to student unrest, could lead to a resurgence of pressures on those committees without great warning.

The system of pressures—through investor letters, meetings with companies, shareholder resolutions, and resolutions or bills in Congress, state legislatures, or city councils—appears established. Companies will continue to feel their activities in South Africa under special scrutiny, and more are likely to sign the Sullivan principles as a demonstration of their responsiveness to investment concerns. Banks similarly will have to answer for their loans to South Africa. The value of U.S. loans to South Africa has declined steadily since 1976, in part because of the economic situation in that country but also as a reflection of political pressures. In 1977, for example, only one of twelve South African loans or bond issues had participation by a U.S. underwriter (Manufacturers Hanover Trust), and in 1978 the only loan to South Africa other than short-term trade credits was a $33.3 million loan to the Urban Foundation for black housing in Soweto. In 1979, two loans were announced: one $8.7 million loan by Morgan Guaranty

Trust for black housing at Crossroads and one by Crocker National and Citibank for $25 million for construction of a black medical school near Pretoria.

Conclusion

An economic boom in South Africa and a decline in visible antiapartheid pressures in the United States has begun to open bank purses, and it certainly encourages new investment. But votes by shareholders during the 1980 annual meetings against involvement in South Africa demonstrate that a strong level of concern remains and can be tapped should events in South Africa worsen. A further demonstration of concern appeared in a 1979 Carnegie Endowment for International Peace poll, which revealed a relatively high degree of popular support for cutting trade with South Africa (43 percent for to 37 percent against) and restricting business investments (48 percent for to 32 percent against).[11]

Such feeling is not likely to be translated into specific sanctions against South Africa, but the polls nevertheless demonstrate that the controversy over the role of American companies in South Africa continues as a strong undercurrent of U.S. relations with South Africa. It dampens enthusiasm for new business ventures in South Africa and is unlikely to evaporate until the changes taking place in South Africa are seen by blacks within and apartheid critics abroad as far more stubstantial than they are today.

Notes

1. *Survey of Current Business* 60 (August 1980).

2. Annual Report and quarterly bulletins, South Africa Reserve Bank.

3. Desaix Myers III, with Kenneth Propp, David Hayck, and David M. Liff, *U.S. Business in South Africa* (Bloomington: Indiana University Press, 1980).

4. Joint news release, Federal Reserve Board, Controller of the Currency, Federal Deposit Insurance Corporation, June 21, 1979. Library of Congress, figures from the Congressional Research Service.

5. *Survey of Current Business* (August issues 1974–1980).

6. United Kingdom-South Africa Foreign Trade Association, London, 1978 figures.

7. Lawrence Franko, "South Africa: The European Connection" (unpublished manuscript, Carnegie Endowment for International Peace, April 1978).

    8. *Report of the Commission of Inquiry into Labour Legislation* (Pretoria: Government Printer, 1979).

    9. Ibid.

    10. "Time of Compromise," *Financial Mail,* November 30, 1979, p. 931.

    11. James Baker, J. Daniel O'Flaherty, and John de St. Jorre, *Full Report, Public Opinion Poll on American Attitudes toward South Africa* Washington, D.C.: Carnegie Endowment for International Peace, 1979).

6 The Black American Constituency for Southern Africa, 1940-1980

Philip V. White

The identification of black Americans with the racial and political aspirations of black Southern Africans is increasingly widespread, and is of relatively recent development. During the twentieth century until the end of World War II, racial internationalism in the black American community was articulated consistently by a narrow elite such as Marcus Garvey, W.E.B. Du Bois, and Paul Robeson, while mass interest was stirred primarily through black churches. Vigorous protests occurred over the Spanish-American War and the Philippine campaign at the turn of the century, the U.S. Haitian occupation (1915–1934), and alleged atrocities committed by the Belgians in the Congo prior to its independence in 1960. Widespread pro-Africa sentiments were aroused by the activities of Marcus Garvey in the 1920s and by the Italian invasion of Ethiopia in 1935. Condemnations of colonial rule and imperialism were particularly common within the pan-African movement in the United States.

Developments after World War II

The decade following the end of World War II witnessed a marked decline in black elite initiative on African affairs.[1] Crucial in contributing to this decline were the combined effects of the cold war, the actions of liberal whites, and the progress of the movement toward civil rights in the United States. James Roark, in a perceptive article about black leadership during this period, observed that black leaders felt obligated to affirm their loyalty to the United States and to demonstrate that their civil-rights campaign was not Communist-inspired at a time when many conservative Americans were ready to believe that Communist instigation lay behind black demands for civil equality.[2] Furthermore, American Communist Party attempts to target

I found invaluable in preparing this chapter the bibliographic essay by Francis A. Kornegay, Jr., "Black Americans and U.S.-Southern Africa Relations," in *American-Southern Africa Relations: Bibliographic Essays,* ed. Mohamed A. El-Khawas and Francis A. Kornegay, Jr. (Westport, Conn.: Greenwood Press, 1975).

black organizations in a united front campaign to fight against European colonialism and American imperialism made continued denunciations by black leaders and black organizations extremely risky in an atmosphere where guilt by association (or common articulation) prevailed.

Although black leaders during this postwar decade urged international racial solidarity and cooperation, they also attempted to forge bonds of interracial cooperation domestically. The evolving civil-rights movement was an amalgam of coalitions with white trade unions, liberal-minded political organizations, some predominantly white churches, and civil-liberties groups. Most of the major civil-rights organizations involved large numbers of white as well as black Americans. Thus, as Roark noted, the strategic placement of white liberals inside and outside the movement enabled them to exert significant pressure on the movement when they took up the anti-Communist crusade in the late 1940s.[3] Black leaders' freedom of action was thereby restricted, and those who refused to modify their publicly expressed views on world affairs risked losing prestige and power. Indeed Roark noted that one white scholar even wrote in a leading black journal that black American agitation on behalf of Africans was retrograde and cast doubt on the loyalty of black Americans.[4]

Also tending to undercut black American links to independence movements in Africa and elsewhere in the colonial world and to reduce the opposition of blacks to President Truman's cold war containment doctrine vis-à-vis the Soviet Union during this period were actions that the president took to foster a measure of racial progress: empowering the President's Committee on Civil Rights to report on the forms and costs of racial discrimination; abolishing racial segregation in the armed forces; supporting the civil-rights plank in the Democratic party platform for the 1948 election; strengthening the civil-rights division in the Department of Justice; and calling for the abolition of poll taxes and the enactment of federal anti-lynching legislation. Responding to a combination of domestic politics, principle, and international pressures, Truman probably did more for black Americans than any preceding president had since Abraham Lincoln. Black leaders focused their attention and priorities on domestic gains and had to ask themselves if they could continue to enjoy Truman's support in further efforts to reduce discrimination at home if they opposed central aspects of his foreign policy such as containment.

So notable indeed was the decline in the leadership of black Americans regarding African affairs that W.E.B. DuBois was moved to lament in 1955:

> This new leadership [of black businessmen, bureaucrats, and white-collar employees] had no interest in Africa. It was aggressively American. The Pan-African movement lost almost all support. . .

Today the American interest in Africa is almost confined to whites. African history is pursued in white institutions . . . while Negro authors and scholars have shied away from the subject which [earlier had been their special preserve].[5]

The 1950s

What DuBois had in mind was the emergence of a new, primarily white constituency for African affairs that predominated during the 1950s, one that was effectively isolated from the mainstream black community. Within the constituency that took organizational form in the 1950s in groups such as the African-American Institute (1952), the American Committee on Africa (1953), the American Society of African Culture (1957), and the African Studies Association (1957), only the American Society of African Culture (AMSAC) had a predominantly black membership. This emergent new constituency was composed primarily of white liberal activists and scholars, corporate elites with African business interests, and church leaders.[6]

Thus the African-American Institute (AAI), founded as the Institute of African-American Relations in 1952, began as an interracial membership organization largely through the efforts of black Washingtonians like the African studies pioneer Leo Hansberry of Howard University, but by the end of the decade it had become largely financed and its board dominated by individuals connected with white-controlled corporations with African interests like American Metal Climax. The influence of blacks in AAI diminished as it strengthened its ties to corporations, foundations and the government, including the Central Intelligence Agency (CIA). The African Studies Association (ASA) was composed primarily of white academics. The American Committee on Africa (ACOA) was principally a vehicle of liberal white activists and advocates, many with backgrounds in the churches. AMSAC was not a broad-based organization but one that defined its mission as the dissemination of knowledge about and appreciation for the diverse cultural achievements of Africans through the efforts of black American academicians, writers, and artists who comprised its membership. It devoted little attention to controversial economic and political issues. Not until the convening of a conference in spring 1963, "Southern Africa in Transition" (the papers from which were published by AMSAC in 1966), did AMSAC address itself to conspicuously political concerns. After a series of revelations about its receiving CIA funding, AMSAC became discredited, was unable to secure adequate alternate sources of funds, and fell into decline after the mid–1960s.

The 1960s

Black Americans' awareness of and interest in Africa was sparked by a series of dramatic developments beginning with the independence of Ghana in 1957, multitudinous attempts by Ghanaian President Kwame Nkrumah to promote pan-African unity, and his appeals to American blacks to participate in the rebirth of Africa. Other states including Guinea, Mali, Senegal, Zaire (Congo), and Nigeria in rapid succession won independence. The disintegration of Zaire into civil war and the murder of Patrice Lumumba riveted the attention of many black Americans. In March 1960, following rural uprisings in Pondoland, peaceful protestors were shot and killed in what became known as the Sharpeville massacre, awareness of the egregious plight of black South Africans burned itself into the consciousness of black Americans in an unprecedented fashion.

As AMSAC was the dominant organization through which black American concerns with African affairs were expressed in the 1950s, so did the American Negro Leadership Conference on Africa (ANLCA) become the prime institutionalized expression during the first half of the 1960s. Although allied with AMSAC, the ANLCA, which was first convened in 1962, was exactly what its name implied: a conference of leaders of the major civil-rights and black social-improvement organizations. Martin Luther King, president of the Southern Christian Leadership Conference; Whitney Young, executive director of the National Urban League; A. Philip Randolph, president of the Brotherhood of Sleeping Car Porters, AFL-CIO; Dorothy Height, president of the National Council of Negro Women; and Roy Wilkins, executive secretary of the National Association for the Advancement of Colored People, were all participants in the first conference, as were representatives from AMSAC, the Negro American Labor Council, and the Gandhi Society of Human Rights.

The ANLCA formed in part in response to the deteriorating situation in Zaire, and it has been argued that a telegram from the leadership to President Kennedy was decisive in persuading him to hold firm in support of the reunification of Katanga with the Congo against the pressures of the Katanga lobby.[7] Resolutions passed at this maiden conference included a call for more vigorous American support of the liberation movements and castigation of public and private American agencies for not giving black Americans greater opportunity for service in Africa. But even at this first meeting signs, which were to become more pronounced later in the decade, were evident of disagreements regarding African issues between the more aggressive and more gradualist elements in the black leadership community; the resolutions that passed were more conservative than a significant minority of those present would have wished.[8]

At the second biennial meeting of the ANLCA in 1964, concerns were wide-ranging, from the need to increase personal and institutional hospitality to Africans visiting the United States, to American aid to African education, to American policy regarding Portuguese colonies. Several strong resolutions against policies of the white South Africa regime were passed. Among them were resolutions urging much stronger U.S. action against South Africa, including prohibition of future investment, discouragement of the continuance of subsidiaries or plants owned by Americans, American support for U.N.-sponsored economic sanctions, imposition of an oil embargo, rigid adherence to an arms embargo, and abandonment of the practice of excluding blacks from the U.S. diplomatic mission to South Africa. The last set of resolutions passed called for establishing a permanent organization to carry out the aims and purposes of the conference; effective use of the black press for disseminating conference findings; raising funds for the establishment of a lobbying effort in Washington in behalf of conference objectives; raising funds for legal defense of the victims of apartheid; and helping the conference's sponsoring organizations to set up Africa watchdog committees to keep congressmen informed on African issues and opportunities for U.S. assistance to African nations. The resolutions also made explicit the links joining the civil-rights struggle, the international image of the United States, and American interests in Africa.[9] More than forty black and biracial organizations were represented at this conference, the importance of which was acknowledged by the Johnson administration's efforts there to rally support for its African policies. Attendants included Adlai E. Stevenson, chief American representative to the United Nations; G. Mennen Williams, assistant secretary of state for African affairs; W. Averill Harriman, under secretary of state for political affairs; and Dean Rusk, secretary of state, who made a luncheon address.[10]

The third and final biennial meeting of the ANLCA, held in January 1967, dealt primarily with southern African issues. The ANLCA enjoyed limited success as a black voice in U.S.-African policy, but it neglected the task of trying to educate more black Americans about Africa and mobilizing mass support for the policies it advocated. The organization soon became moribund after its futile attempts in 1968 to mediate in the Nigerian civil war.

The demise of the ANLCA was symbolic in part of the new directions that domestic black politics was taking and the development of new ways and mechanisms for expressing concerns about Africa. The implicit faith and explicit optimism generated by the Kennedy and early Johnson administrations, by the Peace Corps, and by what seemed to be a new concern with African policy turned sour with the development of new ideological perspectives rooted in the disillusionment of dashed hopes in the civil-rights struggle and manifested in the urban rebellions, and the influence of increasing American black identity with the struggles in the third world. Mal-

colm X patterned his eponymous Organization of Afro-American Unity on
the Organization of African Unity, which he tried to persuade to bring
before the United Nations the treatment of blacks in the United States:
Stokely Carmichael preached solidarity with the third world and counseled
that black Americans would never be free until all of Africa was free; and
H. Rap Brown, a leader of the Student Nonviolent Coordinating Committee, twice approached the United Nations to volunteer black American
troops to fight in the southern Africa liberation struggles.[11]

Identity with Africa particularly and with the fate of the peoples in
the third world more generally became much deeper and more widespread
during the second half of the 1960s. A conflation of events, domestic and
international, reinforced this development: the transformation of the civil-
rights movement into a much more militant, race-conscious movement
advocating black power and its cultural corollary black consciousness; the
strong impact of the ideas of Frantz Fanon set forth in *The Wretched of the
Earth* and other writings; the inspiration of Malcolm X, a consummate
practitioner of pan-Africanism who diligently attempted to educate black
Americans to view their problems in an international context; and the growing resistance to and criticism of American actions in Vietnam by both
blacks and whites. More and increasingly visible protest against South
Africa by black African nations in various international forums and the
growth of viable liberation movements in Guinea-Bissau, Mozambique, and
Angola heightened awareness in the United States of racial conflict in white-
ruled South Africa.

The cultural identification and appreciation that AMSAC celebrated
during the 1950s and that seemed in some respects a substitute for political
engagement, became politicized during the next decade as a growing array
of cultural nationalists, revolutionary nationalists, and pan-Africanists
became increasingly engaged with African issues. Inevitably as racial internationalism intensified and domestic race relations deteriorated, black
American interest in African affairs focused more and more on liberation
movements, especially in southern Africa. These struggles, unlike the complex factors underlying the Nigerian civil war, which colored that tragedy
with moral ambiguity, were stark, easily comprehended, and fitted in well
with the notions of pan-African solidarity that were growing among American blacks.

By the end of the 1960s, several developments were indicative of the
reassertion of black America leadership in African, particularly southern
African, affairs. These included the elevation of Congressman Charles
Diggs to the chairmanship of the House Foreign Affairs Subcommittee on
Africa in 1969 and the formation of the Congressional Black Caucus, which
Diggs was the first to chair in 1971. Creation of the all-black African Heri-
tage Studies Association occurred in the context of the conflict between

black and white members of the African Studies Association (ASA), which raised questions about the status of and opportunities for black Americans in African studies and ties among the ASA, the African-American Institute, and the U.S. Agency for International Development. Black Americans challenged the nonpolitical status of ASA in an attempt to commit it to support for the liberation movements. The widely publicized entrance of blacks into the investment-disinvestment debate through the formation of the Polaroid Revolutionary Workers' Movement (PRWM) in 1970 was another sign of increased black interest in southern African affairs.

The 1970s through 1980

Although black college students had protested in the 1960s what they perceived as universities' complicity in apartheid through holding stocks in companies doing business in South Africa, it was the chain of events set off by demands of the PRWM to end all sales in South Africa and contribute any profits to liberation movements that greatly expanded the visibility of blacks in the movement against corporate involvement in South Africa. Polaroid responded by halting sales of products that could be used directly or indirectly in the pass card system. PRWM, feeling this was a grossly inadequate response to their demands, called for a worldwide boycott of Polaroid and picketed Polaroid headquarters. The company appointed an interracial committee to study its involvement with South Africa and sent some of the committee on a fact-finding mission there. The committee's recommendations were published in several black and white newspapers and journals. Its recommendations called for dramatically increased salaries and benefits for nonwhite employees, training programs for nonwhites, underwriting educational expenses for about five hundred blacks at various educational levels, and helping to upgrade teaching of blacks. Polaroid's advertisement, "An Experiment in South Africa," set forth the committee's recommendations and succinctly summed up Polaroid's philosophy:

> We believe education for the Blacks, in combination with the opportunities now being afforded by the expanding economy, is a key to change in South Africa. We will commit a portion of our profits earned there to encourage black education. . . .
>
> How can we presume to concern ourselves with the problems of another country? Whatever the practices are elsewhere, South Africa alone articulates a policy contrary to everything we feel our company stands for. We cannot participate passively in such a political system. Nor can we ignore it. That is why we have undertaken this experimental program.[12]

The advertisement appeared in major newspapers and black weeklies on January 18, 1971. Unimpressed, the two original black organizers of the anti-Polaroid campaign became the first persons to testify against an American corporation before the Apartheid Committee of the United Nations in February 1971. One of them, Caroline Hunter, was discharged from her job at Polaroid a few days after her testimony; the other, Kenneth Williams, had resigned from Polaroid shortly after the campaign began.

Three considerations were particularly significant about this episode. First, Polaroid publicly committed itself to the argument that enlightened corporate involvement could help end racism in South Africa. This argument was clearly not new, but Polaroid was the first company to assume the challenge of demonstrating that corporate involvement was effective in transforming the structure of apartheid. Second, the Polaroid campaign, spearheaded by the corporation's black employees, enjoyed greater credibility than had previous actions against American corporations. As Jim Hoagland has argued, black Americans with knowledge about the realities of South Africa often can make more formidable adversaries to corporations involved there than can liberal whites who are more easily dismissed as mere "bleeding hearts" working through their own guilt complexes.[13]

Third, and related to the first point, is that Polaroid's position added substantial heat and passion to the ongoing debate between advocates of corporate reform and proponents of disengagement as alternative ways of ending apartheid. Substantial disagreements were fueled in the ecumenical movement against apartheid, with several Protestant denominations rejecting the World Council of Churches' 1972 endorsement of a disinvestment strategy.[14] The engagement versus disengagement debate raged within the black community as well (and has yet to be resolved there). Former foreign service officer (and U.S. ambassador to Algeria during the Carter administration) Ulrich Haynes in the March 28, 1971, *New York Times* attacked the Episcopal Church's decision to apply pressure to General Motors to withdraw from South Africa. Haynes, an Episcopalian, felt that such a position would seriously undermine the economic situation of black Africans and recommended instead that the ameliorative Polaroid example be followed. Haynes's position was roundly criticized by Congressman Diggs, Robert Browne, activist, scholar and head of the Black Economic Research Center, Percy Sutton, the black burough president of Manhattan, and other black leaders. Indeed, the Reverend Leon Sullivan, founder and director of the black self-help organization, the Opportunities Industrialization Corporation, and the first black American named to the board of directors of General Motors, supported the position of the Episcopal Church. In testimony before Congressman Diggs's subcommittee, Sullivan presented a five-point plan advocating total U.S. government disengagement and government insistence that American industry do the same.[15] However, the appeals

that were made to convince skeptics and opponents of the beneficial nature
of corporate involvment would prove themselves persuasive enough to
change the minds of some influential former advocates of disengagement:
Leon Sullivan eventually issued the Sullivan principles for enlightened corporate investment and NAACP head Roy Wilkins, upon returning from
South Africa in 1972, rejected his organization's 1966 resolution to ask the
U.S. government to prevent further private investment in South Africa.

Polaroid later withdrew from South Africa. The costs in time, money,
and energy of dealing with protesting blacks in the United States were far
greater than the limited anticipated profits the company expected to derive
from its South African operations.

Growing concerns by black American leaders about southern African
issues continued to manifest themselves in many different ways. Congressman Diggs, to the cheers of many, resigned from the U.S. delegation to the
United Nations in December 1971 to demonstrate his disgust at what he perceived to be the Nixon administration's retreat on African policy and its
hypocrisy in ritualistically denouncing apartheid while offering unwavering
support to block any U.N. action against minority regimes. Loud protests
were registered in the black community against the Azores agreement,
which gave Portugal almost half a billion dollars in loans and credits over a
two-year period for access to the islands' air bases, when it was well known
that most of this assistance would be channeled into Portugal's colonial
wars in Africa. New organizations were formed, and older ones joined new
tasks. The African Liberation Day Coordinating Committee (later, the
African Liberation Support Committee) sought to raise awareness among
black Americans about the liberation struggles in southern Africa, and
Africa Information Service used films to portray the realities of the struggle
in Mozambique. The quasi-official African-American Scholars Council was
formed in 1971 to give blacks entree into the African economic development
research area long dominated by American whites. The African Heritage
Studies Association's Positive Action Committee attempted to pressure
government into more pro-African stances in its legislative and executive
actions. The Pan African Liberation Committee became increasingly involved in encouraging a boycott of the Gulf Oil Corporation for its support
of the Portuguese in Angola.

In recognition of these activities, the African-American National Conference on Africa was sponsored by the Congressional Black Caucus at
Howard University in May 1972. The meeting epitomized the promise and
the problems (to a certain extent symbolically anticipated in the engage-
ment-disengagement debate) surrounding the growing black constituency
on southern Africa in the early 1970s. The promise was the convening under
two disparate auspices—the black-elected officials symbolized by Diggs and
the Congressional Black Caucus and the pan-Africanists symbolized by

Owusu Sadaukai and the African Liberation Day Coordinating Committee—of a broad spectrum of influential political and professional opinion in the black world, all united by a common desire to overcome the forces of apartheid and oppression and to reestablish transnational linkages. Participants included ambassadors to the United States from several African nations, representatives from liberation movements, leaders from U.S. community-based organizations and pan-Africanists, spokesmen from the Caribbean, and professional Africanists from the federal bureaucracy and academia. Discussion at the two-day conference focused on Caribbean links, economic development, and the liberation of southern Africa.[16] The day following the conference, the African Liberation Day Coordinating Committee sponsored a rally of 25,000 black Americans at the Washington Monument (dubbed Lumumba Square for the day) in what was probably the largest demonstration in behalf of southern African liberation ever to occur outside the African continent. Because 1972 was an election year, both contenders for the Democratic presidential nomination, Senators George McGovern and Hubert Humphrey, acknowledged the conference and the march, with Humphrey calling for strict U.S. observance of U.N. sanctions on Rhodesia and curtailment of American investment in Namibia and for taxes on profits there being paid to the United Nations rather than to South Africa.[17]

Yet the attempt by the caucus to create a unified black constituency on southern Africa, a constituency that perhaps would eventually consolidate a multiracial lobby under its leadership, failed because the conference reflected, but did not overcome, the schisms that had developed in black politics in the late 1960s. Polarization had developed between black elected officials as they grew in number and activist blacks further to the Left, who themselves were fragmented into nationalist, pan-Africanist, and Marxist groupings. The first National Black Political Convention held in Gary, Indiana, just a few weeks prior to the Conference on Africa, was an attempt to foster a measure of unity among these various segments through the development of an agenda for political action and a vehicle, the National Black Political Assembly, through which it could be implemented. The nationalist coalition represented in the Africa conference was not disposed to accepting any ongoing structure's coming out of the conference, preferring that any structure operating as a lobby for Africa should be a creature of the National Black Political Assembly. Thus the unresolved conflict between the elected officials and the nationalists, a conflict in part ideological and in part about the control and direction of the U.S. black constituency on southern Africa, doomed the development of any viable black initiative emerging from the Washington conference.[18]

The Sixth Pan African Congress (SIX-PAC) meeting in Dar-es-Salaam June 19–27, 1974, did little to further the development of the U.S. black constituency at a time following the Lisbon coup and the beginning of the unraveling of the subcontinent when a unified constituency was more crucial than ever. The congress was five years in the planning, yet the North American delegation, which with representatives from the Caribbean was the prime mover behind SIX-PAC, was unable to develop a unified position in Tanzania and merely transferred the increasingly bitter feud between U.S. pan-Africanists and Marxists to African soil. In addition, Tanzania was faced with the delicate problem of recognizing representation among governments and the opposition movements favored by the planners of the conference. It stepped around this diplomatic land mine by limiting participation among opposition movements to those from southern Africa, the Comoro Islands, and one or two other places. But the question of participation in SIX-PAC was the central one from the beginning of the planning, and this question, as much as any other, highlighted the continued fragmentation of the black American African constituency. James Garrett, one of the planners of SIX-PAC and a sympathetic observer, wrote that while the conference planners were wary of including the black elected officials, it was precisely they with whom the Tanzanians wished to deal. Garrett observed that the nationalist and progressive elements in the black community probably have a smaller constituency than they sometimes recognize.[19]

In 1976 southern Africa became an issue in the presidential campaign. Black Americans had been unhappy with Nixon-Ford African policies; many black groups had testified against Henry Kissinger's nomination as secretary of state in 1973 [even before the disclosure of the controversial National Security Study Memorandum (NSSM-39), which advocated accomodation with the white regimes in southern Africa since they would likely continue in power for the foreseeable future]. The general drift of Nixon-Ford policies was perceived as duplicitous and neglectful, with Africa becoming important only when it became a potential arena of cold war struggle. President Ford, through Secretary of State Henry Kissinger, announced during the presidential primary elections in 1976 a major shift in policy away from tacit support of white regimes toward more active promotion of peaceful social change, while Jimmy Carter claimed that the Republicans had never been interested in Africa until the presidential campaign. South Africa was brought up in the second debate between candidates Ford and Carter when Ford claimed that only the highest standards of morality should guide foreign policy.

The Democratic party platform committed the party to "policies that recognize the intrinsic importance of Africa and its development to the U.S.," greater involvement of blacks in foreign policy and in decisions affecting Africa, and increased bilateral and multilateral aid to Africa. The platform also expressed strong support for majority rule: "Our policy must be reformulated towards unequivocal and concrete support for majority rule in Southern Africa, recognizing that our true interests lie in peaceful progress toward a free South Africa for all South Africans."[20] It included pledges to establish normal relations with Angola, terminate the Nixon-Ford relaxation of the arms embargo against South Africa, repeal the Byrd amendment (which allowed the importation of Rhodesian chrome in defiance of a U.N. resolution), deny tax advantages to corporations in South Africa and Rhodesia that participated in apartheid practices, prevent any trade in products manufactured in the United States that could be of military significance to South Africa, and refrain from any actions toward Namibia that would assist or recognize South Africa's illegal control. Some of the subsequent actions of the Carter administration could be interpreted as attempts to fulfill some of these promises, such as the relative weight given to Andrew Young's views in the formulation of African policy and increased consultation with the frontline states Angola, Mozambique, Tanzania, Zimbabwe, and Zambia.

The significance of these Democratic platform planks is that they so closely paralleled many of the important points made in the African-American Manifesto on Southern Africa produced at the Black Leadership Conference on Southern Africa in September 1976. This meeting, called by the Congressional Black Caucus, brought together some 120 black representatives from the NAACP, Africare, Operation PUSH, the Black Economic Research Center, The National Council of Negro Women, and similar organizations. But the manifesto went considerably beyond the Democratic party platform by endorsing armed struggle, if necessary, by the liberation movements and their seeking aid from whatever quarters available, opposing U.S. support for any settlement in Namibia and Zimbabwe that compromised the freedom of blacks, and condemning U.S. political support of South Africa "as ransom for America's hostage private corporations."[21] This African-American Manifesto recommended U.S. support for action under Chapter 7 of the U.N. Charter if South Africa continued its illegal occupation of Namibia and if negotiations failed or were "unacceptable to African liberation leaders and the African people of Zimbabwe, Namibia and South Africa."

The most promising development from this 1976 conclave was the incorporation in July 1977 of TransAfrica, the black American lobby for Africa and the Caribbean, under the leadership of Randall Robinson, lawyer and former administrative assistant to Congressman Diggs. TransAfrica in 1980 had about 10,000 members broadly representative of informed black opinion on Africa. The membership of the group embraces elected officials, academic and professional specialists on Africa, religious leaders, and knowledgeable and interested observers of African and Caribbean developments. The lobby has found the House Subcommittee on Africa its most responsive pressure point in the policymaking process and can use its congressional coordinators around the country to deliver 250 letters or telegrams to any legislator, the secretary of state, or the president within twenty-four hours.[22] By late 1980 Robinson had had several meetings with the president and the secretary of state and regularly conferred with the assistant secretary of state for African affairs and relevant others in the State Department and on the National Security Council. TransAfrica can claim some credit for the firmness of the Carter administration on sanctions against Rhodesia in 1979–1980, particularly in light of intense counter-pressure from conservative legislators to lift sanctions as early as summer 1979. Robinson and a small number of other black leaders, including representatives from the NAACP, the Opportunities Industrialization Corporation, and the National Urban League, met with President Carter in November 1979. According to Robinson:

> In our meeting with Carter, he said unequivocally that the sanctions wouldn't be lifted at the point that the British governor arrives in Salisbury. He said to us clearly that the sanctions would extend up until the time of the elections or the beginning of the electoral process. We take him in good faith and quite seriously on that point.[23]

Nevertheless the fact that the State Department was planning a major public conference on Africa as recently as March 1980, which was postponed under pressure from TransAfrica and other black groups, without significant contributions by blacks, suggested that there still remained much work to be done to make black Americans a major voice in U.S. African policy.[24]

There were at least two other signs of expanded activity within the black constituency for southern Africa in the 1970s and in 1980. The first was the renewed emphasis on African issues indicated by the NAACP's Task Force on Africa, which was charged by its board of directors in 1976 "to study and develop a meaningful and lasting policy on Africa for the guidance of [our] members and the nation." During the period of its work from October 1976 until June 1977, the committee subdivided into teams and visited all regions of Africa. It produced a 500-page report with forty-two recommendations, including the establishment of a structure at the national level that would be responsible for African affairs and the creation of the Committee on International Affairs on the board of directors. The report also made a host of recommendations regarding South Africa, including the imposition of economic sanctions and endorsement of corporate disinvestment. Testifying before the Subcommittee on International Economic Policy and Trade of the House Subcommittee on Africa in support of three bills concerning unfair employment practices, tax credits, and prohibitions of investment by American Corporations operating in South Africa (one of the bills, sponsored by Congressman Diggs to gradual disinvestment), Broadus N. Butler, chairman of the NAACP's new Committee on International Affairs, reiterated strongly the organization's commitment to disinvestment, a commitment that had been modified after Roy Wilkins's return from a journey to South Africa in 1972 to render it less confrontational. This renewed commitment and strong advocacy of other forms of economic sanctions against South Africa were influenced in part by conversations that the task force team held with then South African Prime Minister Vorster and Foreign Minister Botha and Botha's deputy.[25]

The second noteworthy development was the summit conference of black religious leaders in April 1979 joining in an International Freedom Mobilization against Apartheid in New York.[26] Religious leaders from thirty-eight states and fifty-two cities rejected the gradualism of the Sullivan principles, demanded immediate economic disengagement of U.S. corporations from South Africa, and passed a resolution declaring "its unequivocal support of the national liberation struggle waged by the South African people under the leadership of the African National Congress." Reverend Wyatt Tee Walker, secretary-general of the International Freedom Mobilization and pastor of the Canaan Baptist Church in Harlem, observed, before setting forth his list of concrete actions to be taken around the country at the local level, that

> two things are necessary to keep in mind: first, the apartheid system is in a state of profound crisis resulting from international pressure and the militancy of the liberation movement in South Africa; and, second, the Black Church, at this moment in history, has the challenge and the opportunity to bring the Afro-American community into the struggle as a *visible* force in the national and world anti-apartheid movement. The irony is, we are not *now* a visible force in that movement and a major objective of the network we are building is to correct that reality.[27]

In another major address, Reverend William A. Jones, Jr., president of the 650,000-member Progressive National Baptist Convention and pastor of Bethany Baptist Church in Brooklyn, spoke on "A Theological Basis for Armed Struggle," in which he concluded:

> The question in South Africa is essentially one of self-defense against a systemic violence that is pervasive and unceasing. Genocide, on a massive scale, is being practiced in South Africa. To be non-violent in the context of genocide is to affirm violence and is tantamount to alliance with the adversary. To resist, by whatever means necessary, is the only sane and spiritual response of one who calls himself a Christian. Non-cooperation with evil is righteous and redemptive. The task of darker peoples the world around is to tune in to God's judgment already in process against that wicked and nefarious system.[28]

Reverend Jesse Jackson of Operation PUSH advocated that black ministers speak to their congregations about Africa every Sunday, that political and economic pressure be brought against U.S. opponents of African freedom, that public opinion be mobilized against South Africa's participation in sports events, that bond drives be started in the black community to raise money for Africa, and that black ministers work to halt the sale of the Krugerrand in their communities.

Conclusion: Toward a More Unified Black Constituency

As the Carnegie Endowment report, *Public Opinion Poll on American Attitudes toward South Africa,* concluded: "The potential black constituency for U.S. policy toward South Africa is not a figment of the imagination of black leaders; the basic concern and interest is there whether or not it has been realized."[29] The challenge that faces the leadership of this constituency is the extent to which it can influence American policy without itself becoming an instrument of policy with which it may disagree, as happened during the 1940s and 1950s. (In fact, avoidance of the risk of co-optation is one of the reasons that activist nationalist and Marxist black groups eschew attempts directly to influence the foreign policy of the United States, preferring mass organizing and education.) Hence the need for unity on at least some important basic issues is pressing.

This need is particularly crucial now, for South Africa finds itself in an even more precarious international position than it was in the 1960s when it adopted an "outward-looking" policy and tried to establish dialogue with individual African states in the wake of what for it was the frightening, and frighteningly rapid, process of decolonialization. This new policy achieved a measure of success as Ghana under the late K.A. Busia, the Ivory Coast, Malawi, and other African countries began to argue that the policies of the Organization of African Unity (OAU) in support of confrontation by the liberation movements had been ineffective, and that other methods (such as a dialogue with South Africa) might be more useful. Not only was some hostility diverted from South Africa for a time, but disunity and irresolution were sown thereby among black African nations.

There exists relatively greater harmony of interests regarding South Africa among black Americans than among white Americans. What dissension does exist in the black community, moreover, does not arise, as it does among white Americans, in any immediate sense from concrete politico-economic stakes in South Africa but more from organizational, ideological, or career imperatives, which may be more easily moved toward consensus. The creation of a more unified and informed black constituency for South Africa clearly is not solely under the control of black Americans themselves. It is greatly influenced by developments in South Africa and political conditions in the United States. While prediction is always risky, several speculations are in order.

Either the outbreak of sustained guerrilla actions or sabotage by blacks against the South African government, or a striking increase in repression by the government against South African blacks probably would trigger a dramatic increase in the salience of South African issues among all segments of black America. Both Sharpeville in the 1960s and Soweto in the 1970s stood as cynosures for notable increased attention to and interest in South African affairs by black Americans. At one level of commitment, new groups would probably form to channel material aid to South African blacks. At another level of engagement, campaigns for divestiture (the selling of stocks or divesting of other interests in companies that do business in South Africa) and disinvestment (the cessation of all business operations in or with South Africa) would become much more prominent, more effective as vehicles for mobilization, and enjoy wider support. Moderate proposals from established black civil-rights organizations, which had been ignored in the past, would not be nearly as common but would be given more attentive hearings by political authorities. Particular concern would be expressed to prevent the United States from rendering any kind of support to the Afrikaner regime, and indeed some pressure would likely be exerted to have the United States render assistance to the rebels. The outbreak of violence would tend to foster social pressures to constrict the range of opinions publicly expressed by black Americans. Important in this process would be the attempt, in a spirit of unity, to follow the cues provided by rebelling black South Africans and by such influential and passionately interested countries as Nigeria and the front-line black states. Such a probable closing of black ranks would mean that the rhythm of any expressed plurality of views among black Americans would be very much determined by the rhythm of war; second thoughts expressed among black South Africans occasioned (for example) by devastating losses would probably find their counterpart echoed among some segments of black America.

On the other hand, the gradual dismantling of apartheid in such a manner as to prevent the escalation of violence to levels deemed intolerable by Afrikaners probably would result in a greater pluralism of opinion among black Americans. In this apparently unlikely case, black Americans would endeavor to persuade the U.S. government to pressure authorities in Pretoria for more rapid change, but the widespread interest and mobilization that would accompany the outbreak of violence would probably not occur. The black community would speak with voices probably more differentiated than at present as new interests emerged around divergent preferences for the new social order in South Africa, an issue of manifestly secondary importance in the throes of war. In such a scenario, many more American black elites and professionals would be available for recruitment by governmental and private agencies intent on shaping the emerging order in South Africa.

Domestic political conditions set the immediate boundaries of the context in which black Americans form their reactions and opinions. What has been touted as a rising tide of conservatism has achieved its apotheosis with the election of President Ronald Reagan and a notably conservative Congress. The kind of access and indeed rapport that TransAfrica enjoyed in the State Department under President Carter may very well not be repeated in the Reagan administration. Although there will still be some avenues open on Capitol Hill, the perception by blacks that opportunities for political access, influence, and leadership on South African affairs will be markedly limited may tend to decrease the range of acceptable opinion among black Americans. So, too, might the weakening of the liberal alliance of blacks, Jews, and labor. With Jews ideologically immobilized over South Africa and embittered over clashes with blacks about affirmative action, the Middle East, and quotas, and with labor not having made South Africa a priority, black Americans may find themselves almost isolated (possibly along with liberal church elites) as the most important constituency for the liberation of South Africa. But that relative isolation also means not having to make compromises that coalition politics made necessary, as, for instance, during the civil-rights struggle.

Beyond the issue of the effect that lessened political access and erosion of the liberal alliance have on the unification of the black constituency for South Africa is the larger question of the meaning of the empowerment of a conservative legislature and executive for black interest in southern African affairs. Will the attempts to roll back the gains made by black Americans over the past two decades lead to their exclusive preoccupation with domestic politics? This is difficult to assess. The late 1940s offers one alternative answer, although the principal concern of black Americans then was to extend and protect newly won rights. But the 1960s suggests another answer, when concern and involvement with colonial struggles were viewed as another and necessary dimension of the civil-rights struggle. It could develop in the 1980s that defense of the civil-rights gains of the past would coincide with and reinforce identification and commitment to the struggles of black South Africans. The developing support structure (for example, organizations like TransAfrica) for African affairs would then become very important.

The question of the development of a unified black constituency is complex, and there are a number of important dimensions that I have not mentioned, such as the internal politics of the black community and the content and extent of that unity on fundamentals. But it is a very timely question. With profound changes having occurred in the subcontinent during the 1970s and 1980, South Africa will make superficial changes and use every arena to deflect attention from the fundamentals of apartheid. Black Americans are an important constituency, and any black disunity, disagreement over tactics, and irresolution over goals and objectives will surely be exploited by the South African government and its allies in the United States.

Notes

1. The analysis that follows is greatly influenced by James Roark, "Black American Leaders: The Response to Colonialism and the Cold War, 1943–1953," *African Historical Studies* 2 (1971):253–270.

2. Ibid., p. 266.

3. Ibid., p. 268.

4. Ibid., p. 269.

5. W.E.B. Du Bois, "The American Negro Intelligentsia, in *Apropos of Africa,* ed. Adelaide Cromwell Hill and Martin Kilson (London: Frank Cass & Co., 1969), p. 320.

6. Francis A. Kornegay, Jr., "Black Americans and U.S.-Southern Africa Relations," in *American-Southern Africa Relations: Bibliographic Essays,* ed. Mohamed A. El-Khawas and Francis A. Kornegay, Jr. (Westport, Conn.: Greenwood Press, 1975), p. 144.

7. Curtner Mokapele, *Crisis and Change* (December 1966), quoted in ibid., p. 151.

8. William Payne, "U.S. Negroes Discuss Africa," *Africa Report* (December 1962):14.

9. American Negro Leadership Conference on Africa, *Resolutions* of the Second National Conference of the ANLCA, September 24–27, 1964, Shoreham Hotel, Washington, D.C.

10. *New York Times,* September 26, 1964.

11. Locksley Edmonson, "The Challenge of Race: From Entrenched White Power to Rising Black Power," *International Journal* 24 (Autumn 1969):709.

12. Quoted by Jammie L. Hoagland, *South Africa: Civilizations in Conflict* (Boston: Houghton Mifflin, 1972), p. 354. Also see the account by George Shepherd, *Anti-Apartheid: Transnational Conflict and Western Policy in the Liberation of South Africa* (Westport, Conn.: Greenwood Press, 1977), pp. 159–161.

13. Hoagland, *South Africa,* p. 358.

14. Shepherd, *Anti-Apartheid,* p. 160.

15. Kornegay, "Black Americans," p. 155.

16. See Inez Smith Reid and Ronald Walters, eds., *From Gammon to Howard: Proceedings of the African-American National Conference on Africa, May 25–26, 1972, Howard University* (Washington, D.C., n.d.)

17. Bruce Oudes, "The African Liberation Day March," *Africa Report* (June 1972):13.

18. Kornegay, "Black Americans," pp. 159–160.

19. "The Sixth Pan African Congress: A Historical Sketch," *Black World* (March 1975):15.

20. *Congressional Quarterly Almanac* (Washington, D.C.: Congressional Quarterly, 1976), p. 871.

21. Congressional Black Caucus, "The African-American Manifesto on Southern Africa," *Freedomways* 16 (1976):216–221.

22. Michael Shuster, "Advocates for Africa on Capitol Hill," *Southern Africa* (January 1980):5.

23. Ibid., p. 4.

24. *Washington Post,* March 8, 1980.

25. Broadus N. Butler, Statement to the House International Relations Committee, Subcommittee on International Economic Policy and Trade of the Subcommittee on Africa, September 7, 1978, p. 4.

26. See Simon Anekwe's front-page story, "Sullivan Plan Rejected," *New York Amsterdam News,* April 28, 1979.

27. "Where Do We Go from Here" (speech to the Summit Conference of Black Religious Leaders on Apartheid, New York City, April 19, 1979), p. 9.

28. "A Theological Basis for Armed Struggle" (speech to the Summit Conference of Black Religious Leaders on Apartheid, New York City, April 18, 1979), p. 12.

29. James E. Baker, J. Daniel O'Flaherty, and John de St. Jorre, *Full Report: Public Opinion Poll of American Attitudes toward South Africa* (New York: Carnegie Endowment for International Peace, 1979), p. 41.

7 U.S. Religious Institutions and South Africa

Paul Deats

Religion is a major component of all cultures. Even so, religious loyalties in both South Africa and the United States seem to be more than usually important, and religious beliefs and involvement in religious institutions permeate both cultures. Religious institutions play a central role in both societies—sometimes as conservative influences, increasingly as forces for change, or, at least, as communities in which the forces of conservatism and change confront one another in a unique way.

There is a remarkable consensus among church leaders for change in South Africa; it is considered necessary and believed to be occurring to at least some degree. Nevertheless there are certain differences of opinion among American religious leaders:

1. There is disagreement about the pace of change in South Africa—how rapidly it is occurring and how rapidly it should or must occur.
2. There is disagreement concerning the kinds of changes, the scope of those changes taking place, the changes that need to take place in South Africa, and the appropriate priorities that should be assigned. Some American church leaders agree with the argument of some South African whites that economic growth will probably, if not inevitably, improve the education and employment of blacks and their power as consumers. Others interpret such developments as benefiting primarily black elites with little likely benefit for the black majority. The second group, who have become increasingly influential in the churches, argue that the crucial change must be in the system, the political structure, with majority rule in a single South Africa precluding separate development and any homelands policy.
3. There are different perceptions of South Africa in American churches.

I acknowledge gratefully the able research assistance of L. Frederick Allen, a Ph.D. candidate in social ethics at Boston University, and the assistance of Kelly Coleman. Both were funded in part by Boston University. Mr. Allen reviewed documents, conducted interviews in Boston, New York City, and Washington, D.C., and wrote early drafts of several sections. The use of "we" in the chapter indicates shared responsibility for interpretation.

Some South Africans ask searchingly if their country is seen as "beyond the pale and such a moral outrage" that U.S. churches will permit or encourage increased suffering, even a total collapse, to achieve a more egalitarian South African system. Some American church leaders respond by asking whether South African whites will destroy their society in their attempts to save it.

4. There is no consensus in American churches whether the main forces for essential change are within South Africa or outside, or whether U.S. churches, corporations, other private institutions, and government can individually or together bring about constructive change.

5. There is more question than disagreement whether churches in either country have the will or the leverage to influence significantly either corporate or government policy and behavior.

The Churches and U.S. Public Opinion

Attitudinal differences among American Catholic, Protestant, and Jewish religious constituencies regarding South Africa and U.S. policy with respect to it are minor to insignificant.[1] Black Protestants generally are more liberal in their views on South Africa than are whites of any religious preferences. There is no indication that frequency of church going or other indications of strength of religious identification, however measured, have any recognized or acknowledged influence on views held about South Africa.

U.S. respondents to various surveys as individuals share common views, regardless of their professed religious identification. A majority, for example, believe that the system of apartheid in South Africa is morally unjustified. One report suggests "a profound dislike of the present system . . . , a general feeling that the United States should do something, and a strong reluctance to get directly involved." There is a tendency among all religious groups to approve of specific actions that seem to be risk free (such as a boycott of military supplies to South Africa), with greater support for verbal denunciation and decreased trade than for more direct pressure. There seems to be general opposition to any U.S. military involvement or to U.S. actions that seek directly to overthrow the government of South Africa. Many in all major religious groups feel the United States has no right to interfere in the internal affairs of South Africa, a belief in conflict with an emerging consensus in pronouncements and policies of their respective churches. Several interviews provide support for the analysis that suggests that "racial violence in South Africa would trigger disturbances at home, particularly if the U.S. were involved with the white government."[2]

Distinctive Factors Relating to U.S. Churches and South Africa

A conclusion drawn in one analysis makes any distinctive factors related to the churches particularly important for our study. The authors of a 1977 Harris poll suggest that such findings, though accurate, are incomplete because "the consensus is weak, volatile, and readily subject to change."[3] When this situation prevails in public opinion generally, and in church constituencies in particular, the influence of leadership in the future direction of that opinion will be decisive. Several factors make the role of church leaders and of churches as institutions strategic.

Important institutional and personal ties exist between many leaders of U.S. religious institutions and their counterparts in South Africa. Moreover these seem to be growing in salience and number, despite restrictions. Such is the case of South African churches with numerous black and coloured memberships, and especially (but not exclusively) the Roman Catholic Church. Many American churches have a century or more of missionary involvement in southern Africa, such as Lutherans to Namibia and Methodists to Zimbabwe. The U.S. Catholic Conference invited the Peace Commission from Rhodesia to the United States for consultation in the late 1970s. Some leaders foresee that if and as the settlement becomes more stable in Zimbabwe, there is likely to be, and should be, a shift of focus by American churches to South Africa. Church ties mean sensitivity and openness, which means potentially growing influence by South African developments on memberships of U.S. churches, and vice-versa. Such is likely to occur not only among denominational bodies such as the Episcopal (Anglican) Churches but also among ecumenical institutions, such as the National Council of Churches in the United States (NCC), the South African Council of Churches, and the World Council of Churches (WCC). The churches are international institutions transcending national boundaries and open to frank, ongoing communication in matters of common concern in ways that are not as easy for most other institutions or the two national governments.

There also prevails a latent moral sensitivity in the churches that can be aroused and instructed by leaders of U.S. and South African churches. Consider a few illustrations. The Reverend Leon Sullivan came into church and public awareness a decade ago as one of the first public (and probably the first black) member of a major corporate board of directors, that of General Motors. His concern with racism and corporate responsibility led him to the formulation of the Sullivan principles after a 1975 visit to Johannesburg during which he was urged to try to make U.S. corporations agents for change in South Africa. His six points included nonsegregation in eating, comfort, and work facilities; equal pay; fair employment practices for all; training programs that move blacks and other nonwhites into management and supervisory positions; and improving employees' lives outside the work place.[4] Only as many church bodies came to press corporations to adopt and implement these principles did other leaders in both countries come to see them as too little and too late.

An active white South African churchman, Alan Paton, has also done much to prick the consciences of American church leaders and members with his novels. More recently his views have been called into question by some churchleaders as those of a "white liberal." Still more recently, Paton has urged Americans to listen to black voices:

> If prolonged and increasingly bitter conflict is to be avoided, a conflict that will draw in active participants from the wider African and world scene, the voices of black South Africans must be listened to. A groundswell of black political opinion is asserting that the issue is not a matter of marginal, incremental changes within the apartheid system. Rather there must be fundamental change—a matter of black political power *and* the restructuring of the economy, for example, land redistribution.[5]

The important notes here are not primarily the substance of Paton's judgment but that he urges attention to black voices and that he writes in the leading liberal lay Catholic periodical *Commonweal.* Articles with similar messages have appeared in such diverse nondenominational but religiously oriented magazines of significant influence as *Worldview, Christianity and Crisis,* and *Sojourners.*[6]

It is not always easy to get a clear message or a single message from black leaders in South Africa. American church leaders argue that this difficulty is at least partly due to severe governmental restrictions about what South Africans may say about divestment and other controversial issues without danger of prosecution or banning. They also understand that this phenomenon is also partly due to disagreement among black leaders. U.S. church leaders who wish to be responsive to their counterparts in South Africa have had to learn to distinguish among the counsels given by such black leaders as Chief Gatsha Buthelezi, Bishop Desmond Tutu, Dr. Nthato Motlana, and the Reverend Allan A. Boesak. Many have learned from their disappointing experience with Bishop Abel Muzorewa that they can take no single voice without critical inquiry; they thought he spoke for his people, but he was overwhelmingly defeated in the 1980 elections. They have also learned to interpret various statements in contexts of informal private conversations and other indicators. Sometimes unspoken or affective messages are accorded higher priority than spoken or other more direct ones. For example, many American church elites have come to trust Bishop Tutu as a moderate and responsible spokesperson for such a representative group as the South Africa Council of Churches. When Bishop Tutu's passport was withdrawn in March 1980, the government of South Africa gave new emphasis to the bishop's message, further reinforced when he and his wife received prison sentences, albeit brief ones.

Communication is made even more problematic by restrictions on who may enter and leave South Africa. One prominent black leader in a predominantly white church, a top ecumenical officer charged with African affairs, asked South African visitors in 1980 why such dialogue could not take place in Johannesburg rather than New York. Almost all other black church leaders in that discussion had been denied visas to visit South Africa, some repeatedly. Also many black leaders in South Africa who seem to be moderates by U.S. standards cannot leave their country on terms which they can in conscience accept.

The role and voice of black caucuses regarding South Africa have also grown considerably in predominantly white U.S. churches. So has communication on South Africa by important and articulate leaderships in black churches themselves. One influential black official has noted that U.S. black church leaders first responded to southern Africa largely as Americans but that more and more they have responded primarily as blacks. They form a sensitive and increasingly influential pressure point within U.S. churches on issues related to South Africa.

Black preachers in local predominantly black congregations probably have more influence on U.S. black thinking about and concern with South Africa than any other force. Understandably preoccupied with domestic issues, these preachers nevertheless responded with passion to newsworthy events such as Sharpeville in 1960, Soweto in 1976, the death of Steven Biko in 1977, and South African's black and colored protests in 1980. Probably the most significant single illustration of this mounting concern and articulate expression was in the Summit Conference of Black Religious Leaders in April 1979, at which the Reverend M. William Howard, president of the NCC and a black, was a major speaker.[7]

On South Africa, as on other ethical issues, black churches concentrate on eloquent preaching rather than on written resolutions. Moreover, some predominantly black denominations have sister churches in the same denomination in southern Africa with whom they are in rapport. They do not want to get their black sisters and brothers into trouble by their statements in this country. This makes the resolution supporting the struggle for liberation in southern Africa passed by the predominantly black Progressive National Baptist Convention even more newsworthy.

South Africa poses a deep theological issue for the churches. Charles Villa-Vicencio writes for a number of others who have come to realize that in South Africa the theology of apartheid provides a rationale for the system.[8] What he calls a "synthesis of white nationalism and neo-Calvinist theology" provides a fundamental theological challenge, making the responsibility of the churches crucial.

There are other pertinent aspects. One black South African church leader wrote in an unpublished manuscript in 1977 that "most of the support from overseas against apartheid is from, though not exclusively, the churches and their institutions." He criticizes the weakness of this support. The July 1979 South African Christian Leadership Assembly expressed a new note, the responsibility of whites for change in that country, introduced by Professor Ronald Sider, an influential evangelical leader in the United States.[9] Thus there has been an expansion of normal conciliar ecumenical range and potency of the churches' concern with South Africa beyond the Roman Catholic and main-line Protestant denominations of liberal or even moderate theological orientation.

U.S. Church Involvement in South African Issues

There has been more than a century of U.S. missionary activity in southern Africa. Missionary efforts have transmitted the Bible and the gospel message. Churches, schools, and hospitals have been built. Churches with black memberships have developed in many African countries. The struggle for these churches to be autonomous in relation to the sending churches, however, has often been difficult. Even missionaries with a strong sense of the political relevance of the gospel seemed to have an inhibiting sense that they were guests of the existing government and therefore did not wish to risk the continuation of the enterprises or to expose Africans to retaliatory measures. A significant turning point for some churches came in the Portuguese colony of Angola in the revolution of 1961 when missionaries were imprisoned or expelled when they identified with their black parishioners' cause.

The issue of racism has been the continuing central focus of American religious concerns about southern Africa and specifically South Africa. During World War II more Americans became aware of race as a problem, first with the explicitly racist threats of nazism and fascism, and then the awareness that the United States had not solved its own problems during and after the Civil War but rather had followed the ending of slavery with the institution of Jim Crow segregation. Publication of Gunnar Myrdal's *The American Dilemma* in 1944 contributed to a process of consciousness raising and self-criticism, which found expression in a number of institutional challenges. The civil-rights movement of the 1950s, with court battles and demonstrations as well, and the more intense black power and black liberation movements of the 1960s heightened U.S. awareness of its own racism. Although there has been progress, legal victories and legislative achievements have not solved racism in the United States.

In the process of the changes Americans have made concerning race, many in the churches, and especially in the black churches, have come to view South Africa as important symbolically "as the citadel of racism."[10] The ways in which South Africa mirrors and/or distorts our own problems make it "a challenge to America's moral character and its commitment to the principle of racial equality." There is thus a strong symbolic identification with efforts to end apartheid even when there is considerable disagreement over the means to be used in that struggle.

Racism is not just a domestic concern with spillover elsewhere. Insofar as the churches have been part of the developing ecumenical dialogue, they have been aware of racism as a world issue for a longer time. In 1925 the Native Administration Act and the Immorality Acts in South Africa were passed. Also in 1925 the first event in the modern ecumenical movement occurred. The Stockholm Universal Christian Conference on Life and Work reported:

> The modern ascendancy of the white races throughout the world is overwhelming. So often have they used their power for selfish ends and ruthless exploitation of weak and backward [sic] peoples that an ominous tide of indignation, unrest and resentment is arising among all other races.[11]

The development of an ecumenical consensus has been a slow achievement, first in its articulation and then even more in its penetration into the thinking and institutional life of American churches. Not until 1954 was school desegregation declared unconstitutional by the U.S. Supreme Court. Also in that year the Second Assembly of the WCC was held in Evanston, Illinois, readily accessible to U.S. participation and media coverage, especially by American church organs. That assembly declared "its conviction that any form of segregation based on race, colour or ethnic origin is contrary to the Gospel and is incompatible with the nature of the Church of Christ." The assembly urged all "churches within its membership to renounce all forms of segregation or discrimination and to work for their abolition within their own life and within society."[12]

The 1964 Mindolo consultation, the first sponsored by the WCC on racism in southern Africa, noted the increasing gravity of the situation there and observed that for many Christians "the question of possible violence as the only remaining alternative has become an urgent and ever-pressing one."[13]

The developing consensus was brought to a sharp focus in continuing vigorous debate with the establishment by the WCC's Program to Combat Racism and the creation of a special fund for that purpose (1968–1970). In 1972 the issue became investments in South Africa. The WCC published a pamphlet, *Time to Withdraw,* and this call, plus the ensuing series of consultations on "Violence, Nonviolence, and the Struggle for Social Justice," helped bring some debates nearer to center stage in churches in the United States. Probably the most central concept formulated in this series of consultations has been that of systematic or institutional violence. This concept poses for U.S. churches the dilemma of implicitly supporting the violence involved in any existing racist order or government or of supporting the violence threatened or exercised by revolutionary or liberation movements. This dilemma does not make ethical judgments easier. On the contrary, it puts the burden of proof upon those who have thought in the past they were uninvolved or uncommitted.

These two streams of awareness of racism and of ecumenical concern with racism are part of the legacy of the churches in the United States, a legacy of which many are as yet unaware and to which there are vigorously different responses. The legacy and the dilemmas posed, however, have been difficult to avoid in the face of a succession of events in South Africa that have demanded a response from churches: Sharpeville in 1960, Soweto a decade and half later, the banning of newspapers and the Christian Institute, the banning of well-known figures such as Byers Naudé, and the death of Steve Biko. These events have been given prominent media coverage in the United States where public opinion seems to require a crisis for attention to focus on an issue such as racism, whether it is at home or abroad.

Probably the main channel of the churches' involvement has been that of corporate responsibility. Desaix Myers III credits churches as "among the first to raise social concerns before corporations in which they held stock."[14] The Interfaith Center on Corporate Responsibility (ICCR) came into existence as a joint Catholic-Protestant agency under the NCC both as a symbol of this concern and as an institutional means of taking common action on a cluster of issues with which churches came to deal in the 1960s. The ICCR in 1971 published a document, *Corporate Responsibility and Religious Institutions,* which focused on efforts to end the Vietnam war, to continue the gains of the stalled civil-rights movement in the United States, and to deal with related issues of fair employment and equal opportunity (for women as well as ethnic minorities). The agenda of corporate responsibility has expanded over the ensuing decade to include nuclear-weapons production and proliferation, labor policies of the American textile chain of J.P. Stevens Company, nuclear power development, disposal of hazardous nuclear wastes, and infant nutrition.

A significant early component of the concern for corporate responsibility focused on the role of U.S. business in southern Africa. Howard Schomer has written:

> The awakening churches began to ask themselves (as shareholders in U.S. companies doing business in Southern Africa) if they were indeed partners in apartheid and colonialism. . . . Indeed it was possible that more church dollars were involved in Angola and South Africa through business corporations each year than through the modest grants that the American denominations made to help the churches, schools, and hospitals of their oppressed Christian friends in those lands.[15]

The first shareholder resolution filed by a church investor, in 1971, was by the Protestant Episcopal Church asking General Motors to cease operations in South Africa. Members of ICCR now include representatives of 14 Protestant denominations and more than 150 Catholic communities.

Developing Positions in U.S. Churches: Corporate Responsibility

During the late 1960s churches became concerned about the role played by foreign investment in supporting white minority governments and began to press for ways in which they could influence meaningful social change. Some of the early church resolutions dealt with economic sanctions by the United Nations, but these efforts proved ineffective. It was the bank campaign that first developed enthusiastic support in the mid–1960s with seminary protests, as they became aware that ten U.S. banks had a floating credit arrangement of up to $40 million with the South African government. Several religious institutions had accounts in these banks. The campaign began with meetings between church leaders and bank officials, after which came public statements, resolutions, and finally publicized withdrawal of accounts held by church groups in those banks. After achieving some success with the banks, the churches turned their attention to other corporations doing business in South Africa, primarily by filing stockholder resolutions. Church groups renewed protests in 1973 following a WCC move to divest and withdraw funds.

Many of the first resolutions pressed corporations to withdraw from South Africa, but these were so roundly defeated that they could not be resubmitted.[16] (The Securities and Exchange Commission has a rule requiring 3 percent stockholder support for resubmission at the next stockholders' meeting.) Then came resolutions requesting that corporations establish review committees to evaluate the impact of their presence on apartheid and to disclose this and other information (such as the extent of business in South Africa) to stockholders. A third stage in the development came with resolutions that required corporate articulation of a policy on doing business in South Africa and/or subscribing to the Sullivan principles. Further efforts pushed this line to request firm adherence to these principles and to evaluate their effect, with some external monitoring by the consulting firm Arthur D. Little. A new set of church demands urged that corporations not expand operations or make new investments. Finally came a stage which required that if a corporation did not comply with the Sullivan principles, it should initiate efforts to disengage or withdraw, with recognition that this was not an easy or simple process.

Other themes were evident. Specific corporations were asked not to continue to provide products (such as photographic devices and computers) that were understood to be useful in police and military operations that might be applied to blacks. Fact-finding trips to South Africa were conducted to acquire firsthand knowledge of working and housing conditions and to consult with black leaders. Many church leaders became more sophisticated about the structural depth and complex manifestations of racism in South Africa, the problematic impact of what came to be seen as superficial reforms, and the prudence of companies' reducing operations in South Africa because of its instability. In recent years there has been a much-publicized campaign for divestment, urging institutions, especially universities, to divest themselves of stock in any corporation doing business in South Africa. Since most churches had faced this option earlier, there was considerable resistance to the campaign, which was imprecise in the interchangeable use of *divestment* and *withdrawal.* Leaders were aware that divestment was a one-time effort, relinquishing responsibility for further influence on a corporation, and should be a selective approach to be used when corporations continued to be unresponsive to stockholder resolutions.

Finally there was a realization that the real intent of the campaign was symbolic: to focus attention upon the necessity of change in South Africa. Desaix Myers III concludes that "there is no strong consensus among institutional investors in favor of disinvestment," except as a last resort or as a threat. The arguments favoring divestment stress that "the presence of American corporations in South Africa gives moral legitimacy to the white minority regime and . . . creates a vested American interest in the status quo and the stability of the existing political system."[17] Some urge further that churches (and universities) should not receive funds derived from operations in South Africa.

About the time that many corporations were being persuaded to accept the Sullivan principles, some institutional investors, especially educational and religious groups, came to question the effectiveness of these principles in changing conditions for the masses in South Africa. Some doubted whether the principles benefited more than the urban elites among the blacks. This questioning came to a focus when the Reverend M. William Howard, president of the NCC, addressed the Summit Conference of Black Religious Leaders on Apartheid on April 18, 1979. Howard expressed appreciation to Sullivan for raising the consciousness of citizens and corporations, but his address was entitled "Beyond the Sullivan Six Principles." The Howard principles involved:

1. A commitment to no expansion and no new investment in South Africa.
2. No new bank loans to South Africa. (Loans to government, parastatal agencies, and private concerns were included.)

3. No sales to the police or military.
4. No investment inside or on the border areas of Bantustans.
5. An end to trade in strategic fields with South Africa. (These included aircraft, machinery, and computers.)
6. A commitment by U.S. investors to withdraw operations from South Africa unless and until the white supremacist government abandons its apartheid policy and implements steps to provide full political, economic, and social rights for the black majority.[18]

It is too soon to evaluate the acceptance of these principles either by churches or by corporations, except that the sixth principle found expression in a number of 1980 stockholder resolutions. Most of these principles had already been embodied in one or more resolutions earlier. However, it is important to be aware of the symbolic and strategic importance of Howards' challenge as the second black church leader to become president of the NCC and of the emerging consensus that has been articulated in the Council.

In 1980 several stockholder resolutions urged corporations to review operations in South Africa and report to shareholders. Some, such as one addressed to the Caterpillar Tractor Company, focused on the effects of its continued presence in South Africa, including one resolution supported by the American Baptists. A larger number of review, evaluation, and report resolutions were addressed to General Motors Corporation and Ford Motor Company, with a focus on vehicles sold to the South African police and military. Still other resolutions directed corporations (IBM and Sperry Rand, among others) not to sell computers or other products useful to police and military activities, whether for police control or for defense purposes. Statements supporting these resolutions were adopted by the Protestant Episcopal Church, American Baptists, Reformed Church in America, United Church of Christ, United Methodist Church, United Presbyterian Church U.S.A., and several Roman Catholic orders.[19]

There has been a continuing church concern with banks' making loans to the South African government or its agencies, supported by Lutherans, American Baptists, the United Church of Christ, Methodists, and the Church of the Brethren. In related moves, the sale of Krugerrands in the United States was opposed by a number of church groups, including Roman Catholic orders.

Some resolutions continued to urge corporations to adopt the Sullivan principles (Lutherans, Methodists, Union of American Hebrew Congregations), but others focused on pressuring corporations to adhere to or evaluate the effect of these principles. These were addressed particularly to high-technology manufacturers. And several resolutions urged "no expansion—no further investment." They included the U.S. Catholic Conference, Episcopalians, American Baptists, Presbyterians (U.S.A.), and a number of Roman Catholic orders.

Three relatively new developments transpired in 1979 and 1980. One was the insertion of an "unless-or-until" clause in resolutions pertaining to loans, expansion, and other concerns. One resolution fairly typical of those addressed by church investors to banks and oil companies used this language:

> . . . unless or until the system of racist laws and regulations has been revoked and meaningful steps have been taken in the direction of majority rule, including full political, economic, and social rights for the black population.[20]

A second development involved a deadline for compliance with the Sullivan principles by company affiliates. In resolutions addressed to Phillips Petroleum, Dresser, Schlumberger, and U.S. Steel, that deadline was the end of 1981, urging that if there is not compliance, "the corporation shall take whatever steps are necessary to dispose promptly of its ownership interest in its South African affiliate."

A third development has been the adoption of a policy on international investment and human rights as part of a general statement of investment policy for the United Methodist Church by its General Council of Finance and Administration in 1978. The policy statement is directed to general agencies of that church and to local churches and individual church members. Its application to South Africa is explicit:

> Specific reference must be made to the abhorrent system of apartheid as it exists and as it is practiced in the Republic of South Africa. Investments of any unit of the United Methodist Church must be carefully examined with respect to the possible involvement in any business entity whose operations are supportive of apartheid. Agencies . . . should not do business with nor invest in banks which have banking operations in or make loans to the Republic of South Africa, nor should they do business with or invest in banks which make loans to parastatal (government-owned) corporations of the Republic of South Africa.[21]

This policy moves activity regarding South Africa from agencies of mission and social justice to include those dealing with the administration and business affairs of the churches. Expressive of this change is a resolution filed with Ingersoll Rand Company, on behalf of the Board of Pensions of the United Methodist Church, asking affirmation of the Sullivan principles. The potential impact of this development becomes evident when one realizes that pension funds are among the largest stockholders in important multinational companies.

Church Pronouncements and Initiatives

A black Episcopal seminary professor told one group from South Africa in 1980 that the South African racial situation has galvanized the Episcopal Church into a more prophetic and militant stance than usual on most other issues. This church first realized that it could use its invested funds to achieve social ends. Then it moved to policy statements, which reflect a growing conviction that a radical change in the South African power structure is required, not the collapse of the society. He also suggested that churches with financial resources should consider how to achieve a cooperative witness on South Africa with black churches. Other churches, especially the United Church of Christ, have exercised exemplary leadership.

In many ways the NCC has taken the initiative, setting the tone of and the stage for action by other church bodies. In 1963 it adopted a position affirming its commitment to the Universal Declaration of Human Rights. In 1972 its Resolution on the Churches' Policy toward Southern Africa affirmed the principles of liberation and self-determination as applied to the "oppressed black people of Southern Africa." In 1976 the NCC Governing Board reaffirmed its commitment to majority rule and condemned the establishment of homelands "as a device by the South African government to divide in order to control." A November 1977 policy statement supported efforts to end economic and military collaboration between the United States and South Africa, supported the struggle for liberation and racial justice as well as assistance for those who suffer from the denial of human rights (refugees, political prisoners), and continued support for the withdrawal of all funds in financial institutions making investments in or loans to South African government or businesses.

It appears that the 1977 policy statement above and perhaps the position of the Reverend Howard were informed by the work of a convocation, "The Church and Southern Africa," convened by the NCC and the U.S. Catholic Conference, March 7–11, 1977. Four other items in the report of and message from that consultation are important:

1. The peculiar responsibility of the churches requires more education of church constituencies about the current South African situation.
2. The churches are urged to intensify efforts to influence the agencies of the U.S. government to support policies for change toward majority self-determination.
3. The extensive contacts with South African churches and leaders should be continued and utilized.
4. We must point out that the choice by the Black nationals to resort to armed struggle did not come as a first and easy choice."

There have been successive statements of opposition to apartheid and of support for black protest groups, beginning with the Protestant Episcopal Church in 1972 and including the Lutheran Church in America.

At least three statements have been adopted by many major Jewish religious organizations. In June 1976 the Central Conference of American Rabbis, representing Reform congregations, referred to South Africa as a "repressive police state" and found "its present constitution and mode of establishment of its government repugnant and offensive to the sensibilities of humanity." The resolution called on the U.S. government "to refrain from politically or militarily supporting the government of the Republic of South Africa and to embargo voluntarily trade between the U.S.A. and the Republic of South Africa.

In October 1976 the Synagogue Council of America, which bridges Reform, Conservative, and Orthodox Jewry, decried the "growing violence" in South Africa and found that "at the root of the violence is the degrading policy of apartheid which denies blacks the vote and subjects them to a variety of disenfranchisements and repressions." The Council expressed its admiration for both blacks and whites "who have spoken out bravely and at great personal risk in condemnation of their government's repression and injustice." The Synagogue Council also called on the U.S. government to follow a policy "that expresses clearly our repugnance of the racial policies of the governments of South Africa and Rhodesia."

The General Assembly of the Union of American Hebrew Congregations, composed of Reform Jews, in December 1979 urged the government of South Africa to "eliminate apartheid and grant full civil rights to all non-white residents." The resolution commended those who "struggle non-violently from within" for change and urged the United States "to refrain from political and military support of the government of South Africa." This resolution included a final paragraph addressed to any business investing in South Africa, essentially affirming the Sullivan principles, and it included an early "unless-and-until" clause: "If these conditions cannot be met, we urge these companies to terminate their business dealings with South Africa until apartheid itself is ended."

Evangelical churches have not been part of the corporate-responsibility initiative, nor have they addressed resolutions directly to either government. For some, as one Southern Baptist leader put it, there has been a "great silence" in his church's case, reflecting a preoccupation with racism in the life of local communities and congregations. He did venture that a new concern with South Africa may be forthcoming.

One officer of Evangelicals for Social Action interprets their posture as exercising influence opposing apartheid through vigorous nonviolent confrontation and favoring at least corporate adoption of the Sullivan principles. He adds, "If ever there were a case for a just resolution, this is it!"

Another evangelical leader called attention to the Koinonia Declaration, produced by a group of concerned South African Calvinists in November 1977. The declaration supported "equal treatment" and "equal rights" and "the abolition of all statutory and other prohibitions which impede in any way free dealings between people of different races." It concluded: "It is our conviction that the maintenance of justice rather than the maintenance of law and order and state security is the prime God-given task of the government and the governed."[22] Churches in the Reformed Ecumenical Synod have expressed sympathy with this statement and encouraged further dialogue.

The Reformed Ecumenical Synod is a world body that includes three denominations in the United States (Christian Reformed Church, Orthodox Presbyterian Church, and Reformed Presbyterian Church of North America) and eight in South Africa. The Synod has regularly addressed racism, specifically in southern Africa, since 1976. Its address is set within a continuing dialogue among churches that are in ecclesiastical relationship. Concern is first expressed through correspondence, then sending of emissaries, and finally "mutual ecclesiastical admonition." After Steve Biko's death in 1977 and the suppression of dissent, the Christian Reformed Church addressed a letter of inquiry to churches in South Africa "asking what actions they were taking against the Terrorism Act" and calling the churches "to the exercise of love and justice." The letter also praised the Koinonia Declaration, urged the churches to "heed the Testimony," and asked for response.[23]

In August 1980 the Reformed Ecumenical Synod decided to "urgently request the RES member churches in South Africa to do all in their power to work for such changes in their country that remove the structures of racial injustice still present and use their influence with the South African government to effect such changes."[24] Insofar as the theology of apartheid undergirds the present political structure, this may be a very direct method of dealing with the issue for Christian churches.

Characteristics of Church Responses

The shifting, rather amorphous quality of U.S. opinion has left the public, and especially the churches, open to influence by committed leaders. Resources for change are found in the personal and institutional contacts between church leaders in the United States and in South Africa, the at least latent moral sensitivity of church constituencies, the influence of black caucuses, and crucial issues of theology. But the general consensus regarding a commitment to demand change in South Africa does not yet include agreement on effective means of moving toward that change.

Church people, including most of their leaders, typically are reluctant to approve in advance resort to violence. Whether because of theological or ethical reasons or due to personality characteristics or cultural conditioning, we prefer orderly, evolutionary change within a system. But this caveat requires qualification. At least as much as their more secular compatriots, church members have been outraged by events such as Sharpeville, Soweto, and the death of Steve Biko. This sentiment is reinforced by the reluctant but growing understanding of the systemic violence of the existing order, which refuses to place the burden of proof upon those engaging in revolutionary violence as a last resort. Many church leaders can understand the resort to violence even when they cannot endorse it. A number of leaders acknowledge that they are fully aware that few countries in black Africa have achieved freedom without the threat of or the resort to armed violence, even when they also acknowledge the costs of that violence. If church constituencies have difficulty supporting the armed struggles of liberationist groups, they may well be torn apart over the support of more overt repressive violence exercised by minority governments, especially in the unlikely event of U.S. involvement on behalf of that government.

Moreover, church bodies, members, and even leaders tend to react to events rather than to initiate action on their own. They are fairly easily distracted by events at home or by internal institutional dynamics from sustained and creative dealing with policies and struggles overseas.

Most church leaders nevertheless are convinced that there is a large reservoir of potential commitment to action supporting significant change in South Africa within U.S. churches. This potential awaits informed and persuasive leadership. Information and commitment are now unevenly distributed among churches. Not all are as far along as the NCC, the Protestant Episcopal Church, and the United Church of Christ Board of World Ministries. And even within these churches, there are different levels of awareness, concern, information, and commitment. Church members can respond to situations of human need, but only with persistent educational efforts can they resist the current pressures to turn within (personally and institutionally) and sustain attention to such ethical issues as are raised in South Africa, Chile, and elsewhere abroad.

We are persuaded that the churches have a role beyond their own membership and institutional actions. Church leaders often overestimate their potential influence on governmental decisions on issues of religious social concern.

But educated and committed church members are also citizens, voters, stockholders, and jobholders in other institutions, and some hold positions of considerable corporate and government power. We also believe that the churches can, and often do, exert a subtle influence on the ethos and general moral sensitivity of the nation, which can extend far beyond their influence on specific decisions of governments or corporations.

What Can We Expect from the Churches

The churches, especially their leaders, should and will expand their dialogue with their counterparts in South Africa, white and black. They will be responsive especially to black voices from South Africa and within the churches in the United States. One illustration is the address of the late Bishop Mandlenkhosi A.I. Zwane of the Roman Catholic diocese of Manzani, Swaziland, on "Human Rights Role: The Church in Africa." He said:

> One of the most exciting developments in the last decade has been the way Christians in a number of different countries have played a practical role in providing information about human rights. In countries with strict governmental control of the mass media, the churches have at times been the only alternative source of news and data for the outside world.[25]

The bishop noted that the gathering and dissemination of such information are dangerous exercises, especially in states that attempt to limit human rights in the linked causes of the common good and national security.

More U.S. church agencies, including pension boards and local and regional units, should and will exert pressure on corporations, resorting more to "unless-and-until" clauses in their resolutions. Church bodies will become more supportive of the Howard principles and of the earlier Sullivan principles.

Churches will continue to respond to human needs, especially where these have relief dimensions. Some churches will seek alternatives to the WCC Program to Combat Racism Special Fund and will provide direct support to institutions to which they are related, such as the South Africa Council of Churches and their respective denominational channels.

A few churches are already committed to a sustained process of informing and educating their own constituencies. This education will likely be coupled with focused pressure on the U.S. government, both executive decision and legislative action, as church leaders come to see the limits of influence through corporate channels and the necessity to resort to political expression.

Notes

1. See chapter 2 to this book for a more detailed analysis of public-opinion data. Note especially Hero's interpretation that "cause versus

effect relationships between religion and international thinking. . . are indirect, amorphous, and probably complex.''

2. Deborah Durfee Brown and John Immerwahr, ''The Public Views on South Africa,'' *Public Opinion* (January–February 1979):54–59.

3. Ibid., p.55.

4. See chapter 5 to this book.

5. Alan Paton, ''A Patriot's Dilemma: Why I Stay in South Africa,'' *Commonweal,* November 11, 1978, p. 717.

6. *Worldview* is published by the Council on Religion and International Affairs (funded by an endowment established by Andrew Carnegie) and aimed at a sophisticated readership. *Christianity and Crisis* is a journal founded by Reinhold Niebuhr and continuing his interest in Christian realism. *Sojourners* is a relatively new periodical combining evangelical or conservative theology with liberal social views. All three are moderate rather than radical in the American context.

7. See chapter 6 to this book in which Philip V. White stresses the importance of this summit conference.

8. *Christianity and Crisis,* March 13, 1978, pp. 45–49. This article was part of an issue devoted to South Africa.

9. ''Evangelical'' refers in the United States to a large and growing body of Christians who are conservative, even fundamentalist, in theology. Many evangelical bodies have not belonged to the NCC. Most are self-conscious about political responsibility. Some are conservative in politics; others are more liberal, following the lead of Evangelicals for Social Action. The periodical *Sojourners* is one manifestation of liberal social and political thought among a significant fraction of evangelicals.

10. James E. Baker, John de St. Jorre, and J. Daniel O'Flaherty, ''The American Consensus on South Africa,'' *Worldview* (October 1979):12–16.

11. Elisabeth Adler, *A Small Beginning: An Assessment of the First Five Years of the Programme to Combat Racism* (Geneva, Switzerland: World Council of Churches, 1974), pp. 72, 75, 77.

12. Ibid.

13. Ibid.

14. Desaix Myers III, with Kenneth Propp, David Hauck, and David M. Liff, *U.S. Business in South Africa: The Economic, Political, and Moral Issues* (Bloomington: Indiana University Press, 1980), pp. 12–15ff.

15. Howard Schomer, ''The Role of Transnational Business in Mass Economic Development,'' *Forum for Correspondence and Contact* 7 (October 1975):84. Schomer is the executive officer of the United Church Board of World Ministries and has led United Church of Christ efforts at corporate responsibility.

16. See chapter 5 to this book.

17. Myers, *U.S. Business in South Africa,* pp. 275–276, 285.

18. *Corporate Examiner* 8 (May 1979):2.

19. The American Baptist Convention is a national body, whereas the much larger Southern Baptist Convention is more regional in its membership.

20. This resolution was addressed to American Express, Bank America, Wells Fargo, Citicorp, Allegheny Ludlum, Borg Warner, Exxon, and Eastman Kodak. This and the two succeeding resolutions are taken from *Church Proxy Resolutions* (January 1980):54–116, published by Interfaith Center on Corporate Responsibility, 475 Riverside Drive, New York, N.Y. 10115.

21. United Methodist Church General Council on Finance and Administration, *Statement of Investment Policy* (Evanston, Ill.: A78), pp. 6–7.

22. "The Koinonia Declaration," *Journal of Theology for Southern Africa,* no.24 (September 1978): pp. 58–64.

23. Letter from Dr. John Bratt, Secretary of the Interchurch Relations Committee of the Christian Reformed Church, September 2, 1980, to the author.

24. *Reformed Ecumenical Synod News Exchange,* August 12, 1980, #1577.

25. *Origins,* 9, no. 46 (May 1, 1980).

8

American Universities and South Africa

Lawrence F. Stevens and
James G. Lubetkin

In the late 1970s the internal troubles of a distantly located country at the southern tip of Africa became the focus of student interest unparalleled since the activist days of the Vietnam war. It must be a matter of particular interest to South African observers, if not of some puzzlement, to try to understand why groups of students at American universities (indeed universities in a number of countries) felt so strongly about an issue that they confronted their respective administrations and demanded that those institutions adopt policies and take punitive steps in response to the operations of a government thousands of miles away.

With a broad array of domestic and international problems to choose from, what prompted students to occupy the offices of several university administrations in order to force them to recognize and respond to the problems posed by South Africa? What aspects of the situation in South Africa prompted 294 students at Stanford University to act in a manner that brought about their arrests in 1977 and caused 3,000 students at Harvard University to take to the streets in 1978 to express their concern? What conditions needed to exist in order to encourage the administrations, faculties, and student bodies of many of America's more prestigious private and public liberal educational institutions to spend countless hours formulating institutional responses to the problems of a country that almost none of them had visited, or were likely ever to visit?

It seems clear that no single event, either in the United States or in South Africa, was responsible for the rise in student concern that was experienced most dramatically in the 1977–1979 period. Instead a number of factors came together during that period to produce a dramatic surge in student concern over a situation with which few members of the academic community had direct experience.

American Universities and South Africa, 1960

Some have speculated that the racial confrontations that occurred in South Africa's townships in 1976 were the major causal factor. Clearly these

123

events did play an important role, yet in 1960, the events surrounding Sharpeville (which in many ways, at least to the foreign observer, were comparable to the later events) did not produce widespread or persistent concern on American campuses. To understand why Sharpeville did not create a crisis on campuses in 1960 but Soweto (1976) and the death in detention of Steve Biko (1977) did, one must examine the differences and changes that existed and took place in the United States between 1960 and 1976.

To be sure, the Sharpeville incident did not go unnoticed in the United States; it was widely reported. However, the events at Sharpeville were viewed from an American perspective that was focused on rising concerns about domestic civil rights. Sharpeville produced a response on American campuses, but it was limited.

Americans generally, and students in particular, were living in a rapidly changing period of emerging civil rights and were developing their community attitudes. The U.S. Supreme Court's decision in *Brown* v. *Board of Education,* which declared "inherently unequal" all racial segregation in public schools, had occurred only six years previously, in 1954. Accordingly the focus of concern was a still new and active examination of cases of systematic discrimination. Many American schools and colleges were admitting black students for the first time, in some cases with protection provided for them by municipal, state, and federal authorities. Also for the first time, large numbers of blacks and whites, many of them students, were working together in acts of civil disobedience, primarily in the South, to test the constitutionality of state and municipal laws that barred blacks and whites from such routine and daily activities as eating together in restaurants or traveling side-by-side on public conveyances. Those who were concerned about the definition and protection of individual civil rights were actively involved in the process of integration. They were promoting change in racial attitudes and were taking the steps necessary for the revision of discriminatory laws and practices. In short, the early 1960s produced a steady stream of racial incidents in the fifty United States, occasionally violent, which were part of understanding and seeking to diminish the widespread existence of institutional racial discrimination.

Therefore when the incident at Sharpeville occurred, it was interpreted on American campuses in the context of the racial dynamics that were ongoing in the United States. It was seen in part as an act of civil disobedience not dissimilar to actions in the American civil-rights experience. There was sympathy on American campuses and elsewhere for the struggle of South African blacks against the white government, but there was also the perception that such struggles were simply part of the process by which entrenched attitudes were changed.

In retrospect, a fundamental lack of American understanding regarding the major differences between the nature of the racial struggles in the United States and in South Africa at that time led to a misinterpretation of the significance of Sharpeville. Clearly, though some perceived it as such, Sharpeville was not one of the steps along the way to racial integration. Instead it and subsequent events were a demonstration of the commitment of the South African government to enforce its governmental system of racial differentiation and separation. The most profound effect was not the identification of legal mechanisms that were in need of modification or abolition in order to promote racial harmony; rather Sharpeville constituted a statement by the South African government that racially discriminatory laws, no matter how inequitable, would continue to be made and enforced by the white-controlled government; the policies and practicies of apartheid were to remain in place. Had the members of American university communities understood better the significance of Sharpeville and followed more closely the events that later took place, up to and including the arrests at Rivonia in 1963, it is not inconceivable that there would have been a more lasting concern exhibited and a firmer foundation established for understanding the importance of Sharpeville and the events in South Africa that followed.

Campus Developments, 1960–1976

Between the early 1960s and the mid–1970s, a great number of developments contributed to the strong and persistent university reactions in the post-Soweto era. In terms of national and worldwide events, the progressive decolonization of Africa, the emergence of a definable African bloc at the United Nations, the civil-rights movement in the United States, the tarnished American self-image brought about by the war in Vietnam, the trend toward national self-criticism, and even the recognition of international interdependence brought about by an oil crisis were elements in this equation. Yet two developments that took place on American campuses during this period seem particularly important to an understanding of the manner in which the South African issue was raised as a subject to be addressed by the U.S. educational community.

The first was the emergence in the 1960s of student activism as the means by which students demonstrated their concerns over matters of social, institutional, or ethical importance. Students who were frustrated by their inability to effect the changes they thought were necessary adopted a new activism and began to express their views through acts of overt confrontation with their respective university and college administrations. Initially the focus of the issues was internal. The free-speech movement at the University of California at Berkeley, institutional policy and community-relations problems at Columbia University, and military recruiting and ROTC programs at Harvard University were typical of the topics that resulted in major on-campus confrontations. Gradually, however, the confrontational model became the almost-standard manner by which students expressed their frustration and anger with respect to matters of policy, internal or external. The vast number of campus confrontations that took place during the height of the war in Vietnam show how formidable a force students had become. Many university administrators had to add a new unwritten first law to the practice of administration: a university ignores the legitimate concerns of its students only at its own peril.

The second development was more subtle but no less important to an understanding of the way in which the issue of South Africa emerged as a focus of campus debate. This development was the growing belief, initially by some students and faculty and later by administrators and trustees, that universities did not exist independently from the country's economic system and that by virtue of their ownership of corporate securities they were inextricably involved in the actions of the corporations in which they held investments. Increasingly members of the educational community believed that since universities were beneficiaries of corporate profits through dividends and were fractional owners by virtue of shares of stock held in their portfolios, they also had an ethical responsibility to express concerns, where warranted, over the manner in which the corporations conducted their operations and earned their profits. The specific concerns that led to the formation of the ethical investor model varied somewhat from campus to campus. For some (Princeton University, for example) the issue, even as early as 1970, was that of U.S. corporate involvement in South Africa. At other campuses the defining issues involved questions of environmental concern, alleged discriminatory practices, production of military equipment, equal-opportunity employment, ties with the military-industrial complex, and others of a primarily U.S. domestic character.

The manner in which institutions responded to these concerns differed from campus to campus. Some institutions merely recognized these issues as legitimate concerns, while others set up elaborate procedures to ensure that these issues were thoroughly and thoughtfully considered. The most important factor in this development was the general acknowledgment by university trustees that their institutions had a responsibility to invest endowment funds in a manner that was not inconsistent with the values of educational institutions. The acceptance by trustees and university administrations of the ethical responsibilities involved in the institutional ownership of corporate securities created a point of intersection between student concerns over South Africa and institutional involvement in South Africa that did provide initially, and continues to provide, the focal point for campus debate over this issue.

Student Concerns over South Africa, 1976-1977

The riots in Soweto in 1976 followed, among other events, by the death in detention of Steven Biko and the bannings and detentions of a number of government critics in 1977 once again focused world opinion on South Africa's racial policies in a manner that demanded attention. The generation of American students then on campus was the product of a substantially different period in American history from the generation on campus in 1960 when Sharpeville occurred. For the most part, the later generation had been raised during a time when American racial attitudes and practices had become considerably liberalized and when there existed a general presumption that the full force of law would be used to enhance and protect the rights of individuals. Accordingly the racial disturbances in South Africa highlighted the general perception that little had changed in South Africa and appeared in sharp contrast to the values and ideals that many U.S. students of the latter 1970s held.

With the incidents in South Africa serving to focus attention on the racial aspects of South African society and given the general sensitivity of U.S. college students to issues of race, it is not surprising that on a number of campuses, students who shared a common perception of the situation formed organizations to express their support for the struggles of South African blacks in their attempts to gain political and economic freedom. However, the sharing of a common perception is rarely a sufficient force to bind groups together if there is neither a continuing direct focus for those concerns nor the means to secure some change. For most student groups concerned about South Africa, the immediate focus was the ownership by their institutions of shares of stock in the 350 or so U.S. companies that maintain direct links in South Africa through subsidiary or affiliate companies. Means to secure change were also available as students first formulated demands and then presented them to university trustees or administrators. In some cases, such as at Stanford and Harvard Universities, these presentations were quite forceful.

In order to understand the students' position, it is useful to examine the nature of their demands, recognizing that the manner in which the issue of South Africa arose at different institutions varied depending on the size of the student group that pressed for change, the willingness of university administrations to debate the matter, and the extent to which students, administrators, and faculty were knowledgeable of the current problems of South Africa. Nevertheless, the substance of the demands placed before most schools did have common characteristics, and the positions later adopted by schools more often than not shared a number of common points. It is in these common characteristics that one can understand most clearly the nature of the debate and the appropriateness of its resolution.

Students' arguments in favor of U.S. corporate withdrawal from South Africa generally were based partly on ethical grounds and partly on political and economic grounds. The ethical argument usually stated that the manner in which South African laws are written and South African society operates makes it impossible for any American or other organization to operate there in a way that does not exploit blacks and support the status quo. Since there is an assumption (indeed, a reality) that a company which treats blacks and whites equally in all phases of employment is in violation of South African law, no company that operates within the law can operate in a manner consistent with a basic policy of equal opportunity. Therefore, students reasoned, the only way a company could relieve itself of the ethical dilemma of operating under one set of principles in the United States and another set of principles in South Africa was to withdraw from South Africa.

The political and economic argument was based on the assumption that white South Africans (or at least the majority of white South Africans who have been successful in keeping the Nationalist Party with its apartheid policies in power continually since 1948) have too much at stake in the maintenance of the current system to permit significant evolutionary change to occur. Therefore students rejected as an ultimately ineffective mechanism for change the argument frequently presented by corporate managements that they can encourage gradual change by operating in South Africa in a manner that tends to ameliorate the effects of apartheid on their non-white workers in the work place. To arguments by the companies that they were adopting changes in employment practices to enhance the opportunities for black workers, the students responded that it was too little, too late. To claims that withdrawal by U.S. firms would only make it easier for the multinational corporations of other countries to invest in South Africa, students responded that U.S. firms should serve as an example that the South African system was too repugnant to operate within. In short, student groups adopted the position that the only responsible activity that U.S. companies could follow was that of withdrawal from South Africa and thereby setting the stage for an unheaval in the South African economy that would sufficiently weaken the government of South Africa to enable blacks to gain political and economic rights through revolution.

Regardless of whether the basic argument was moral, economic, political, or a combination thereof, the conclusion reached by students was the same with respect to their views on what U.S. companies should do: withdraw from South Africa until such time as that country had abolished all aspects of apartheid.

At virtually all campuses where student groups were formed around the South Africa issue, the focus of student discontent was the investment policy of the institution. Students generally demanded that the institution sell the securities of the companies that have operations in South Africa and the banks that were continuing to grant loans to the government of South Africa.[1]

In making their divestment demands, students used a line of reasoning similar to that which they had used in reaching the conclusion that American companies should withdraw from South Africa. In some cases the demand for divestment was primarily economic: that such sales would lead to a depression of the securities' values and that the companies would dispose of their South African operations in order to restore investor confidence in the companies. In other cases, the student demand for divestment was ethical: that it was inconsistent with the values of the university to finance its operations from profits that had been gained, in part, from the exploitation of black labor in South Africa. Regardless of the reasoning, the demand was consistent. Of the 150 institutions surveyed with respect to investment policy changes as a function of concern over South Africa, there was no instance in which a student group made demands of the institution that did not include at least the possibility of divestment of some securities.

Educational Institutions

The Problem of Response

The problem posed to educational institutions with respect to the manner in which they should respond to student demands regarding South Africa proved to be quite complex. At those institutions where demands were presented, controversy over what the institution ought to do was common.

The basic issues in South Africa that caused student groups to take the actions they did generally were not a matter of controversy. University administrations concurred with student groups that the inequities and injustices of the South African system constituted a cause for special concern. Many institutions have addressed this point. The following statement by the Yale Corporation (the governing board of trustees of Yale University) in June 1978 is a particularly clear example of the position taken by most boards of trustees:

> The [Yale] Corporation has earlier stated publicly its abhorrence of the policies of the present government of South Africa and hereby reaffirms that statement, unanimously and without qualification. In our opinion, it is unacceptable for any nation to ground its political and social system on distinctions of race. It is equally unacceptable for any racial group to impose such a system upon a whole country, to institutionalize it in every aspect of its laws, and to enforce it daily upon others by force. We believe that the system of apartheid now in effect in South Africa must and will change. We believe the University has an ethical duty to contribute to the process of peaceful change rather than see that process deferred so long

that change can only come about through massive racial and civil warfare. We know that social injustice exists in many nations. And we do not presume to infringe upon the proper responsibilities of the United States government. But apartheid in South Africa is so distinctive in degree as to require special attention.[2]

South Africa and its racial policies were not a source of controversy between students and their institutions; rather the controversies developed over what actions the institutions should take in response to student demands for action.

At the heart of the controversy was the fundamental conflict over the nature of a university and its role in a free society. Derek C. Bok, president of Harvard University, summarized the nature of the conflict in an open letter in March 1979 to all members of the Harvard community:

> Universities are designed to achieve particular purposes. Their special mission is the discovery and transmission of knowledge. . . . Nevertheless, unlike other organizations, such as political parties, environmental associations, or civil rights groups, their institutional goal is not to reform society in specific ways. Universities have neither the mandate nor the competence to administer foreign policy, set our social and economic priorities, enforce standards of conduct in the society, or carry out other social functions apart from learning and discovery.[3]

For most institutions, then, the problem was one of deciding what they could do in recognition of the special circumstances of South Africa and still act in a manner that was consistent with their special educational purpose. Again, Derek Bok, in another open letter to the members of the Harvard community in April 1979, stated the problem facing Harvard in attempting to respond to student demands for divestment:

> The distinctive aspect of many of the proposals is that they seek to have Harvard respond, not by academic means, but as part of a pressure group using the leverage of our purchases, our endowment, and our prestige as a university to push for social or political ends. These efforts do not fall within our traditional educational activities and threaten to conflict with institutional restraints that have long been considered important to the preservation of academic values and pursuits.[4]

Recognizing that these conflicting issues were important to educational communities and that their resolution would require considerable time and effort, most institutions that considered the issue did so by assembling a committee to investigate the varying points of view within the community and to report back to the president of the institutions or their boards of trustees with their findings, including any recommendations for actions to be taken by the institution. The groups represented on these committees varied somewhat, but most included some faculty members and some students. Occasionally they also included administrators, alumni, and/or trustees. Because of the high level of interest in this topic, these committees were very active on most campuses; in many instances they were the most active of any other university committees in operation during this period. Most committees were composed of people whose knowledge of South Africa was slight; therefore members spent much time learning about the country, its history, and the development of its policies. Additionally, since the demand for divestment hinged at least partly on the economic issues of corporate disinvestment, substantial effort was made to become familiar with information with respect to both U.S. corporate involvement in South Africa and the composition of the institution's investment portfolios, including the costs associated with any major portfolio changes. Usually, after several months of study and debate, these committees reported back to their administrations and, following suitable study by them, recommendations were accepted or rejected and policies were adopted.

The Policies Adopted

In general, the policies adopted by educational institutions in response to student pressures fall into one of three broadly defined categories: divestment, selective divestment, not divesting but taking other appropriate actions instead. Two observations, based on a review of policies, are striking. First, there have been few, if any, instances in which an institution has studied this issue in any detail and decided to take no action. Institutions that reported no specific investment policy with respect to U.S. companies with operations in South Africa also reported that this concern had not been raised by students on their campuses and they had not, therefore, been required to consider policy changes. Second, the policies that have been adopted by institutions within each of the major categories are remarkably similar to each other. The actions that have been decided upon, as well as the supporting rationale for these actions, show many more similarities than differences within categories.

Divestment: A small number of institutions decided to adopt policies of selling all of their investments in companies that maintain subsidiary or affiliate operations in South Africa. With rare exceptions, these institutions indicated that the basis for the action was primarily ethical; the institution decided it was inconsistent with the values of the university community to receive dividends from any company that derives part of its income from direct operations in South Africa. These institutions, which are primarily public and have small endowments, do not depend on endowments to pro-

duce an appreciable percentage of their annual operating budgets. Therefore divestment was unlikely to affect the ability of the institution to carry
out its primary function. In addition, many of these institutions noted that
their holdings in individual companies were small and unlikely to be influential in encouraging changes in corporate behavior. Finally, some of these
institutions acknowledged that the controversy surrounding their continued
holding of these companies in the portfolio was likely to do more damage to
the educational process than would the slight loss in income as a function of
divestment.

Selective Divestment: A somewhat larger number of institutions decided
upon policies that combined their recognition of the ethical aspects of
investments with an assumption that their roles as investors gave them an
opportunity to influence corporate behavior in constructive ways. These
institutions indicated that they would continue to hold investments in companies that operate in a way that the institution believes to be appropriate
and constructive. One differentiating aspect of these policies is the criteria
used to determine appropriate and constructive. On one end of the con-
tinuum, at least one institution defined appropriate behavior as an indication from companies that they have made or are making plans to cease
operations in South Africa. This has turned out to be tantamount to a
policy of divestment since very few companies (if any) have revealed plans
to disinvest from South Africa. For most of the institutions in this category, however, appropriate behavior was defined as following progressive
employment practices such as the Sullivan principles or the European Economic Community Code of Conduct. The administrative problem that this
policy has caused is in developing a mechanism to determine whether companies in the portfolio are in compliance with the institution's policy. Some
universities and colleges have determined that the periodic reports issued by
the Sullivan organization are sufficient for their purposes. Accordingly
these institutions maintain their investments in companies that have signed
the Sullivan principles, provided that these companies make reasonable progress toward implementing the Sullivan goals. A few schools have created
more complex mechanisms that rely on the institution's initiative to gather
pertinent available information, including correspondence with individual
companies, to arrive at an independent evaluation. In all cases, if a company consistently fails to meet the criteria set by the institution, that company's stock will no longer be held or purchased by the institution.

Actions Other than Divestment: A majority of the institutions that have
considered student demands have rejected the notion of divestment as a
means of either influencing corporate behavior or relieving the institution
of its ethical dilemma. Typically these institutions have adopted the policy

that they will continue to invest in companies with South African operations, but as a condition of doing so they will communicate their views to the companies that have subsidiaries or affiliates in South Africa that such operations pose ethical questions of which the company should be aware. Some institutions in this group advocate U.S. corporate disinvestment from South Africa, while others emphasize implementing progressive employment practices there. Virtually all have indicated that they will vote a shareholder resolution in a manner consistent with the institution's position even if such a resolution is opposed by management. A few institutions have chosen to sponsor shareholder resolutions regarding corporate activity in South Africa. Nevertheless, these institutions have rejected the concept of divestment either because they believe it would be ineffective as a method to induce change in corporate behavior or because they believe that such action is inconsistent with their fiduciary obligations.

Lack of Policy: There is, of course, a fourth category: that of institutions which have not adopted special or new investment policies as a function of South Africa-related concerns. In a few cases, the lack of policies shaped by the ethical investor model is a matter of principle. These institutions have declared that the sole purpose of their endowments is to support the educational enterprise and, as such, should be free from restrictions that are not primarily financial in nature. For most, however, the reason such policies have not been articulated is that there has not been significant pressure on these institutions to do so from their constituents.

Most of these schools are either small, private institutions with relatively modest endowments or public institutions that are dependent on their endowments for only a very small percentage of their annual operating revenues. In addition, many of the institutions at which there was little student pressure are located in the South, Midwest, or Southwest where student groups were less well organized and student demands were less forceful. Many of these educational institutions have indicated a willingness to address these issues, if and when they are presented, but for the time being other items of priority occupy their attention.

The Policies: Some Observations

Because the focus of student concerns has been directed at stock holdings, it is not surprising that the majority of private colleges with relatively large endowments have particularly felt the effects of student pressure. Most of the more active, organized student concern has been among institutions with high standards of faculty appointment and student selection, institutions with a relatively large endowment per student, and institutions whose reputations are national, if not international in scope. Indeed of the ten wealthiest private institutions, eight have adopted investment policies as a result of their investigations into the South Africa concerns raised on their campuses. Five of these eight have adopted policies of selective divestment based on an assessment of corporate adherence to progressive employment policies. The other three schools have adopted policies of communicating their views on appropriate behavior in South Africa to their portfolio companies.

There has also been some regional variation based, in large measure, on the nature of the institutions clustered in the area. For example, the Northeast contains a relatively large number of private, liberal-arts colleges and universities with significant endowments. Such institutions, due to the interests and views of the students they attract, proved more likely than larger, public institutions (which are more prominent in the South, Midwest, and Southwest) to have had South Africa become a major campus concern. Thus of the institutions that were surveyed, a higher percentage of those in the Northeast had adopted policies than had institutions elsewhere.

The primarily black colleges in this country were not silent on the issues of South Africa. Although the student pressure for divestment was most visible at colleges and universities with a largely white student body, students at America's black colleges felt, and continue to feel, a deep concern for the problems of South Africa's blacks. But for the most part, the predominantly black colleges in this country, roughly one hundred located primarily in the Southeast, are institutions with small endowments, if any. Most are state or federally supported, with few investments in private industrial concerns. Accordingly although there existed strong sympathies on black campuses for the struggles of South Africa's blacks, the same focal point, stock holdings in U.S. companies with investments in South Africa, did not exist. In those few black colleges with significant endowments, policies often were adopted. In the case of one, a decision was made not to hold stock in a company doing "substantial business" in South Africa. In the case of another, its investment managers were instructed "to the greatest extent possible to avoid companies that have not signed the Sullivan Principles." Black universities and colleges were concerned, but the pressure, for primarily financial reasons, was only infrequently visible on black campuses.

Effects of Institutional Concern

It is difficult to know with precision what effects the South Africa-related activities on campuses have had. Some matters seem apparent, however. As a direct result of the focus of student concern, many more students, faculty, and others on campuses have a much improved knowledge of South Africa and its racial policies than would have been the case had the controversies not been raised. In addition, many trustees who hold influential positions across the spectrum of American institutions beyond their university roles have been pressed to study the issues posed by South Africa in a way that they probably would not have had to do in their primary activities. For many of these trustees, the university and college debates on this subject have brought them to recognize publicly that South Africa's racial policies are so repugnant that they form a basis for special attention. It would be naive to assume that trustees would not be affected in their activities as corporate leaders, government officials, lawyers, media executives, and the like.

The pressure placed on American companies as a function of the concerns of a major class of shareholders with the public visibility of distinguished universities has, in part, caused many companies to consider in detail the nature and quality of their operations in South Africa. Many companies are taking steps in South Africa to upgrade their employment policies and practices. It is difficult to ascertain the degree to which university and college concerns have caused these changes, but no doubt they are among the most influential factors.

Finally, the translation of student concern into institutional policy means that the continuing sensitivity regarding the South African operations of American companies is now independent of student interest. Academic institutions that have adopted policies are under their own obligations to implement these policies until such time as the policies are changed (which seems unlikely unless there is a dramatic alteration of circumstances in South Africa). Should universities and colleges fail to implement their own policies, they will subject themselves to the just criticism that their policies were cynical in the extreme. To the extent that students learn from the actions of their educational institutions, such would seem to be a poor lesson indeed.

The Future

It is risky to speculate about what developments are likely to occur on campuses in the near future; however, based on the issues that have been discussed over the last several years, some trends seem likely.

The extensive discussion on some campuses over formulating university positions on South Africa that are consistent with the university's central purposes of teaching and research seems likely to cause institutions to look beyond financial avenues of response. One clear alternative is that of making the educational resources of the school available to South African blacks for whom equivalent opportunities are not readily available in South Africa. Already some universities have organized special programs to recruit black South Africans for undergraduate- and graduate-level study. For schools that cannot afford special recruiting efforts, a program currently in its initial phases at the Institute of International Education in New York will provide a recruiting and coordinating function to match capable students with American educational institutions that have an interest in such students. With sufficient financial support, this and similar programs should expand.

The richness and diversity of the U.S. educational community could also be made available in other appropriate ways. Faculty exchange programs offer one such possibility. Teaching opportunities for American academicians at South Africa's black colleges offer another possibility. Such programs are not likely to be undertaken alone by most institutions, but mechanisms might easily be developed through foundations or professional organizations if sources of financial support became available.

Finally, the future will almost certainly see South Africa and apartheid as a continuing concern for American students and the institutions they attend. The intense debates that have taken place recently on American campuses have served to sensitize many people to the moral issues of South Africa's system of racial separation and exploitation. It is unlikely that the misinterpretation of the significance of Sharpeville will be repeated. The policies of South Africa's government are now better understood and the pessimism regarding the prospect of near-term meaningful change is much more pervasive. The reaction of the vast majority of academic institutions thus far has been moderate and has expressed hope that change can and will occur.

Whether that change occurs is not a matter to be decided on U.S. campuses, but until it does occur, South Africa will be a matter of importance. American educational institutions and their students will not lose sight of South Africa. The level of concern may rise and fall, but as long as the situation there remains basically unchanged, the topic will continue to be addressed in various ways by the U.S. educational community.

Notes

1. The issue of loans to South Africa shows a great deal of variation by university and appears to be related to the expertise developed by student groups regarding the nature and extent of U.S. financial relationships with South Africa. On some campuses, the demand for divestment extended to banks that were making loans to either the public or private sector on the basis that both types of loans had been very important to South Africa's

economic recovery in the post-Sharpeville period. At other institutions the demand was confined only to banks that were making public-sector loans on the basis that this limitation was consistent with shareholder initiatives seeking to prohibit such loans. At the remaining institutions, the demand for divestment was limited to the banks that had a physical presence in South Africa and could be said to have a subsidiary operation in that country.

2. "Statement of the Yale Corporation on Ethical Investment Policy and South Africa" (New Haven, Conn., June 1978).

3. Derek C. Bok, "Reflections on the Ethical Responsibilities of the University in Society: An Open Letter to the Harvard Community." (Cambridge, Mass., March 9, 1979).

4. Derek C. Bok, "Reflections on Divestment of Stock: An Open Letter to the Harvard Community" (Cambridge, Mass., April 6, 1979).

9

The U.S. Policy Process and South Africa

Chester A. Crocker

South Africa and southern Africa have risen to a place of some prominence on the U.S. foreign policy agenda since the mid–1970s. Moreover, it is quite possible that these issues will grow in importance in the next few years. Given the intractability of the South African question, the likelihood that it will be around for a long time, and the domestic political equations in our multiracial society, it is predictable that South Africa will rank as one of the top two or three regional conflict issues of the 1980s.

Or almost predictable. It is possible that other foreign concerns will preempt more of the agenda: a heightened focus on East-West tensions and a renewal of U.S.-Soviet arms competition; a major economic crisis triggered by energy, inflation, or trade rivalry; or a regional blow-up in some other area (such as Yugoslavia, the Middle East, the Caribbean, or Northeast Asia). Thus it may be unwise to adopt a straight linear projection of domestic U.S interest in South Africa's problems. Should other issues push their way before U.S. opinion and decision makers, South Africa as an issue will be downgraded. The degree of attention given it would reflect more closely the degree of the crisis in South Africa. In sum, Americans may not be able to afford to deal with South Africa as though there is a crisis when other crises demand attention unless, of course, South Africa does begin to enter the crisis phase itself.

Nevertheless the conventional wisdom is that the domestic heat on the South African issue will continue and probably grow gradually. Further, it is commonly assumed that any major flare-up of rioting, strikes, or Crossroads-style controversy would provoke a quantum leap in domestic U.S. attention to South Africa.

Another point to keep in mind is that the uncertain state of U.S.-Soviet relations as of late 1980 affects all other policy issues. While the current climate lasts, there is reduced interest in African regional issues in the American policy process, except insofar as African issues pertain directly to U.S. interests in the U.S.-Soviet relationship. In general, Washington's preoccupation with the central strategic balance reduces the foreign-policy resources for dealing with other issues.

This chapter was written in May 1980 and revised in December 1980. Except where otherwise indicated, its conclusions apply to the era of the 1970s and are not to be taken as timeless judgments or forecasts. No effort has been made to take into account the implications of the Reagan Republican victory of November 1980.

The practical effect of the current international climate on American perceptions of South Africa can be summed up in terms of several distinct trends, not all of which are necessarily consistent with each other.

First, senior policy levels in the White House and State Department have less time and energy for activist diplomatic initiatives on secondary problem areas; African specialists and officials will have more difficulty gaining the attention of top officials.

Second, public opinion is less fragmented along the lines of special interest, narrow topical concerns, or ethnic politics because the White House and national media concentration on the "big issues" preempts the stage. The perception of foreign crisis has a broad unifying effect on opinion, and debate focuses on central issues rather than those perceived to be peripheral. Issues become ranked more clearly, and public opinion is concerned mainly with a few major priorities.

Third, in policy areas such as southern Africa, U.S. diplomacy is likely to be reactive and sporadic and less likely to seek to manage secondary problems on a continuing, day-to-day basis. Major policy reviews and reassessments on African issues are less likely; the path of least resistance will be to do nothing or continue current policy. In practice, this may give regional and working-level officials some scope to operate according to their own preferences, but only within a narrow range of policy parameters.[1]

Fourth, a more polarized East-West climate will mean that the policy community, Congress, and public opinion think more clearly in terms of basic categories such as friend or foe. Africa will get attention to a greater degree in these terms—as a function of U.S. needs for military facilities (as in Kenya and Somalia), for diplomatic support (for the 1980 Olympic boycott, for example), and for vital raw materials. This does not mean that Washington will suddenly start looking at South Africa as a potential member of NATO, but it does mean that heightened East-West tensions make U.S. participation in trade sanctions less likely since both the United States and its key NATO allies are more sensitive to their African (including South Africa) raw material dependencies. In sum, such a climate means a greater focus on security issues.

Bearing in mind these trends during 1979–1980, we can return to the main thread of the analysis on the perhaps-debatable assumption that U.S.-Soviet tensions will decline and a détente atmosphere return.

Executive Branch

The point of departure in considering attitudes of policymakers is to ask how much autonomy the executive branch has in devising South Africa policy. The answer is, it depends. When African-policy issues (including South Africa) are out of the media spotlight and policy can be made in a routine, everyday fashion within the State Department's African Bureau, the executive branch has considerable autonomy. Few Americans in Congress, interest groups, or the press know enough or care enough to seek to shape policy outcomes. Many of those who do will probably share the preferences of African specialists in the Department of State and in the U.S. mission to the United Nations.

However, when Africa assumes a more crucial importance and decisions concerning it are treated as high foreign policy, the African specialists quickly lose control of policy. Under any president, the natural instinct of career Africanists will be to steer a liberal to moderate course, which smooths the way for American diplomacy in black Africa, avoids inflaming domestic groups, and makes clear U.S. abhorrence for racism.

In fact, however, there is little domestic support for this liberal-moderate line because the political center in the United States does not know much about Africa and cares little about it. Thus, as in any other policy field where there is little interest or support from the wider public, moderate policies on South Africa are inherently fragile. Although opinion poll data may point to substantial passive sentiment of a liberal-moderate nature on South Africa, this sentiment does not translate into sustained and effective pressure on the policy process. Rather the ideological fringes are often the loudest and best-organized voices.

Once African issues are taken from the Africanists because of pressures from outside the policymaker community, the political extremes seize the initiative. The twin poles of East-West theology and black-white theology tend to take over African debates at this point. The net result, given our system of government, will be nasty debate followed by compromise, inconsistencies, public-relations posturing, and, at times, a paralysis of policy. The United States, in sum, may be destined by its own complexity to be an ineffective actor in southern Africa. Or to put it more accurately, the U.S. government may be so destined by the nature of American society and politics. A few examples will illustrate the point.

At the height of the Nixon administration enthusiasm for closer ties with Africa's conservatives, the Portuguese, and the white minority governments, it was never considered feasible to provide public rationale for such a policy. A conservative administration apparently judged that the policy would not stand up to public scrutiny or that the domestic fight necessary to sustain the policy would not be worth it.

Despite wide agreement among both liberal activists and more conservative ones that more U.S. aid dollars are needed to support African policy, the outcome year after year is tokenism. It is easier to agree to do little than to have the debate about what we are trying to do. While this argument applies primarily to policymaking toward black Africa, it also applies by analogy toward South Africa. Moreover, U.S. policy in Africa generally has a direct effect on what Washington is able to do in its relations with Pretoria.

The Carter effort to retain Rhodesian sanctions and to threaten Pretoria with the risk of sanctions over Namibia was difficult to sustain. The government in Pretoria knew this and used the knowledge. South Africa is often referred to as "a house divided," but the divisions at home in the United States are also fairly obvious.

A second aspect of executive-branch policy toward South Africa is its hard-core pragmatism whenever tough choices arise. South Africa cannot be isolated from the broader fabric of U.S. interests, and this reality is given further weight by the lawyer-like or technician approaches of many U.S. diplomats and foreign-policy elites. This quality may explain both the strengths and weaknesses of worldwide American diplomacy, but the important thing to note is the effect in terms of policy toward South Africa.

Washington elites believe that they cannot afford to adopt a consistent or rigorous human-rights policy. Selective indignation will be applied globally because policymakers can get away with it. In the 1977–1979 period an exceedingly tough standard was applied to political change in Zimbabwe-Rhodesia and a tougher one toward South Africa than to other offenders for comparable offenses. But this may not always be the case. Depending on how South Africa and the United States develop their relationship in future years, Washington's attitude toward human-rights issues in South Africa could vary. As a result, the United States will apply that standard which is politic to apply in the circumstances.

By the same token, Washington elites know they cannot devise policies toward South Africa in a vacuum. The black African dimension of U.S. deplomatic interests will play an important role, perhaps an increasing one, in the formulation of policy for South Africa. In practice, this means an effort to avoid offending African sentiment, even when it may be clear that U.S. effectiveness would be possible only if Washington is free to antagonize and bring pressure on all sides to a conflict. As the Namibia talks clearly demonstrated, it may not be possible to mediate lasting solutions to deep-seated political conflicts when one is more concerned about one's image with one side than with the other. For both domestic and African reasons, Washington policy elites may continue the recent pattern of finding it easier to scapegoat Pretoria than to deal with it. The tendency is reinforced by Pretoria's habit of doing exactly the same thing in its relations with the West.

Ironically U.S. policymakers are also sufficiently pragmatic to tread very carefully in southern Africa's economic waters. They suspect, with good reason, that public tolerance for policies that cost something may be far lower than for policies based on rhetoric and diplomatic negotiations. The case for taking it easy on South Africa because of the minerals it supplies is gaining credibility at a time when political awareness of South Africa's racial inequities is also growing. Similarly executive departments appear to be aware that there are limits in how far the United States can go in applying restrictions on trade and investment when our industrial competitors are not doing so. America's economic pragmatism, in short, cuts directly across the grain of its political and diplomatic pragmatism. As of late 1980, the growing salience of the minerals issue in Washington did not translate into consensus about the importance of South African minerals or about their policy implications. Diametrically opposing conclusions were still being aired in this increasingly visible debate. However, there could be little doubt that during the 1980s U.S. economic interests would be seen as strategic, perhaps just as strategic as the question of sea lanes and naval bases.

These general observations about the parameters of U.S. African policy have several quite specific implications for future policy toward South Africa. First, there can be no turning back of the clock in U.S.-South African relations. The days of "business as usual" with South Africa are gone, and so are the days when U.S. rhetorical opposition to apartheid was contradicted by a covert cooperation with South Africa. The U.S. system will no longer permit this sort of behavior on any issue that arouses strong feelings among an important constituency. This change has the further implication of probably ruling out for now a U.S.-South Africa rapprochement in the defense field. If Washington's interest in Indian Ocean and South Atlantic strategic-naval questions continues to grow, as it probably will, that interest probably will be served without reliance on South African cooperation (except in the event of a major East-West crisis), apart from the field of indirectly shared intelligence data.

Second, it is highly unlikely that the United States will develop the flexibility of policy to compete with the Soviet Union over the orientation of guerrilla movements in southern Africa. The logic of East-West theology would rule this out even if it seemed attractive in purely regional terms. The United States cannot operate in Africa as the French have done, because they are less ideological in their domestic political debates than we are. By the same token, most Americans will probably continue to view freedom fighters as terrorists for some time to come, and U.S. aid will be confined to refugee assistance.

Third, policymakers may continue to find it expedient not to recognize fully the extent of change that may take place in South Africa. It will be easier to soft-pedal progress in South Africa than to lay the groundwork for persuading Americans of the actual complexities and dilemmas there. Policy elites are shrewd enough to recognize that no amount of persuasion will bring around the domestic radicals and activists who trade on the currency of crisis and polarization. The White House will also find it easier not to tell Americans to stop being so parochial and so arrogant about other peoples' problems. There may be solid foreign-policy reasons for not reducing pressure on South Africa when it finally begins to move toward meaningful racial change, but that is a separate subject. We are dealing here with a syndrome of deliberate obfuscation of foreign events for domestic American reasons. South Africans, in turn, will conclude that each time they take a step forward, Washington raises the price for respectability. Thus there are no solid grounds for predicting an improvement in the long-term character of U.S.-South African political relations.

On this point, however, it is possible that significant attitudinal and stylistic differences might develop between Democrats and Republicans or liberals and conservatives. The concept of constructive engagement put forward in some Republican quarters necessarily implies a readiness to back and recognize change that can be considered meaningful. The political feasibility of this approach—in both Africa and domestic arenas—remains unknown.

Fourth, the U.S. government will not be permitted by the broader American political system to move much further down the road of official limits on U.S.-South African economic relations, barring major incidents or crises within the Republic. The evidence for this judgment is quite clear. Official spokesmen from the State, Treasury, and Commerce departments are on record as opposing investment sanctions. State Department personnel are aware of the difficulties of applying current Commerce regulations on exports to the police and military and of becoming involved in monitoring the affirmative-action performance of U.S. or South African corporations. It was thus predictable in early 1980 that State would oppose legislation on investment issues (except, reluctantly perhaps, for monitoring) in the April–June 1980 congressional hearings, in large part because of the broader implications and precedents of such action for U.S. economic interests elsewhere.

Foreign service officers working on South African issues are quick to concede that the threat of sanctions over Namibia is very different from threatening them over South Africa's own internal policies. The judgment at high levels in our South African mission and in Washington seems to be that the United States would not readily consider sanctions on internal matters. It must also be questioned whether the United States and other Western nations would cooperate with mandatory economic sanctions initiatives (under Chapter 7 of the U.N. Charter) even in the case of open South African defiance over Namibia. Threatening sanctions as a policy instrument to persuade Pretoria to cooperate is quite different from imposing them. In this regard, it is significant that some consideration was given in 1979 to unilateral Western measures of a limited kind outside the U.N. framework. The distinction is a crucial one: U.N. measures are irreversible in practice, whereas Western or U.S. measures are not. Pragmatists in the foreign affairs bureaucracies are aware of these points, and they also recognize the limited effectiveness of sanctions and dilemmas regarding their use.

By the end of the Carter administration, Western diplomats working on Namibia continued to express concern that lack of progress would eventually lead to an African diplomatic insistence of pushing mandatory U.N. sanctions. Beneath the surface, however, was a continuing effort among the Western five in the Contact Group (Canada, The Federal Republic of Germany, France, the United Kingdom, and the United States) to determine which country was prepared to veto serious sanctions measures. There was little doubt that someone would have to do so if African states were not prepared to live with modest, partial measures. Moreover, it was also clear by late 1980 that the American domestic mood made U.S. support for U.N. sanctions a barely credible threat at best.

None of the above rules out more limited steps in the direction of pressure on Pretoria, but the likelihood is that the executive branch will continue to be without coercive tools in its policy arsenal. In sum, barring miscalculations and overreactions (always a possibility), it appears likely that U.S. private-sector caution on conventional grounds of economic and political risk is likely to remain more effective and more substantive than official actions in the next few years.

Fifth and finally, U.S. government has at its disposal neither the potential carrots nor the sticks required for a coherent and effective policy. It will be unable seriously to threaten major economic damage, or to hold out the promise of substantive rewards such as nuclear cooperation or resumed arms sales. Moderate policies will be fragile, but compromise will prevail in the end.

The structure of policymaking within the executive branch tends to reinforce my comments on the substantive limits of policy. Traditionally the African Bureau within the State Department has been the leading bureaucratic actor on South African issues, and this remained the case at the end of the Carter administration. The White House (National Security Council), the Defense Department, the intelligence community, and the economic agencies (the Export-Import Bank and the Commerce, Treasury, Labor, Interior, and Energy departments) have seldom taken the lead in interagency policy debates or reviews of African questions. By the same token, however, the African Bureau (known in the policy community as AF) has traditionally been weak in terms of bureaucratic politics. For years Africa has been the stepchild of the regional budgeting process for economic and military assistance, in large part because AF has not been effective in arguing its case with competing interests. Morale in AF has seldom been high, the two exceptions being in the short-lived Kennedy period and the first few years of the Carter presidency. AF has tended not to attract the most aggressive and ambitious officials because the African field all too often has appeared to them to be a dead end. AF has controlled jobs in the field (because there are many small posts in Africa), but few of AF's slots in either Africa or Washington, D.C., offer their incumbents a sense that they are shaping important matters in U.S. foreign policy.

Within the State Department, AF has tended not to be a launching pad for careers at the pinnacle of the diplomatic service. Within other executive departments, especially the economic agencies and the Defense Department, there is a long-standing habit of viewing AF as a weak bureau staffed with romantics and experts on obscure countries. Officials outside State believe that AF has consistently ignored U.S. economic and military interests in Africa, focusing instead on vaguely defined political-diplomatic concerns. This attitude has been summed up in the view that AF's only interest is to maintain the maximum number of diplomatic slots in Africa by maintaining smooth relations with as many African countries as possible. Because AF is so preoccupied with the task of managing minor posts in Africa and conducting bilateral relations with minor countries, it may have spent less time than it should in choosing priorities and considering Africa's strategic place in the broader context of U.S. global interests.

Within AF, South Africa historically has been a special case. Because South Africa is a unifying symbol and target for black African criticism, it is also commonly defined by AF's African specialists as a major obstacle to smooth U.S. relations with the rest of Africa. There are many strands to the AF view of South Africa: the Republic is seen as an embarrassment for the West, an anachronism, a source of long-festering conflict that attracts Soviet attention and manipulation, an evil society whose white minority is both sick and doomed. Few AF officials know much about the Republic or have any direct acquaintance with it. This is not surprising, because only a small minority of AF officials will ever see service in the Republic, there are few incentives to develop substantial expertise about the country. AF's pool of officials with expertise on South Africa has been and remains thin. Those who develop such knowledge seldom retain it for long since their career incentives all point toward getting assignments elsewhere in Africa lest they become typed as simply "South Africa hands," another dead end. Consequently there is little institutional memory on South Africa in the U.S. government. The net result of these factors has been:

1. A strong tendency toward a highly critical view of South Africa in AF that translates into a preference for the United States to dissociate itself from the Republic.
2. An interest in seeing the United States make a "good record" for itself

on southern African racial issues for use in black Africa and in the United Nations.

3. A belief that the United States must make a record with the black majority in South Africa so as not to alienate South Africa's future ruling majority.

4. A lack of focus on how to encourage South Africa to move toward a more just society and a tendency toward posturing and rhetoric instead of more substantive policy formulation. A chasm of credibility exists between AF's definition of the problem and the measures it has available to deal with it.

This description of AF's views and roles, however, needs some qualification for the Carter period. AF as a bureaucratic entity was less isolated from 1977 through 1980 because a number of senior officials outside the bureau strongly supported its general views on African policy questions, including those of southern Africa. The head of the Policy Planning Staff, the U.S. ambassador to the United Nations, the secretary of state, and the president all devoted more time and interest to Africa than their predecessors did. Some participants estimate that Secretary Cyrus Vance spent from 25 to 33 percent of his time on African matters during much of his tenure. In addition, one of the State Department's three ambassadors at large spent considerable energy on the question of South Africa's possible adherence to the Nuclear Nonproliferation Treaty. The incumbent of another top job at the Department of State, the under secretary for political affairs, was widely experienced in African affairs and a former incumbent in the top AF post (assistant secretary). Measured by these standards, the Carter State Department was quite African oriented, and far more so than under any past administration.

This recent pattern had several results. First, AF had important allies within State in the International Organizations (U.N.) Bureau, in the new Bureau of Humanitarian Affairs (not always an ally, but often one on southern Africa), in the Policy Planning Staff, and among the most senior officials. Thus, instead of AF's being the lonely champion of African causes, the Department of State itself became the advocate for an activist U.S. role on the African continent. However, this important shift did not basically change the pattern in the rest of the bureaucracy. The economic agencies and the Defense Department continued to be relatively minor actors on African issues. Although officials in other departments often grumbled quietly at State-determined policies they did not endorse, the resistance was passive and low key. The White House, the ultimate point of coordination in most interagency debates, seldom challenged State's lead (and that of Ambassador Andrew Young and Donald McHenry at the United Nations) on Africa in the 1977–1980 period. As a result, it set a tone of deferring to State that was mirrored elsewhere. This was particularly true during Ambassador Andrew Young's tenure at the U.N. mission since the president's instinct on many African questions was to seek Young's personal judgment. As a cabinet member and senior Department of State official, Young shaped both the department and administration viewpoints.

Young's departure closely coincided with a growing shift in U.S. domestic opinion on foreign policy. McHenry, his successor, had a more contentious domestic climate with which to deal and a less politically solid base of support. Nonetheless, he continued Young's pattern of personally dominating key African issues, albeit with different style.

The growing Department of State interest in Africa meant that this region received higher priority than previously among intelligence agencies whose African staffs have grown in recent years. Because of the paucity of career analysts with an African background, non-Africanists and Africanists from the academic world helped fill the void. Intelligence agencies, however, do not make policy. Their lack of a large pool of seasoned South African specialists has confirmed their secondary role: to provide current intelligence on demand, to anticipate emerging trends where possible, to improve the decision-making data base on countries and individuals, and to prepare longer-term analyses on selected problem areas. These functions gave them only limited influence in shaping State Department initiatives, except when State specifically requested their analysis.

By the November 1980 election, a number of conclusions about the policy process in the Carter era could be reached.[2]

1. State's primacy was confirmed. Other agencies could resist, raise questions, or complicate the picture, but they could not make policy themselves or directly challenge the substance of policy by raising issues to the White House level and expect to reverse State's preferences.

2. In some economic areas such as Ex-Im credits and export licenses to South Africa, the executive branch made policy by obfuscation. The absence of clear guidelines and regulations had the effect of limiting U.S.-South African economic relations since the U.S. private sector was unable to get a clear reading on where it stood regarding South Africa under federal policy.

3. As time has passed, it became progressively clearer to officials in the State Department and other agencies that the United States has very narrowly limited leverage over South Africa. The bold rhetoric of the first twelve to eighteen months of the Carter administration was overtaken by a quieter style and a more pragmatic substance. Attention focused largely on specific policy issues pertinent *inter alia* to South Africa—nuclear relations and the NPT, Zimbabwe, Namibia—rather than a broad agenda of pressure for reform in South Africa itself. Much of the burden on reform issues fell to the private sector and congressional initiatives.

4. As part of this increasingly visible trend toward greater realism about what outsiders can achieve, the officials who monitor South Africa closely spent more effort trying to understand the country. Some of this effort took the form of the social psychology of Afrikaners. More germane, perhaps, were its studies of the Afrikaner political community, of key Afrikaner factions, and the South African government's decisionmaking structures. Although it is too early for high confidence, any trend toward greater official U.S. understanding of the South African environment and key actors within it is likely to be positive from the standpoint of both realism and effectiveness.

5. As the lead agency on Africa, the Department of State remained in need of a domestic constituency for its policies. The base for conducting a moderate policy of U.S. engagement, carrots and sticks on specific issues, and a readiness to play this role over the long term remains weak—both in the government and the broader American society. The number of officials in State with an in-depth understanding of South African political dynamics remains far smaller than it should be.

Congress

It is in Congress that America's strange schizophrenia about Africa is evident in the most exaggerated form. At a time when some other American elites and the intelligentsia are gradually waking up to Africa's real roles in the framework of basic U.S. interests, most congressmen and senators remain uninterested in African issues. No more than three or four senators regularly keep abreast of African issues; perhaps a half-dozen are prepared to fight on specific African questions. The House may be proportionately worse off. The level of interest, like the level of ignorance, is appalling. Yet because congressional support is required for so many aspects of foreign policy today, the potential for mischief, shortsightedness, or simple emotional display is large and growing. Potentially useful diplomatic efforts in Africa repeatedly die in one house or the other for want of a single strong voice to champion them. Moreover, these and other problems in Congress will not soon disappear. African issues are the victim of a noisy chaos on the Hill that reflects structural and leadership weakness in the legislative branch of government. Our legislative system is dangerously weighted down by information, decision requirements, and egos in search of media attention. Congress is capable of paralyzing governmental action, but it is not equipped to lead in any direction or even to help shape the national debate on key public policy issues except by distorting and oversimplifying them.

The implication for South African policy is that there is no political center or mainstream capable of holding the middle ground for a consistent line of policy, except perhaps by inaction. This is fine when congressional inaction is what is needed, but we cannot be confident that a policy of no policy will always be the wisest one, if indeed it is today. Second, it means that the main vehicles for congressional interest in South African questions are those of racism or communist threat. When these themes are combined with the motif of "no more Vietnams," we have the perfect formula for an inconsistent, unpredictable, and ineffectual congressional input to policy formulation. In such circumstances, initiative passes to legislators on the fringes of American politics. Whenever tough choices are presented, the fringes will cancel each other out, leaving the field to a bored and uninformed mass of compromise-oriented legislators. Only when a straightforward issue arises—such as Biko's murder in 1977—will the Congress be capable of a sweeping and broad-based symbolic act of censure.

Nor does the rise of congressional interest in strategic-minerals policy between 1979 and 1980 necessarily imply an improvement in congressional coherence or effectiveness. On the contrary, it could further fragment concern, priorities, and authority on important aspects of the South African question.

Congressional disinterest means that African issues tend to be dominated by lesser political figures, ambitious young legislators seeking to make a record for themselves, and a handful of long-standing "Africa hands". The established senator or congressman with serious national aspirations seldom seeks service on either the Senate or House African subcommittees. Persons anxious to influence major national issues look for other assignments. Predictably someone who gains a certain degree of prominence for African activities may decide to use them as a launching pad for "bigger" things—such as the Soviet Union, Western Europe, China, or economic issues. This problem has three implications. First, it implies that there will be a continuing tendency to exploit South Africa in the Africa subcommittees when occasions present themselves. Second, these subcommittees are likely to be bypassed and overruled when serious questions present themselves for decision. This has the benefit of avoiding ill-considered actions of one kind but the disadvantage of encouraging simplistic and hasty compromise in other congressional forums. Third, most initiatives on South Africa die in subcommittee. The subcommittees, however, have been able to block many initiatives from other sources and to intimidate their State Department counterparts who look to them for support on necessary legislation.

Lest this assessment be considered unduly negative, we should look at the matter from a congressional standpoint. Legislators and staffs have careers to build and elections to win. Why should they be immune from the same kinds of incentives others have in other arenas? They are simply playing the game according to rules they did not invent. The activists on African questions genuinely believe that if they have a role to play at all, it is by pushing and pressing the executive branch toward actions it could not take alone or by blocking undesirable actions.

In the late 1970s the House fitted this above desciption much better than the Senate, where liberals (such as Senators McGovern and Tsongas) have had their backs to the wall, moderates vainly suppress their yawns, and conservatives have a field day embarrassing the Administration on one foreign policy issue after another. Nonetheless, the basic pattern may remain similar over time. The discouraging fact remains that if and when South African issues grow in prominence, the likelihood is that Senate and House Africa watchers will fight over the action, get much attention from the media and the State Department, and serve generally to magnify the contributions of single-issue pressure groups. Another possibility is that other congressional committees will begin to express greater interest in South Africa. This would have seemed implausible a few years ago, but the visits to South Africa of representatives interested in South African strategic-military and minerals questions in 1979–1980 could signal a shift away from the previous monopoly held by the African subcommittees.

The implications of this description are fairly clear. First, the issue of U.S. corporate involvement in South Africa will continue to draw fire, not because of its intrinsic importance but because it is one of the few tangible linkages available on which U.S. pressures can focus. The effort to discredit the legitimacy of corporate presence in South Africa will be echoed in Congress because this cause will appeal to some legislators, but they are not now a majority, and there is no reason to suppose they will be in the foreseeable future. Efforts to impose a thorough investment boycott (no new investment, actual disinvestment, or no new loans) are unlikely to gain majority support barring major new outbreaks of violence in South Africa or a reversal in Pretoria's current reformist stance. To the extent that further legislation could emerge from Congress, it is more likely to be a sloppy compromise, causing endless problems for corporate and executive branch officials, than a purposeful and coherent measure aimed at influencing Pretoria to change its policy.

Second, the congressional climate favors further domestication of foreign policy toward Africa—that is, emphasis on U.S. domestic political linkages. Few legislators will have any political interest in speaking up for the South African government or for black and white moderates inside the country, and many will wish to appear to be supportive of black American concerns about apartheid. Opponents of legislative pressure on South Africa probably will distort the issues just as much as advocates of pressure in order to win over uncommitted support from their colleagues. Future debates are likely to revolve around superficial slogans—racist repression, vital strategic minerals, the Cape route, U.S. investment "propping up" apartheid—rather than a serious review of how much influence the United States has on Pretoria and how best to use it.

Third, many participants—political exiles, activist groups, U.S. firms, academicians, South African officials, and executive branch officials—will seek to push Congress in one direction or another. Congress probably will continue to reflect prevailing views and emotions within the highly complex U.S. society. A major shift in the center of gravity of public opinion will quickly translate into votes by legislators who cannot be expected to take the lead in shaping U.S. policy. South Africans, in their diversity, will serve in the end to help magnify the diversity among Americans. The quality of South Africa's diplomacy in Washinton can make a difference by putting events and issues in their South African context, but there is no overt "South Africa lobby" for it to play upon, as the Rhodesians did so successfully for years. In fact, South African diplomats are more likely to be effective to the extent that they reach beyond the type of U.S. conservatives who can be accused of holding racist attitudes.

The structure of the house encourages greater specialization and expertise (albeit among a small number) than in the Senate. This means that one would expect the House to be more activist than the Senate on South African issues. This point is underscored by the fact that the conservatism evident in the Senate is not as pronounced in the House. Prior to the 1980 election, the prospect was for the House to take the lead. However, not so long ago the picture was reversed, and it could reverse again as a function of personalities.

Finally, although the Congress has constitutional prerogatives in foreign policy, it also has severe handicaps concerning specific and mandatory guidance to the executive branch. Yet the U.S. constitutional system is in a transition in defining the proper foreign policy roles of the two branches of government. Many, if not most, legislators are well aware that 535 people cannot make U.S. policy toward South Africa, but they will affect it in direct and perhaps even decisive ways nonetheless. Congressional sentiment will rule out some kinds of State Department action and prevent some options from being considered. Constraints from both the Right and Left could increase, further inhibiting diplomatic flexibility. But there is a constructive side to this process: over the longer term, these constraints could begin to set the limits of something approaching a public consensus. In the meantime, domestic political reasoning will take precedence over diplomatic reasoning in Congress. The timing, style, and tactics of U.S. policy will have as much to do with fragile congressional coalitions, personal ambitions of key legislators, and the annual legislative calendar itself as with the current status of U.S.-South African relations. A sophisticated policy can be expected only when the Congress in not heavily involved in it. In this, of course, South Africans should not see themselves as uniquely victimized. The phenomena described here apply to a wide range of foreign-policy topics, including some of greater importance to U.S. national interests.   .

Public Opinion

Recent research about public U.S. attitudes toward South African issues points to two clear conclusions.[3] First, there is a high level of sentiment that South Africa's policies (as described by survey researchers) do not merit U.S. support and that the United States should endeavor to bring about change. In studies of both average adults' attitudes and elite opinion, there is little sentiment (quantitatively) for U.S. support of white South Africans in the event of Soviet involvement against Pretoria. Second, there is little public support for U.S. measures of the sort that might bring significant pressure on the Republic. In other words, Americans have preferences but cannot be considered to be strongly supportive of activist policies of pressure. This ambivalence is perhaps most clearly reflected in questions asking whom the United States should support in the event violence increases and the Soviets intervene with arms or troops. Only 11 to 20 percent of average adult Americans favor U.S. support for either whites or blacks, and a substantial plurality has no preference or opinion. Of those who do favor U.S. alignment with one side, those who favor support of the whites outnumber supporters of the blacks by five to one, and the margin increases as the possibility of Soviet involvement increases.

When the matter of specific policy choices is raised, American ambivalence becomes still more notable. Narrow majorities of average Americans favor U.S. adherence to potential U.N. trade embargoes and cutting off trade with countries that violate our sense of right and wrong. But opinion is evenly divided on the proposition that the United States should mind its own business on how other countries are governed. The prevention by the U.S. government of all new U.S. investment in South Africa received 42 percent support in one Harris Poll (with 58 percent opposed or unsure), whereas only 24 percent favored trade sanctions and 21 percent favored mandatory disinvestment.

A third and highly significant set of conclusions from poll data concerns the division between elite and mass attitudes toward South African policy issues. Although elite opinion is twice as anxious as mass opinion for Western countries to press for change, elites are far more cautious than average Americans about specific policy measures. These tendencies are typical of most controversial fields in U.S. foreign policy. Data from a recent Council on Foreign Relations study suggest that 70 to 80 percent of elite opinion would go no further than the current U.S. policy of public opposition to South African policies while maintaining existing economic and political relations. Seventy-five to 80 percent of elite opinion opposes restrictions on new investment, while 90 to 95 percent of elite opinion opposes trade cuts and mandatory disinvestment. Explanations for the elite-mass divergence probably can be found in greater elite awareness of the limits on U.S. coercive power through such instruments, the difficulty of actually implementing economic restrictions, and a less-emotional approach to distant foreign-policy questions. Again, the elite-mass divergence is by no means unique to opinion about South Africa.

Whatever the explanation, it is clear that opinion is ambivalent or opposed to dramatic new measures. Relatively small numbers have strong opinions, and even among those there is real division. Nor is the black-white disparity of view as wide as one might surmise. Whereas 50 to 60 percent of Americans in general favor "doing something" about South Africa, the figure for blacks is only 67 percent. Average blacks are only marginally more supportive than average whites of such measures as trade cuts and disinvestment.

Two further observations are in order in judging public attitudes. First, mass attitudes on a question as remote to Americans as South Africa are unlikely to be reliable over time. Specific reactions to particular questions in concrete future circumstances could swing wildly. Events, media coverage of them, and the focus and wording of the questions asked all shape the answers in such surveys. In this kind of opinion climate, public-relations efforts by activist groups can make a substantial difference. While a great majority will oppose racist governments or U.S. support for them, a great majority will also oppose violent solutions and U.S. support for hastening the revolution.

Second, activist groups have a long way to go before they would convert a clear majority to a position favoring strong economic measures, especially among foreign-policy elites. But it is quite possible that they will make headway if their arguments go unchallenged.

Public-Interest Groups

Any assessment of the impact of domestic groups should start by asking about their motives and goals and their possibilities for action in light of funding, staff, and institutional access. The various groups that are or may become active on South African issues differ widely in these respects, and it cannot be assumed that there is widespread agreement and compatibility among them. Nor can it be assumed that all activist groups will be on the political left; conservative groups that have been relatively inactive on South Africa to date could become more active.

The major sources of pressure for U.S. disengagement from South Africa are academic and foundation researchers; the traditional white activist liberals in church groups and Africa-focused lobbies (such as the American Committee on Africa); civil-rights groups and other black activist organizations focused specifically on Africa (such as TransAfrica); neo-Marxist or outright Marxist fronts oriented toward support of liberation movements, socialist transformation of African Marxist governments, and attacks on Western business interests in Africa; organized labor, including individual unions, the African-American Labor Center, and the AFL-CIO structure; and specialized bodies that study, service, or coordinate student disinvestment efforts or shareholder initiatives. There is some common ground among them—they share the view that South Africa has a bad regime with which the United States should be less closely associated—and there are important differences, which probably will become more apparent over time.

Such groups differ in their goals, tactics, organizational structures, and the personal motives of their key personnel. All activists require an institutional and financial base of some sort with which to operate. In the case of church-based activists, the internal structure of the mainstream church bureaucracy often gives a small band of determined and committeed individuals a free hand to adopt international stances on behalf of the national church or interfaith coordinating body. Such stances bear little, if any, relationship to the views of the largely apathetic chuch membership or to the domestic functional arms of the church.

This tendency has become controversial in the case of U.S. affiliates of the World Council of Churches, which has increasingly adopted a pro-liberation posture in southern Africa. Church-based activist minorities probably will continue to manipulate the name of their churches to advance such causes as the antiapartheid campaign. But it appears likely that some denominations will come under increasing pressure to curb controversial actions such as rhetorical and financial support for nationalist guerrilla movements because these postures are so blatantly political and unrepresentative of rank and file. Moreover, strongly anti-Communist church groups have become vocal in stating other sides of the story. As and if emotive conflicts continue in southern Africa, it is only a question of time before groups connected with American churches argue more openly with each other. Even then, however, church elites rather than the largely passive and locally oriented membership will set the tone.

Black civil-rights groups and lobbying efforts will focus increasing attention on influencing African policy. For the past twelve years since black pressure was successful in obtaining the cancellation of the Cape Town visit of the aircraft carrier *John F. Kennedy,* there has been a steady if gradual expansion in black focus on Africa. South Africa is the most emotive and sensitive issue in Africa for these groups. Although the influence of specific groups such as the Urban League of TransAfrica cannot be accurately predicted, there is still little question that the black voice in African policy issues will continue to grow.

On the other hand, it seems predictable that the number of black voices on Africa will also grow, and for a variety of reasons: the natural differentiation in the black community, political and organizational opportunities for leadership, the career goals of individuals working within various groups, and the functional interests of various constituencies. It would be shortsighted to assume that the Reverend Jesse Jackson's recent foray into South African politics will be the wave of the future; it generated a host of ambiguities and a mixed response among South African blacks. It generated, moreover, mixed reactions in the U.S. black community. As both American and South African blacks become more sophisticated in dealings with each other in future years, it is possible that black opinion leaders in the United States will become more clearly differentiated: some will provide generalized black viewpoints on South Africa before Congress and within political parties; some will take part in day-to-day monitoring and lobbying efforts aimed at pressing policy in specific directions; some working in South Africa itself will push for improvements such as those argued by Reverend Sullivan. To the extent that this happens, the range of black opinions could become more varied.

It would be a mistake, however, to assume that black Americans will soon start debating each other in public about South Africa. Like Afrikaners and other groups in the United States as well, American blacks are instinctively reluctant to air internal differences for fear of splitting the community. The instinct to stand together at least nominally on an issue of symbolic importance is strong. Unless growing numbers of blacks gain first-hand experiences in foreign policy (including African policy) and greater knowledge of South Africa itself, simplified and extreme positions could continue to go largely unchallenged among the small minority of black Americans who focus on Africa as a political issue.

The future of specialized activist groups such as campus coordinating groups and specialized monitoring bodies such as the Investor Responsibility Research Corporation or the Sullivan effort will depend almost entirely on the future political salience of the South African investment issue. In a sense, therefore, these organizations are highly dependent on opinion patterns, which they cannot control. Because careers and organizational health are at stake, these bodies have a vested interest in continuing public debate over South African investment. Therefore much will depend on the salience of South Africa as a cause relative to others such as nuclear energy, rearmament and disarmament, inflation and unemployment, and other less predictable possibilities. Much the same could be said about university- and foundation-based African activists whose prospects will be a function of how controversial South Africa itself is.

Two final categories should also be mentioned. Organized labor is in a state of disarray about South African issues at present. The AFL-CIO structure is formally committed to a mixed set of positions that are neither consistent with each other nor with the basic principles of American labor history. Labor has not determined which black leaders and black strategies are legitimate to support. This cannot last indefinitely. Either the mainstream of U.S. labor will become more radicalized as an action instrument on South African questions, and more likely to write off internal improvements and internal labor issues; or it will become more pragmatic and join the struggle against the externally based and socialist-communist representatives of the black working class. The history of U.S. labor involvement in international affairs to date points clearly to the second alternative, but this cannot be assured for the future.

Far Left activist groups such as the U.S. affiliates of the Liberation Support Movement play a distinct role among interest groups that are active on South African issues. Their dual links with the exiled nationalist parties and with the American and European Left more generally provide them with at least two networks of information and personal contacts that give such groups a potential influence far out of proportion to the numbers of people involved in them. On the one hand, they function as sources of information (or disinformation) that is produced and distributed through journals, academic meetings, and non-Marxist activist circles. On the other hand, by providing legitimate outreach vehicles for nationalist movements, they widen the audience that is reached by exiled party leaders and thus can be considered as the propaganda dimension of exile politics. The increasingly clear pattern of Marxist terminology and rhetoric among activist groups reflects these relationships.

It would be a mistake to assume the existence of a monolithic Marxist Left organized on democratic centralist principles to fight on southern African issues. There are enough Marxist-oriented individuals (or more commonly liberals who adopt terminology and clichés of Marxist origin, consciously or otherwise) in universities, foundations, media, and research or lobby groups to explain the similarity of conclusions and language that one finds in publications on South Africa. But it would also be a mistake to assume that the Far Left anti-South African lobby is a wholly benign and spontanous outpouring of American concern. For some activists, the attack on U.S. corporate involvement in South Africa goes so far beyond any rational assessment of South Africa's actual dependence on multinational corporate (MNC) capital or technology as to suggest that the underlying motivation is an attack on capitalism itself. In this sense, the anti-South African campaign on the Left should be viewed in the context of the anti-

nuclear drive, the campaign to limit or control MNC activities abroad generally, and other such efforts. Thus over time it is possible that left-wing
activism on South Africa will fluctuate according to which issues make the
best targets for propaganda, campus organizational efforts, and the like
rather than according to developments in South Africa or in U.S.-South
African relations. In addition, because of personal, organizational, and
financial links across the Atlantic, it is likely that there will be some degree
of correlation between the ebbs and flows of anti-South African activity
in various Western countries. Of all the factors that help to explain and
account for domestic U.S. efforts to limit or terminate ties with South
Africa, the Marxist-oriented activists are by far the most international in
their linkages, sources of support, and methods of operation.

It is not easy to gauge the impact of such interest groups on the policy
process in the United States. A quick glance at the list of those asked to
testify before congressional committees on South Africa might suggest that
American academicians, liberal activist organizations, and black or civil-
rights groups are the only elements in our society with a clearly articulated
viewpoint. When hearings concern U.S. investment, corporations with
exposure in South Africa should also be added to the list. However, this
short list is highly misleading. The list is short because the relevant com-
mitte chairmen seldom seek out a wider range of viewpoints. Another factor
is that many powerful U.S. interest groups with a potential viewpoint on
South Africa do not choose to seek out public platforms for their views on
this sensitive question that most still regard as low priority and eschew.
Given the very limited leverage, in most cases, of the Africa subcommittees
in the congressional power structure, it is not surprising that mainstream
interest groups would seldom seek out such vehicles for expressing whatever
views they may hold. Thus, the impression is created that black and liberal
activists, academics, and a few corporations are shaping congressional
action. In fact, the picture is far more complex. The general opinion climate
toward the United Nations, the Soviet Union, Africa, or the third world sets
clear parameters for such esoteric discussions. Major initiatives to sever ties
with South Africa are dependent on a favorable general climate of opinion
or on incidents in South Africa. Neither African-oriented congressmen nor
public pressure groups can do much by themselves to shape those variables.

Interest groups operate less openly in influencing the executive branch.
Much depends on the broad political orientation of a given administration.
Telephone calls from liberal activists are more likely to be returned by officials working in an administration that defines itself as liberal. In the Carter
era, the prominent role played in Africa policy by Vietnam era liberals and
by Andrew Young and Donald McHenry assured an instinctive responsiveness to the views of activist groups. However, this too can be misleading. To
the extent that African policy moved in directions favored by such groups,

it was less the impact of their influence that counted than the representation of their viewpoint within the government. At best, the existence of concerned activists and Africanists served as evidence of public support to enable officials to win their internal debate within the bureaucratic political context. But at bottom the real political process within the government depends on the bureaucratic clout of officials with the State Department's Africa Bureau relative to other policy elites in State and in other agencies and the external political climate affecting foreign policy at the highest political levels. To date, pressure groups specializing in Africa have little ability by themselves to shape either the internal bureaucratic process or the external climate. Moreover, there remain other avenues and channels for interest groups with other views—the White House, the economic agencies, and the Interior and Defense departments—to get their opinions across.

What, then, is the influence of public-interest groups on U.S. policy? First, they have the ability to develop a public viewpoint that can be expressed in major news media, in lectures before communities and public interest forums, and before Congress. Other things being equal, a clear trend of opinion generated by such activity is unlikely to influence policy directly, but it can shape public and popular perceptions against the background of which all decision makers operate. If enough apparently well-informed people reiterate the same view without rebuttal in enough different channels, there is bound to be some effect on the way Americans think and talk about South Africa (to the extent they do so at all). The very use of language can be subtley influenced by a sustained and one-sided message.

Second, there is a tendency in the vast U.S. information and communications industry to rely on the sharply defined opinions of experts and interest groups. The busy programmer of a radio talk show or the journalist with multiple assignments instinctively looks for shortcuts to get reactions to events, to get viewpoints for stories, and the help buttress his or her viewpoint. Given the exotic nature of South Africa as a topic in U.S. public discussion, it is not difficult for a miniscule research enterprise or a two-person lobby to get its view into major media. Most people in media are in no position to check thoroughly the authoritativeness, the representativeness, or the accuracy of whatever they obtain from such sources, even assuming they wished to do so.

Third, activist groups and individuals on the liberal or Left side of the U.S. spectrum have a built-in network available to them on many prestige (and not-so-prestige) university campuses. Given the fact that the overwhelming majority of Africanist professors sympathize with the liberal to Left message on South Africa, it is simple to place publications, audiovisual materials, and speakers on major university campuses. The influence that derives from these links is hard to measure. Reading lists for students who study Africa are selected by professors from among those titles and authors they recognize and respect. While students do not make foreign policy, universities are important institutions in American life. When they become noisy, administrators and the news media tend to listen.

Interest groups, however, do not necessarily agree with each other any more than news media do. In most fields of public policy, the ability of interest groups to shape opinion in one direction tends to encourage other voices to respond in order to move opinion in other directions. Foreign policy is no exception to this generalization. To date, the bulk of public-interest-group activity on South Africa has tended to argue for greater punitive pressure for change or for actual disengagement. This may continue to be the case, especially if the reformist stance of the Botha government proves to be unproductive of real movement. There is already clear evidence of more sophisticated thinking, more awareness of complex trade-offs, and more articulation of opposing arguments in the years since 1976–1977. This is due in part to the hints of reform from South Africa and to a new climate of opinion about world affairs generally. But it also reflects the willingness of some groups—public-affairs groups, research groups, industrial lobbies, and specialized information services—to fight back. The struggle for the American mind on South Africa has only begun.

What Difference do Events in South Africa Make?

Events inside South Africa may not be the principal influence on American policy concerning South Africa. The United States has a highly domesticated foreign policy, as well as a geographical and historic sense of uniqueness, apartness—some would say parochialism. Americans by and large find it more natural to have feelings about foreign countries than to think pragmatically about how to advance their interests in relationship with them. Moreover, the United States is a complex political system and a complex society, far more so than South Africans who tend to indulge in their own complexities may realize. The American political system is difficult for anyone to govern. The U.S. foreign-policy process spends the majority of its energies reaching the point of decision and spends less time calculating the merits of concrete choices than it should.

But South Africans would do well to place these comments in a broader perspective. At another level, American elite and mass attitudes cannot avoid being influenced by what happens, or does not happen, in South Africa, especially concerning the big, open questions affecting South Africa's future: Reform toward what? Change how soon? Who is allowed to participate in moving toward a new system? It is in our nature as a distant, often naive, and historically optimistic society to ask questions like these. Close observers of South African affairs and U.S.-South African relations become impatient at the tendency of the U.S. system to ask only such basic questions, just as they are impatient at the refusal of most persons in the South African political establishment to answer them. The expert wants both societies to focus more narrowly on how the two countries can coexist and work toward a future both can support. The bulk of Americans are not policy tacticians or political scientists. In considering the effect of events in southern Africa on American attitudes and actions, South Africans should bear in mind some basic points.

For all our idealism and naiveté, the United States is also a practical country. Both our economy and the evolution of our multiracial society demonstrate this. It is obvious to most thinking Americans that South Africa is a country of enormous potential and considerable regional importance. The United States would like very much to be able to embrace South Africa as a close friend and partner. It cannot do so now, but this is both the goal and the inspiration. The number of Americans who wish to see South Africa destroy itself, who believe in the necessity of violent solutions, or who are committed to the notion of Marxist-style transformation is infinitesimal. The number of influential Americans who want these things is minuscule.

Hence it is far from too late for South Africa to reconstruct its American image. Hostility toward South Africa and public pressure for U.S. disengagement is still a fairly new development, confined to a small minority. That minority will grow steadily as long as key opinion shapers in U.S. society continue to believe that the South African government is postponing important decisions. But the American system remains open on the question of South Africa's future. Firm evidence of meaningful change will have an effect. The question of corporate codes of conduct is a case in point. When and if South Africans devise the legal, administrative, and political capacity to remove race discrimination from the work place, it is predictable that American groups will lose interest in external codes. So far, however, even favorably disposed American observers are reluctant to argue that U.S. firms can simply follow local law and practice.

Dramatic incidents, including outbreaks of violence in South Africa, will often produce dramatic reactions in the United States. Lacking a firm base of knowledge about conditions in South Africa, many, if not most, Americans will repeat their earlier erroneous predictions of impending revolution. Others, less persuaded about the revolution but more certain of their tactics, will be quite prepared to manipulate South African incidents into new calls for U.S. action. In the event of future violence, it is the U.S. corporate connection that will continue to be the most exposed and visible target for critics. A sustained pattern of growing violence would strengthen the case for disengagement and other economic measures. In sum, the level of violence (and the way it is handled by the government and described by world media) will play an important role in shaping U.S. attitudes toward South Africa.

America is a diverse society, and some of its diversities remains barely digested. One result is a still high degree of racial sensitivity. The white majority among congressmen and policymakers are reluctant to challenge publicly the views of major black figures on South African issues, even when they disagree, because the racial nerve is a sensitive one. No public official wants to be accused of opposing the black viewpoint on a racial matter. To a very high degree, though not exclusively, South Africa is viewed as a racial matter. Only South Africans are able to change this. When they do, not only will black and white Americans speak more clearly and openly to each other, but also the natural diversity among blacks will be more evident in their publicly expressed views.

Short of basic political change, lesser forms of change in South Africa under appropriate conditions may make some difference in U.S. attitudes and actions. Such lesser changes, including those already announced or implied, may affect the context, or climate, of U.S. policy insofar as they may suggest the direction of future events. The climate of moderate reform in 1979–1980 without doubt has been reflected in media coverage, policy deliberations, and public and congressional viewpoints. But the positive (from Pretoria's standpoint) effect of lesser change depends on momentum, an absence of major incidents, and the perception that such change is not just a series of minimal concessions made under pressure. In sum, the effect could be temporary.

Notes

1. The Western Five/U.N Contact Group initiative on Namibia, undertaken in 1977, continued to receive steady and senior-level backing through 1980.

2. These conclusions apply to the Carter era. They are not put forward as predictions of the policy process in the Reagan period.

3. See chapter 2 to this book for a fuller treatment of this aspect.

10 The American Scene: An Overview

Alfred O. Hero, Jr.

American Public, Group, and Elite Behavior Concerning South Africa, 1980

Only a rather limited minority of American voters, concentrated particularly among the university educated, are more than vaguely aware of the basic issues confronting South Africa and the United States regarding South Africa. However, this is also the case with respect to most foreign-policy issues other than those of clearly direct import for war versus peace and long-standing, traditional American interests regarding Europe and the Soviet Union. Indeed developments in southern Africa in the late 1970s and 1980 generated more attention, concern, and actively held and expressed American opinion and more controversy than did those of Canada, Mexico, and Central and South America—areas objectively of much greater economic and strategic importance to the United States where major developments and issues pertinent to vital U.S. interests were evident.

In all segments of American society, and particularly among the politically alert and active minority, South Africa has generated increasing concern, a trend likely to continue short of major changes in South African governmental behavior toward accommodation and compromise with the minimal demands of most black leaders. Southern Africa has become more salient in both general and more informed opinion than most of the rest of Africa—even the Horn, Nigeria, and erratic Libyan behavior. South Africa is of particularly high and growing relative salience to blacks, church leaders, politically active university and college students and their professors, administrators, and trustees, and intellectuals and the minority generally interested in world affairs.

The central issue for the majority of the American public, for most of the minority who follow international affairs, and especially for blacks, intellectuals, church leaders, university communities, and political activists is race relations. Concerns about access to raw materials and other economic considerations, naval and military considerations, and/or potential influence of governments and ideologies hostile to American interests are of lower priority among the general public and most groups within the population other than some of those who are actively involved in economic relations with South Africa or U.S. defense and security policy, and/or are well

163

to the right of center politically and ideologically. Most Americans who follow foreign affairs think that Communist and other radical influences inimical to American interests are more likely to develop due to resistance of the South African government to racial change than if it accepts concessions toward meaningful black political participation.

Although Republicans and those who vote for Republican presidential and congressional candidates, self-identified conservatives, southern whites, business leaders (particularly those with economic interests in South Africa), and professional military officers on the average attach more relative importance to such nonracial aspects than do Democrats and voters for their candidates in national elections, liberals, people in the U.S. Northeast, those in the liberal professions, and particularly educated blacks, such differences are of moderate magnitude for the most part. Even among Republican, conservative, southern white, business, and military elites, those who assign priority to security, anti-Communist, or mineral or other economic interests over racial considerations do not predominate.

Apartheid, homelands, separate development, and other political, economic, and social situations and institutions entailing racial separation and de facto discrimination based on race are rejected or regarded unfavorably by overwhelming majorities of blacks and of better-educated, more politically active whites, the foreign-policy community, and majorities of most other groups insofar as they are aware of white-dominated rule and the basic racial policies of the South African government. Short of much more credible movement by the Pretoria government than that perceived so far toward dismantling such structures based on race and acceptance of political participation by nonwhites, negotiated and accepted at least by such black leaders as Chief Buthelezi and Dr. Motlana who are still willing to negotiate compromise with white authorities, it is very unlikely that fundamentally critical and unfavorable reactions of most Americans with opinions will become more favorable. Such are also apt to be the central criteria for significant substantive changes in U.S. policy toward expanded cooperation with South Africa in economic, technological, and particularly defense fields.

Prime Minister Botha's limited actual and projected reforms have had little positive effect on U.S. opinion at large or in most groups holding opinions. The great majority of Americans who are aware of them regard Botha's proposals as peripheral or at best initial steps toward much more important changes, to include effective black participation in election of national as well as lower-level governmental decision makers. While acceptance of the one-man, one-vote concept in a unitary state probably is not required for appreciable changes in effective U.S. opinion, at least not at the onset, termination of racial discrimination and negotiations involving the spectrum of leaders of major segments of black opinion and working toward black political participation within a decade or so are probably essential to changed perceptions and policy preferences among most Americans with opinions about South Africa.

Most of those Americans regard eventual control of the South African government by the black majority as inevitable. Thus minimum changes by that government that reject the perceived reality are likely to have little effect on the U.S. body politic. South African arguments for separately governed black and white states, linked in a constellation, have gained little support in the United States.

A majority of Americans advancing opinions on national attitude surveys, and a still larger proportion of the 10 percent or so of the public relatively attentive to world affairs and generally politically aware, are pessimistic about the likely outcome in South Africa in light of South African governmental behavior so far. They envisage accelerating conflict and escalating violence between the National Party government and the black majority and its leadership, resulting in widespread destruction and bloodshed and eventual establishment of black rule under circumstances and with results much more undesirable for both South Africans and Americans that those probably still achievable through early negotiations toward programmed change. Relative optimists in the spectrum of Americans who know much of South Africa hope its government will become sufficiently flexible and astute and feel able politically to negotiate and compromise toward black political participation under pressure of gradually increasing black demonstrations, strikes, and violence short of massive guerrilla warfare, and before it is too late to avoid the latter. However, this minority optimism has decreased over the last several years. More now argue that rather than being brought to the negotiating table by growing dislocation and violence, blacks and whites will be further polarized as moderates of both races lose their bases of support to increasingly intransigent extremes and South Africans slide into all-out racial and civil war, which will end in the black majority's forcible taking of power. Most American who follow international developments feel pessimistic and frustated about the inability of the United States, even in concert with Britain, continental Europe, and moderate black African states, to affect this apparent South African trend.

Thus Americans holding views tend to be more sympathetic with African blacks than with the government and its supporters. Most Americans familiar with the demands of such black groups as Inkatha and the Soweto Committee of Ten regard them as reasonable points of departure for discussion toward an eventual settlement. Many aware Americans are concerned that failure by the government to negotiate a viable program with leaders of such groups in the near future will result in their displacement by younger, on the whole more radical, revolutionary, and probably more antiwhite, anti-Western elements, and within a relatively few years. Pessimism that the government will act with sufficient flexibility and dispatch to avoid such an eventuality is widespread and growing in the United States.

Americans acquainted with South Africans and/or with the racial situation in that country tend to identify more with and feel more sympathetic toward whites of English-speaking and other non-Afrikaner backgrounds than with Afrikaner supporters of the National Party government. Americans familiar with the program and/or personalities of the Progressive Federal Party opposition tend to regard them as more constructive. Rapport by Americans, including the foreign-policy minority, with Afrikaners who support the policies of the National Party government is typically strained. Many educated Americans, especially those interested in foreign affairs, find communication stiff and otherwise difficult and the Afrikaner value system and priorities overly defensive, unrealistic, inward looking, and/or otherwise negative. Although these generalizations apply to communication and general rapport of Americans interested in world affairs with representatives of other cultures that have been relatively isolated, closed to outside thinking, priorities, and values, and homogeneous (such as French-speaking Quebec residents and Japanese), those with Afrikaners tend to be particularly so.

A small minority in the two houses of Congress, a number connected with the mineral and manufacturing industries that consume South African minerals, and a few others, particularly among those involved in mineral exploitation in South Africa, argue for the establishment of more normal, less conflictual relations with the Pretoria government to help ensure continued access to South African chrome, manganese, vanadium, platinum, gold, and other strategic minerals for which the principal alternatives are under Soviet control or influence. Among the foreign-policy community, the more politically aware in general, and those particularly interested in U.S. relations with South Africa, most argue that South African minerals are much more important to Britain and Western Europe and that the United States could, through stockpiling, alternative sources of supply, recycling, conservation, and substitution, do without South African resources for a considerable period. These arguments are felt to apply especially to coal, asbestos, iron ore, copper and its by-products, and uranium. But most argue the American economy could also manage, albeit at higher prices, for some years without the others and without overdependence on Soviet bloc sources. Most who participate in this debate argue that though supply might be disrupted during violence and disorder, virtually any South African regime, including a black one, will need markets in the West for its minerals. This issue continues to be debated, with no generally accepted view except perhaps that it is the most important Western concern pertinent to South Africa other than race relations, though much more for European allies than for the United States.

A majority of those aware of this debate and interested in resources believe that the current South African policies are likely to lead to confrontation and violence and are thus much more likely to result in reduced access to minerals than would be a more flexible policy of negotiation leading to black political power sharing under circumstances likely to be less violent. More feel that ongoing policies are likely to be counterproductive in the long run, if not also the intermediate term.

Other economic interests are of lower priority except among the few corporate executives with relatively direct involvements. U.S. economic interests generally are of much lesser absolute and particularly relative (to GNP) importance than Britain's. American trade with Nigeria alone in Africa is twice that with South Africa, mainly due to oil imports as or more vital to the U.S. economy than South African minerals. Moreover, Nigeria constitutes a significant balance-of-payments problem that the United States hopes to alleviate through expanded exports of capital goods and other manufactures to that country. Nigerian reactions to American behavior toward South Africa thus are of growing concern to the foreign-policy community.

Under the relative boom conditions of 1980, South Africa continues to attract U.S. capital, though considerably less than that from Western Europe. However, American anxieties about instability and accelerating conflict over the longer run are developing, and unless there are changes in South African racial policies, these fears will generate more uncertainty about whether longer-term investments will return capital and reasonable profits within a decade (or an even briefer period). The problem of disproportionate time and resources expended to defend economic relations with South Africa at stockholders' meetings and elsewhere also tends to discourage investment. Most corporate leaders and their advisers who invest in and trade with South Africa have views similar to their British (and South African) counterparts: they are generally to the left of the Botha government and more favorably inclined to their Progressive Federalist opponents. In other words, they are flexible pragmatists rather than ideological conservatives. Without more significant progress toward resolving South Africa's racial problems than those apparently envisaged by the Botha government, new U.S. investment will probably slow even under existing U.S. laws and their application by the Reagan administration.

Political and strategic concerns of interested Americans are generally perceived as closely related to South Africa's central racial problems. Few accept white South African arguments about the dangers of Soviet bloc or other Marxist ideological influence on black leaders in South Africa. Most think that the racial frustration, confrontation, and violence likely pursuant to current South African policies are more likely to result in increased Communist influence than active negotiation with black leaders toward black political participation and termination of discrimination. This perception, with some variations, prevails well to the right of center in American thinking, including probably most with views on this matter who voted for Ronald Reagan.

Attitudes on U.S. security interests in the area parallel those about the likelihood of Communist influence in the black opposition. Violence is perceived as likely to bring South Africa's black neighbors into the fighting. They and indigenous blacks might well appeal for Soviet bloc assistance if the West did not provide it. The small minorities who fear sufficiently for U.S. security interests to argue for active support of the current government are concentrated among the defense establishment and the right of the political spectrum. Probably they will not prevail under likely circumstances.

Only a relatively small minority of the public, and particularly of politically influential elites, favor major changes in U.S. policies toward either the left or right under current circumstances. Support for termination of further investment, a trade embargo, or other economic actions much more drastic than policy in the Carter years is limited to articulate minorities, mostly among blacks, church elites, self-identified liberals, and intellectuals (modest minorities of liberals and intellectuals). Support for such more punitive U.S. policies is considerably less among the foreign-policy community and political activists generally than among the general electorate. Support for active assistance, particularly military, to black opposition in South Africa and among its neighbors, or particularly such drastic U.S. action as blockade or military intervention, especially among those interested and active in foreign affairs, is miniscule.

On the other hand, approval or significant relaxation of demands that the South African government change its policies is also a small fraction of the public, including among the more politically effective minority. Those who would change U.S. tactics and tone away from the more open confrontation of the Carter administration to quieter pressures are considerably more numerous. But even in the corporate community, the defense community, and those to the right of center in the body politic in both major parties, only minorities feel the United States should be more cooperative with and less demanding on the South African government. Most even in these groups agree that though the South African government may succeed in preserving more or less the status quo within acceptable levels of violence for the next few years—even a decade or so—the long-run prognosis is for black majority government either under relatively peaceful or more violent circumstances.

Differences toward more conservative views on South Africa among Republicans than Democrats and among white Southerners than among other regional groups are noteworthy but still relatively limited. Most among each of these groups, insofar as they hold opinions, are within the moderate spectrum that would change current policies other than under quite different circumstances only rather marginally, and more in style than in substance.

Blacks have become more interested in and outspoken about South Africa over the last two decades. They have increasingly demanded tougher policies to induce change in South Africa. Although only minorities of blacks agree with arguments for sanctions, disinvestment, and generally escalated pressures, growing minorities, especially among the university-trained black middle class, are agreeing with such policy alternatives. U.S. black activism on South Africa will probably continue to grow, its rate of increase depending mainly on developments in South Africa.

Church elites and university groups have also become increasingly active and critical of South African governmental policy and of U.S. behavior regarding South Africa. Church concern has been concentrated at national denominational and ecumenical leadership levels, particularly in Protestant denominations affiliated with the National Council of Churches (NCC), in certain Catholic orders, and in the U.S. Conference of Catholic Bishops. In recent years some leaderships of even more evangelical or fundamentalist groups not affiliated with the NCC have expressed views comparable to those of the theologically more liberal denominations. Jews have become more ambivalent, perhaps because of Israeli linkages with South Africa. But church attendance and other involvements in religious bodies have little connection with attitudes about South Africa among the general public.

Activism against South Africa and for more punitive U.S. policy in universities is most prevalent in more selective, elite, private institutions, especially in the Northeast and on the West Coast. However, these institutions, their trustees in their primary careers, and their graduates have influence on media and on policymaking itself greatly disproportionate to their numbers.

With some exceptions, the main-line press at both the elite and mass levels also reflects approximately the above views; they provide little support for the National Party government's racial policies since few papers feel the policy changes it is considering are likely to be significant. The sporadic coverage on television and somewhat greater coverage on radio is of similar tone. Even relatively conservative papers such as the *Wall Street Journal,* the *Chicago Tribune* and *U.S. News and World Report* are not much impressed by the government's measures. Only a few magazines on the Far Right of very limited readership support the Botha government. On the other hand, except for the Left press of rather small readership (such as the *Nation*), several black publications, and a few religiously related magazines, few argue for sharply harsher pressures to achieve change in South Africa. Most of the press, like most of the better-informed public, argues that a viable solution must be worked out primarily by South Africans, especially Afrikaners, but with active encouragement from abroad.

South African issues have been accorded relatively low priority and attention at the policy levels in the U.S. government. Except when racial confrontations or other events in South Africa attract unfavorable international attention, relations are handled by the Africa Bureau of the Department of State and middle- and lower-level officials in other pertinent parts of the executive. Otherwise issues regarded as more central to American interests—relations with the Soviet Union, the Middle East, and the like—absorb much of higher-level attention most of the time.

Thus correlations and linkages between mass opinion on South Africa as indicated by national surveys and media content with public policy and private action in America are low, indirect, and difficult to trace. Even voter opinion on such foreign-policy issues in most congressional districts has little bearing on the behavior of most congressmen once in Washington. Mass opinion on South Africa is too amorphous, little informed, and of low priority to most voters to have much impact. It does, however, provide a context in which more-interested and generally better-informed groups attempt to influence policy and within which congressmen and federal officials debate and determine policy.

Patterns of influence by nongovernmental groups on policymaking are complex and vary from issue to issue, from one federal agency to another, from one actor in the process to the next, and from one presidential administration and one Congress to another. The number of forces, groups, and individuals among diverse elites who influence most particular policies is typically large, varied, and in equilibrium affected modestly, mostly at the margins, by a particular extragovernmental group or by influential individuals attempting to change policy.

Therefore short of major changes in South Africa, particularly growing violence, moderate policies that diverge substantially only to a degree from those of the half decade ending in 1980 seem likely. Policies of the recent past represent compromises around a near consensus among the majority of policymakers and of the forces operating on them.

Some Contrasts with British Reactions

American involvement and interest in South Africa are both much more recent and much less in absolute as well as in relative terms than Britain's. America, of course, has had none of the involved British history beginning with important settlements and developing economic interests, including diamond and later gold, over a century ago; the Boer War; empire, dominion, and then commonwealth relations terminated by the National Party government in 1961; and continuing British migration into the mid-twentieth century. The many Britons at all levels of society who have relatives in South Africa from whom they hear and whom they may even see from time to time have very few counterparts in the United States. Direct British contacts with South African visitors on visits to see their kin, as tourists, in business, in sport, and in many other contexts are unique to the United Kingdom, as are long-standing relationships of churches, voluntary organizations and other institutions. London is still the favorite cultural, intellectual, amusement, and economic center outside South Africa for Afrikaners, as well as for English-speaking and educated black South Africans.

The British economy is much more dependent on imports of South African minerals than is the United States. U.S. investment and trade with that country are sharply smaller proportions of overall American GNP and international investment and trade than are Britain's. British bankers and businessmen understandably are generally more interested and better informed than their American counterparts other than the few with important economic interests in South Africa.

South African developments are covered more regularly, in greater detail, and in more depth in the British than in the American press. Americans who follow South African affairs feel obliged to read serious British newspapers and other periodicals.

Thus South Africa has a considerably higher profile in Britain at the mass level, as well as among those influential in economics, business, and international affairs, than among equivalent groups in the United States. Average middle-class Britons are much more likely to hold differentiated views and to be able to carry on a reasonably informed conversation on South African matters.

South Africa assumes higher priority in British than in American foreign political and especially economic policymaking. The American constitutional system of separation of executive from legislative powers also results in more influential roles of local and other particular interests, especially in Congress, and in greater diffusion and complexity of policy formulation and decision making than in Britain.

Otherwise the thrust of general and most informed opinion in Britain does not seem to differ greatly from that in the United States. Particular American groups—blacks, mainline religious institutions, major universities and colleges, foundations, voluntary agencies, corporations and others with salient economic interests, media of national import, and intellectuals—are increasingly interested and active regarding South Africa. Concern tends to rise among them with each noteworthy incident involving nonwhite confrontation with the South African authorities. Each new such experience results in increased concern and more firmly held views over the previous one.

Potential Future Trends

Return of U.S. public opinion to its relative quiescence about South Africa prior to 1976 seems unlikely. The combination of the coming to power of black governments in Zimbabwe and earlier in Angola and Mozambique, and South Africa's strained relations with them, South African unwillingness to proceed toward independence for Namibia under a democratically elected regime, growing black pressures for change within South Africa itself versus the apparent unwillingness of the government to accept minimal concessions, and thereby the likelihood of further racial incidents suggests accentuation of American concerns instead.

Growing interest and activism of American blacks regarding South Africa also seem very probable under likely South African developments. Although not yet of the intensity of American Jewish feelings regarding Israel, sentiments among blacks, especially the growing educated, politically active minority, are likely to continue to evolve in that direction. Growing numbers of able blacks will also enter upper and middle levels of government and corporate decision making pertinent to South Africa.

The general rise of concern depending on developments in South Africa will also be reinforced as the younger generation of university-educated Americans more committed than their seniors to racial equality assumes roles of greater influence across society. Concern will grow even among relatively conservative groups about implications for U.S. interests if violent prognoses for South Africa become increasingly widely accepted. In that eventuality, sensitivity among the foreign-policy community is likely to grow further in respect to implications for American relations with Nigeria and other black African states important to American interests.

Both public and governmental reactions, however, will be more a function of events in South Africa than such trends in the United States. Thus slow but accelerating reforms, fueled by growing black pressures, labor demands, strikes, general racial unrest, and increasing violence that threatened to get out of hand, resulting in movement of the government to negotiation of a step-by-step program toward black power sharing, would transform aware and influential U.S. opinion and greatly reinforce the influence of pragmatic moderates vis-à-vis groups calling for punitive measures.

Such is perhaps the most optimistic of the likely scenarios for both South Africa and for the United States.

Increasing sporadic, unpredictable violence (such as Soweto in 1976) growing into more widespread bloodshed that polarized whites around harder-line policies and blacks around more radical programs under younger, less accommodating leaders before the government liberalized its posture and too late for incremental concessions to be acceptable to influential blacks would also polarize American reactions among blacks, churches, intellectuals, activist students, and other liberal groups and moderate to conservative whites in corporations, government, and the politically active minority. An extended period of violence leading into widespread guerrilla warfare aided and abetted by neighboring black states; related South African military intervention into these states; accelerating emigration of more-liberal, particularly English-speaking and younger whites and growing conflict between those whites who stayed and more uncompromising Afrikaners would be very divisive across American society.

Increasingly repressive measures by the South African government likely under this scenario, followed by growing black violence and general turmoil, would sharply accentuate negative reactions and political pressures for more forceful U.S. policies vis-à-vis the Pretoria regime. The likelihood of U.N. sanctions seems to have receded because of world economic malaise. However, should it be faced with a U.N. Security Council resolution calling for major economic sanctions supported by the black African states, most of the less-developed world, and the Soviet bloc, the United States probably would not exercise its veto but rather would abstain or even vote with the majority. A vote with the majority by the Mitterand French government would render a like U.S. vote still more likely. Decision making would move from the middle-level bureaucracy, knowledgeable about the issues, to the Congress and the White House. Mass publics and more typical politicians would be greatly swayed by symbols and clichés argued by the media, other poorly informed politicians, and charismatic leaders of particular groups. Decisions would depend more on particular personalities and other factors difficult to predict. U.S. action probably would also be influenced by the British government in light of Britain's more important involvements. However, U.S. intervention on the side of the South African government in such a context seems among the least likely American decisions.

Major South African military intervention into Zimbabwe due to deterioration of the moderate regime toward civil war or possible control by more radical elements, or such intervention on a comparable scale in one or more other neighboring black states with or without growing racial violence in South Africa itself could also place the United States in a major dilemma in the U.N. Security Council regarding sanctions. The failure of the conference at Geneva in January 1981 to agree to put into effect a proposal for Namibian independence with U.N.-supervised elections, accepted by South Africa in principle nearly three years earlier, was widely attributed in the United States primarily to South African intransigence due to likely defeat of its preferred Democratic Turnhalle Alliance at the polls by the South West Africa's People's Organization. Since South African behavior in respect to Namibia is regarded by much of the U.S. elite concerned with South Africa as a bellwether of its overall flexibility and reasonableness toward its black neighbors and its own domestic racial problems, continued refusal to accept meaningful compromise for resolution of the Namibia issue probably will result in furthering hardening of American attitudes.

Finally, American behavior toward South Africa will be affected by extra-African international consideration receiving central policy attention at the time. Even dramatic racial incidents in South Africa will not receive priority U.S. attention when other critical issues face policymakers in Europe, the Middle East, and particularly U.S.-Soviet relations at the same time.

U.S. Policy under the Reagan Administration

American policy under President Reagan, the Republican Senate, and the House with a more conservative majority than previously that took office in January 1981 will continue to be basically reactive to events in southern Africa. The context of underlying interests and prevailing opinions of relevant groups of the United States is not likely to be much influenced by the results of the election. Reagan policies in a given context probably will differ more in style, tone, and perhaps tactics than in substance from those of the Carter administration.

Reagan administrative style will probably emphasize more than its predecessor quiet persuasion and involve less public verbal confrontation with the South African government and less rhetoric about human rights. Public denunciations by Carter era officials are not likely to be repeated or approved by their counterparts in the Reagan administration, at least short of major provocation and frustration of more subtle and quieter efforts. But pressures behind the scenes on Pretoria for negotiation with black leadership in South Africa toward scheduled changes regarding meaningful nonwhite political participation undoubtedly will continue and probably become more intensive should the internal racial situation deteriorate further without such changes in South African policy widely deemed appropriate among Americans who follow such developments. Only a limited minority of President Reagan's supporters likely to have some influence probably will oppose such pressures.

Globally there may be some shift toward the greater tendency during the Kissinger years than under Carter to consider Africa a peripheral area of U.S. interest to be dealt with mainly in terms of its supposed relevance to U.S.-Soviet bloc relations rather than of its intrinsic problems. Secretary of

State Alexander Haig's experience and basic inclinations lie more in that direction than those of Secretaries Edmund Muskie and Cyrus Vance. However, the relatively few more conservative elites concerned mainly with defense and collective security and their influential supporters in the Congress and elsewhere who argue for permitting arms shipments or more active military collaboration with South Africa are likely to lose out in the policy process under conditions other than significant liberalization of South African racial policies.

Business and other interests who argue mineral priorities with respect to South Africa, more prevalent among Republicans and supporters of the Reagan administration than Democrats and supporters of Carter, probably will have more access to the policy process than previously. But short of strong urgings by British and continental European governments much more dependent on South African minerals than is the United States, it is unlikely that this minority will have sufficient influence to change the basic U.S. stance regarding South Africa, except under a much intensified crisis atmosphere with the Soviet Union.

Other business interests involved with South Africa also tend to be Republicans rather than Democrats and to receive more sympathetic hearing in the Reagan administration than they did in the Carter administration. The new administration may devote somewhat higher relative priority to U.S. economic relations with South Africa, leaving application of the Sullivan and similar principles to private American enterprises. But neither did the Carter administration propose nor did the Congress attempt to formulate legislation around such principles. Some laws and regulations regarding trade that are difficult to apply, ineffective, or both may be modified or even repealed. But unless the South African government provided a meaningful quid pro quo related to dealing more effectively with its racial problems, it is unlikely that the basic U.S. governmental stance on economic relations will be much relaxed.

Moderate Republicans, such as Senator Charles Percy as chairman of the Foreign Relations Committee and most senior officials in the Department of State, the National Security Council, the Export-Import Bank, the Department of the Treasury, and the Department of the Interior who will have significant roles in determining policy toward South Africa are likely to be considerably more influential than those further to the right on such matters. Many of the influential civil servants dealing with these problems and advising their policymaker chiefs will be of similar backgrounds, values, and policy views to their predecessors under Carter.

Overall the relevant policymaking officials and their assistants in the Reagan executive are as professional in their respective fields of responsibility as were their predecessors. Although on balance more conservative, especially in their preferred styles of operation, they are empiricists and pragmatists in contrast to the more ideological conservatives to their right interested in African affairs who also favored Reagan over Carter. The political base of the new administration and Congress is more conservative, more Republican or southern Democrat, than their immediate predecessors, whose policy preferences regarding South Africa were also at least somewhat less conservative. The relative weight accorded by the new administration and Congress to this more conservative thinking on such issues as South Africa among the Reagan political base probably will increase, while that of the liberal press, most Africa specialists and others in the foreign-policy research and teaching communities, churches, intellectuals and universities, and blacks will decline commensurately. But any substantial policy shift toward the former would result in widespread criticisms, demonstrations, and other opposition by the latter, which the Reagan administration and its moderate congressional supporters would not feel it prudent to ignore. Moderate Republican politicians, perhaps as much as their moderate Democrat contenders, would not wish to discount the possibility of winning some of their votes during the next election. And while a Republican president and Republican congressmen cannot hope to win many black votes in any likely event, their Democratic predecessors could accord black views on South Africa but modest priority since most blacks would vote for Democrats in any event.

Changes in style and tactics and those in substance, if any, may thus shift U.S. behavior regarding South Africa toward that of the Conservative British Thatcher government and its foreign minister, Lord Carrington. Although that government did not usually disagree with Vice-President Mondale, Ambassador Donald McHenry, and others of the Carter administration on substance, it too has felt that quieter pressures would be more likely to succeed in the long run. Perhaps closer collaboration by the Reagan administration with the Thatcher government will more effectively facilitate the racial progress both feel it in their interests to achieve than did the rather different, sometimes divergent styles of Britain and the United States during the previous U.S. administration.

11 The Magic Moment? South Africa between Past and Future

Hermann Giliomee

In mid-1980 I was a member of a group of fifteen black and white South Africans who spent two weeks in the United States at a series of discussions with prominent Americans in diverse walks of life, all concerned about American relations with South Africa. The South African group was impressed that so many influential opinion formers and decision makers were prepared to discuss cordially and candidly many aspects of the U.S.–South African relationship and the prospects for peaceful change in South Africa. On more than one occasion we South Africans wondered why so many doors were open to us that only two or three years ago would have been firmly shut. Then on the last day of the last meeting Donald McHenry, at that time chief of the U.S. mission to the United Nations, explained the reason: "To us Americans, this looks like the magic moment for South Africa. There will never again come such a golden opportunity for South Africa to extend civil rights to all her peoples. Is there anything we Americans can say to persuade you of the need to seize this chance and by so doing to save yourselves from sure destruction?"

This is the theme of this contribution by a South African to a book mainly concerned with American attitudes. Have South Africans arrived at the tide in their affairs where they have this ultimate chance to move away from political oppression and the denial of civil rights to a more just society with political and civil rights for all, as many concerned observers overseas expect? For McHenry, as well as for other knowledgeable and interested Americans, a combination of developments seems to point to a magic moment. The gold bonanza has lifted South Africa's level of disposable wealth to unprecedented heights. The amount of pressure that Western governments have been prepared to exert upon South Africa has decreased considerably. In South Africa a fair measure of internal stability has returned since the upheavals of 1976–1977. South Africa is no longer the obstinate pariah of the world of the 1960s and early 1970s, nor the cornered wild cat of the years 1976 to 1978. To McHenry and others the South Africa of 1980 must have looked rich and confident. Moreover, they thought they saw evidence that the South African government itself had realized the need for fundamental reform. What could have been clearer than the words of

177

P.W. Botha to the 1979 Natal congress of the National Party that "apartheid was a recipe for permanent conflict" and that "the only alternative revolution" was change?[1]

This leads to a supplementary theme to be considered in this chapter. Under what conditions do societies characterized by discriminatory practices and other human-rights violations embark upon an extension of rights across previous political and racial barriers? Was McHenry correct to assume that conditions of prosperity and political stability were conducive to the institution of fundamental political reforms by an exclusive ruling minority? A look at the battle for the extension of civil rights in the United States yields some general lessons that could be applied to South Africa in analyzing the question whether these conditions in themselves will produce a broadening of the base of civil rights and political representation.

Conditions for Racial Change

In his recent study, *Race and State in Capitalist Development,* Stanley Greenberg focused on political change in ethnically divided societies such as Israel, Ulster, the American South, and South Africa.[2] He concluded that a serious dismantling of the structure of racial oppression occurred only if a society experienced what he named a crisis of hegemony. It was only after the traditional racial hegemony had been seriously challenged, as for instance in Alabama in the late 1950s and early 1960s, that businessmen especially, but also other local and regional leaders, began successfully to insist on a new hegemony. This is a hegemony in which force is tempered by consent, in which arbitrary state and local action by the police and political administration gives way to law, and in which the state forsakes its racial character and emerges as an "educator" and the "motor force of the development of all the national energies," to use the words of Antonio Gramsci.[3]

Greenberg isolates three critical factors that induced Alabama, between 1958 and 1965, and Northern Ireland, between 1967 and 1973, to dismantle the structures of discrimination and oppression. First, the civil-rights campaigns in these countries were able to rely on strong outside intervention: the federal government in the case of Alabama, the British government and army in the case of Northern Ireland. Second, influential manufacturing and commercial interests came down strongly on the side of the reformists in insisting that the society move beyond the existing ethnic stratification. Third, the state in both Alabama and Northern Ireland had too little autonomy and was too weak to defend the traditional hegemony.[4]

Consider in contrast the South African situation between 1976 and 1980. The United States is arguably the only nation in the world that may have both the inclination and the resources to become an effective external force and could link up with any civil-rights movement in South Africa and through both force and suasion promote the dismantling of apartheid. (There is no doubt that there is wider concern in Britain about South Africa because of closer historical and economic links. But the very fact of the closer relationship, particularly the economic interdependence, and also the limits on British power in the world make it unlikely that Britain could become an effective external influence on South Africa.) Between the beginning of 1977 and the middle of 1978, the Carter administration gave the impression that it was tempted to play a significant interventionist role, similar to that of the federal government in the American South fifteen to twenty years before.

In the end the Carter administration's promise of an activist policy toward South Africa turned out to be more posturing than substance. Under Carter the United States supported the U.N. arms embargo, refused to cooperate with South Africa in the production of synthetic fuels and nuclear energy, and expressed concern to the South African government about human-rights violations. The administration, however, stopped short of any action that would seriously harm U.S. interests in South Africa. It refused to support the demand for economic sanctions against South Africa and resisted the implementation of the so-called mild economic options, such as a ban on new investment or statutory enforcement of the Sullivan principles on employment practices.

There are several reasons why the Carter administration was not prepared to do more to meet its pledge to promote vigorously the cause of human rights in South Africa.[5] First, it soon realized that it had greatly overestimated its ability to influence events in South Africa. Shortly after taking office in 1977, for instance, President Carter stated privately that the United States had greater leverage over South Africa than South Africa had over Rhodesia. Vice-President Walter Mondale reportedly told Germany's Helmut Schmidt that the United States would "lean" on South Africa until apartheid collapsed.[6] Such naiveté gradually disappeared in the light of experience, so that well before the end of the Carter administration there was a much clearer perception in Washington of the ability of South Africa to withstand international pressure and maintain its existing political order. Second, it became obvious that there was little enthusiasm in the United States for a more activist policy that tilted toward black Africa and against white-ruled South Africa. Opinion polls indicated that only a 20 to 30 percent minority in the United States favored measures like ending U.S. trade with South Africa and forcing U.S. businesses to close down operations to bring about peaceful change. A third element in America's retreat from an activist policy toward South Africa was the concern among its European allies that this would threaten their economic interests, particularly the supply of strategic minerals from South Africa. The Carter administration soon came to realize that governments, industrialists, and labor leaders in the export-oriented industries of Europe would accept only a cautious, carefully planned and multilaterally coordinated initiative to change South African society.

Thus clearly one of the three critical factors in the breakthrough of the civil-rights movement in the American South (including Alabama) and Northern Ireland has been absent in the case of the movement for black political rights in South Africa: there is no outside agent upon which it can rely. What about the other two: a state too weak to defend the traditional hegemony and strong business support for fundamental reform?

Let us deal briefly with the first factor. While hostility to apartheid, both external and internal, helped to slow down economic growth between 1976 and 1979, the external and internal opponents of apartheid have not yet seriously challenged the autonomy of the South African state. The uprisings of 1976 shook the complacency of the ruling group and frightened away some foreign investors, but there were no sustained strikes and industrial production was maintained. The uprisings eventually were put down by the police without the help of the army, and by mid–1979 foreign investment was back to its previous levels, although new investments tended to be short term. The dramatic increase of the price of gold in 1979 and 1980 brought a windfall in foreign exchange and has greatly diminished South Africa's demand for foreign capital, which has been one reason for South Africa's concern about the campaign against human-rights violations in South Africa. Moreover, South Africa appears to have switched successfully from borrowing heavily from American sources to raising loans in the European capital market, which is much less subject to pressure about lending to South Africa, particularly the public sector. The decision in 1980 of Citibank in New York to join some European banks in granting a loan of approximately $200 million for the erection of black housing and schools suggests that South Africa is breaking out of its former isolation and has gone some way toward regaining the approval and trust of international bankers. There is thus little evidence to suggest that the South African state does not have the autonomy and resources to defend the traditional hegemony.

The third critical factor, the insistent championing of civil-rights and structural reforms by manufacturing and commercial interests, only with qualifications can be said to be present in South Africa today. Certainly business in South Africa during the past two years has been much more vocal in propagating the free-market ideology and the need to co-opt a black middle class in the South African system, but there are as yet no clear and insistent demands for black political representation in the central government, for the opening up of selected schools and residential areas, and for the abolition of influx control and the pass laws. Business may believe that in the long run the black middle class need also be accommodated politically and socially, but it sees little need to risk a confrontation with government to speed up this development.

Recent Labor Reforms

Thus the three critical factors for fundamental change in the American South are largely absent from South African history. This looks hardly like the magic moment when one would expect the government to move purposefully to extend political rights to all peoples without distinction of any kind. But if this is the case, how does one explain the recent extension of industrial human rights across racial barriers in South Africa? In my view this is the one reform of the 1970s that could be called fundamental. *Industrial human rights* is used here to refer to the right enunciated in Article 23 of the Universal Declaration of Human Rights that everyone has the right to form and to join trade unions for the protection of his or her interests. Following recommendations of a government-appointed commission, headed by Nic Wiehahn, which issued its first report in 1979, the government not only recognized black trade unions and brought them into a common system of industrial negotiations but also removed race, color, and ethnicity as criteria or statutory factors to be considered in labor relations. In essence this has amounted to the first government admission that the urban blacks are a permanent, integral part of South African society; they are industrial citizens, if not political citizens.

For those inside and outside South Africa working for change it is important to analyze the true dynamics of the labor reforms and come to a general understanding of the set of conditions in which the South African government finds itself able and willing to extend real rights across apartheid lines. It is also important to assess the extent to which external and internal pressure was instrumental in bringing about this change. A cool appraisal is needed, for on this issue we are confronted with conflicting propagandistic claims of both the Right and the Left. The government claims that external pressure played a minor role, if any at all, in influencing the formulation of the new policy. On the other hand, the wing loosely called the Left in South Africa insists that external pressure was the primary influence.

Before analyzing the major factors in the labor reforms, it is necessary to state a simple but cardinal proposition about change in South Africa. In a nonviolent context, rights, as distinct from ministerial exemptions, will be extended across the apartheid barriers if external and internal pressures reinforce structural shifts in the South African economy, demographic changes in the South African population, and modifications in the Afrikaner nationalist ideology. It is useful to examine briefly the reasons why the government decided to extend industrial human rights to blacks and abolish the statutory protection that white workers enjoyed previously.

Structural Change in the Economy

During the three decades after World War II, South Africa entered the stage where manufacturing and commerce increasingly became dominant in terms of their contribution to the national income, labor, employment, and economic thought and influence. On the eve of World War II agriculture and mining combined still contributed more to the national income than did manufacturing and commerce together, which contributed less than 30 percent of the national income. By 1975, however, manufacturing and commerce contributed nearly half of the national income and twice as much as farming and mining.

There was some time lag before the government attuned itself to this new configuration. For nearly two decades after the war, it gave special consideration to the farmers, who formed an important class and electoral base of the National Party. A new system of influx control was erected in the 1950s mainly to serve their interests and labor needs. In the 1960s the government gave notice of its intention to build the urban economy on contract labor. In this it was influenced not only by the ideology of separate development but also by the pattern of labor employment in the extractive industries. Only by the late 1970s did the government recognize that in order to generate faster growth and accumulate capital in the manufacturing sector it had to permit the development of a stable and contented labor force. The strategy behind the reports of the Wiehahn and Riekert commissions aims at building up a black "labor aristocracy" that can meet this demand.[7] At the same time it is hoped that these blacks will become allies of the whites as people with the same bourgeois orientation, a growing and similar stake in the capitalist system, and a common interest in keeping the unemployed of the rural sector out of the urban areas.

Demographic Changes in the South African Population

In its decision to train blacks as skilled laborers and to recognize them as such, the government's hand was forced by a decline in the increments in the white labor force. As a result of declining white fertility, the sharp drop in immigration, and the extension of the period of military training, the annual expansion of the white labor force dropped by over a third in the last three years of the 1970s alone—from 41,000 in 1976 to 26,000 in 1979. Even before this sharp downturn, there was a considerable net outflow of whites from the semiskilled blue-collar jobs to white-collar jobs. Between 1971 and 1977 there was an increase of 65,700 fully employed, skilled blue-collar workers. Of this the white male population contributed a scanty 15,600 (or 24 percent) compared to the 50,100 (or 76 percent) that the black, brown, and Asian population contributed to the increment in artisans.

The limited number of whites, together with the statutory and extra-legal barriers to the training of nonwhites, created a skilled labor shortage in the 1970s that spurred inflation and retarded growth. In 1977, at the end of the most severe recession the country has experienced since 1933, some 45 percent of a sample of leaders in the manufacturing sector considered difficulties in acquiring adequate skilled labor as causing a bottleneck in production. By early 1980 this figure had risen to 80 percent. Projections in 1980 indicated that by 1990 there will be a shortage of 758,000 skilled workers unless these positions are filled by nonwhites who have been trained for them. To a large degree future economic growth will depend on the availability of black skilled labor. To maintain a growth rate of 5 percent per year during the next two decades, about two-thirds of the increase in the skilled labor ranks will have to come from the black population. The labor reforms amount to a refusal by the government to allow white-dominated unions to prevent members of other ethnic groups from occupying jobs they (the white unions) cannot fill from their own ranks. This attitude of white unions has always been the major obstacle to the most efficient filling of available jobs. However, because of their structural and numerical decline, the right-wing white unions have been unable to counter the new government initiatives in the labor field.

Internal and External Pressure

The growing dominance of manufacturing and commerce in the economy was accompanied by the rise of an African industrial working class. Like other African workers, they suffered severe restrictions: they could not become members of officially recognized trade unions, they were prohibited from striking, job reservation obstructed their upward mobility, and the pass laws curbed their geographical mobility. The only recourse these African workers had was a system of in-plant bargaining through works committees liaising with regional committees and a central council. However, this system hardly served to bolster African labor power.

In 1972 the relative industrial peace that South Africa had enjoyed was shattered by the Durban strikes. While the number of African workers involved in industrial disputes was never higher than 10,000 per year in the 1960s, this rose to 100,000 in 1973. During the 1976 Soweto upheavals there were several unofficial limited strikes by African workers. The 1970s also saw the rise of the independent African trade union movement, which began to assert itself.

Increasingly the government realized the need for a unified system of industrial relations, both to control black unions and to give black labor a sense of identification with the system. It believed that Africans should be allowed formally to join trade unions to enable them to bargain in an orderly way and to impose the same obligations on them as those under which white or "coloured" trade unionists operated. It was also hoped that by the removal of the crudest racial barriers to black upward mobility, an orderly incorporation of blacks into the middle class and capitalist system would be set in train.

International pressure was another contributory factor. During the 1970s foreign opposition to South Africa's labor policy steadily mounted. A whole array of international organizations, multinational companies, overseas trade unions, and disinvestment lobbies insisted that South Africa move toward the establishment of equal opportunity and treatment for all and toward the repeal of statutory discrimination on the grounds of race in respect of the right to training, employment, and collective bargaining.

The most serious of these external pressures were exerted through U.S.-based multinational corporations. In the 1970s South Africa's scarcest resource, apart from entrepreneurship, was capital. It was estimated that the country had to attract between 7 and 10 percent of its capital needs from abroad in order to maintain a growth rate of 5 percent, which would also keep black unemployment at acceptable levels. In the year after the urban upheavals of 1976, South Africa experienced a sharp reduction of foreign investment. Long-term foreign capital inflow dropped from about $2,311 million to $7 million during 1979, and there was a net outflow of $1,438 million in short-term capital and $147 million in long-term capital. In 1978 South Africa's foreign-exchange position deteriorated sharply. In December alone foreign-exchange reserves fell by about $278 million, leaving a balance of only $483 million. Direct investment by U.S. companies came to a near standstill toward the end of the 1970s. According to U.S. Department of Commerce sources, most of some $230 million flowing into South Africa in 1979 was money reinvested by companies already there, while there was a net divestiture of $164 million in that year.[8]

It is now quite clear that foreign pressure in the form of threats of sanctions, boycotts, and disinvestment played a significant role in the deliberations of the Wiehahn commission (appointed in 1977) and in the decision of the National Party to accept most of the commission's recommendations, which flew in the face of its traditional labor policies.[9]

Foreign capital left South Africa not only because of the political risks but also as a result of decreased profitability due to the relatively low productivity of labor. Thus it became necessary to remove some of the causes that produced the instability, while at the same time stepping up production. During the 1960s it was still possible to "float the color bar." This meant that white workers were paid higher wages and that they assumed better positions, usually supervisory, in return for permitting cheap black labor to fill skilled jobs previously done by whites. These jobs were then reclassified so they were no longer reserved for whites or for skilled workers. Blacks who entered them were not properly trained or accepted as artisans. In the parlance of the trade, these jobs became "fragmented" or "diluted." This process of floating the color bar was costly, but because black labor was paid such low wages, profitability was not seriously affected. From the early 1970s, however, strikes, together with political and moral pressures, caused black wages to rise sharply. In order to maintain profitability, companies had to have the required qualified labor. It became more and more costly to delay proper training of blacks as artisans and recognizing them as such.[10]

Accepting the Wiehahn-Riekert recommendations, the government abolished formal racial discrimination in the labor market. In doing so it hoped to take the wind out of the sails of groups pressuring multinationals to disinvest and in fact to increase the supply of foreign investment and enterprise in South Africa.

Changes in Afrikaner Nationalist Ideology

The central concern of the government in the 1960s and the early 1970s was the implementation of the apartheid policy: to protect white workers, to decrease the number of blacks in the white homeland, and to curb the economic mobility of blacks through pass laws and the color bar in industry.

From the early 1970s the political outlook of Afrikaner nationalism began to change. It is tempting to reduce this change to a simple economic or class explanation. This interpretation argues that notions of undiluted Afrikaner supremacy and segmented ethnic groups were welded into an ideology, when the leadership of the Afrikaners was still in the hands of a petty bourgeoisie. However, over the past three or four decades the class structure of the *volk* and the party changed substantially as a result of the rise of manufacturing and commerce. In the 1950s the party was based primarily on farmers and the white working class; by the mid-1970s it had become more oriented toward general business interests and much more receptive to calls for higher production and faster economic development. Because most Afrikaners have entered the bourgeoisie, notions of an exclusive identity are fast losing their appeal, while at the same time the call for growth and equal opportunities is falling on more fertile soil.

This class explanation is, however, too simplistic. Among the Afrikaner people, there had always been an undercurrent of moral unease and disquiet about the injustices of the apartheid policy. By the early 1970s it was evident that the homelands would never become alternative places where blacks could enjoy all political and industrial human rights. Also it no longer made economic sense to continue discriminating against all black workers in the urban areas. What should not be underestimated is the extent to which there was a moral imperative: that it was no longer possible to justify racial discrimination in the labor field through the ideology of separate development.

Since the mid-1970s a new conception of what was in the best interests of whites has begun to take its place alongside separate development. This is the goal of growth, which in the capitalist system is based on the free market and equal opportunities. A new conception of a state founded on an ideology of growth and nondiscrimination against the black insider in the urban heartland is now being developed, while separate development remains the ideology for the South African periphery, in terms of which vigorous influx control is practiced with respect to those blacks who do not have offers of employment in the cities.

Linkages of Labor Reform with Social and Political Changes

The question that arises immediately is whether this new labor policy could spearhead major political and social changes that would effectively dismantle old-style apartheid. The new labor policy cannot be seen in isolation from the current emphasis on growth and the ascending ideology of free markets. For the first time since the 1950s and 1960s when apartheid and separate development mesmerized the Afrikaners, important sections of the white population are spellbound by a new panacea. In Afrikaans as well as English business circles, in the Afrikaans and English popular press, and in important academic quarters one today encounters a fervid belief that unfettered capitalist growth will not only generate enormous wealth but will also produce political and civil liberties and lessen racial and ethnic conflicts. For instance, a well-informed South African political journalist expounded the new faith with almost evangelical fervor writing (after the 1980 budget) a long essay under the caption "Go for growth and apartheid falls away:"

> The economic forces unleashed by growth will create political change that, in turn, will create a new set of white attitudes—to Government spending on blacks, to skilled black participation in the work force, to their membership of unions, and presumably to the final liberty, the free movement of

labour. . . . The market shall set you free. And not only you, but Mr. Fanie
Botha, his acolytes and a whole government struggling to escape from its
old, discredited philosophy.[11]

Discussing the government's acceptance of the Wiehahn commission's proposals, this same journalist had earlier remarked:

> It [white South Africa] finally recognised its dependence on its black
> worker, it has accorded him his first basic civil rights and recognised his
> right to bargain with his vote. Only the naive will believe that this will not
> lead to participation in other spheres of South African society. It was a
> naivete which did not afflict the Wiehahn Commission which stated that
> "steps taken in the field of labour must have consequences, whether
> directly or indirectly, in the fields of commerce, politics and many others."
> This week the Government and the Commission took those first hesitant
> steps . . . and started a social revolution.[12]

These comments closely reflect the views of some of the "new men" in
South African politics, the technocrats and academicians in Pretoria, who
increasingly are making their influence felt upon government thinking and
planning.

It would be interesting to trace the ideological genealogy of the belief,
which has now taken root among the Afrikaner business and technocratic
elite, that there is an intimate connection between capitalist growth and political freedom. One branch is, of course, the view long held by English business interests in this country that capitalist development and apartheid are
incompatible. Sometimes loosely referred to as the Harry Oppenheimer the-
sis, this postulates that the growth of the capitalist sector makes separate
development "less and less plausible" and is "best calculated to end racial
separation and discrimination." This view has received some intellectual
elaboration from Michael O'Dowd, a senior executive of the Anglo American Corporation of which Oppenheimer is chairman. O'Dowd stated in
1974 that if South Africa is to continue the normal pattern of capitalist
development, one could expect the present period of political confusion to
continue for another ten to fifteen years, accompanied by a steady improvement of the position of the black working class, while at the same time there
will be a steadily growing demand for more radical reform. He forecast that
in the 1980s one could anticipate radical constitutional reform correspond-
ing to the Second Reform Act and that by the turn of the century South
Africa should reach the era of the welfare state and universal franchise.[13]

Another influence is the philosophy of Milton Friedman. Friedman
believes that an ever-bigger government would destroy both the prosperity
that we owe to the free market and the human freedom proclaimed so elo-
quently in the U.S. Declaration of Independence. However, if government

activity in the economy is discouraged (by limiting its taxing and spending power, abolishing tariffs, prohibiting wage and price controls, and reducing the taxation of corporations) and free market activity is encouraged, capitalism will create political freedoms. On his visit to South Africa during the mid-1970s Friedman unambivalently expressed the view that "free-market capitalist policies are the only way to a free and reasonably peaceful South Africa."[14]

These claims of the free marketeers should be tested carefully in both the universal and South African context, lest South Africa forsake one chimera for another. A universal perspective casts serious doubts on Friedman's contention that capitalism and political freedom always go hand in hand.[15] It is true that the world's mature democracies like the United States and Britain have capitalist economies; however, one should not infer from this fact that capitalist economies necessarily produce mature democracies. There is disturbing recent evidence from rapidly developing third world countries, like Brazil, Chile, the Philippines, and South Korea, that capitalism and free market ideology go hand in hand with political exclusion and repression of large segments of the population.

In Western democracies, market freedoms have powerfully supported political liberty especially because workers had acquired the right to enter and leave economic life without permission and the right to strike. However, in the third world countries, the tendency has been for ruling elites to suppress political and civil liberties while stimulating growth through capitalist development. A crucial question here is whether growth is of the kind that absorbs or generates surplus labor. If a large supply of surplus workers resists their exclusion from the market, the need for repression arises. What capitalist development in this setting does is to create modern or first world enclaves within a pool of third world poverty and underdevelopment. There emerges from capitalism in this context little or no broad political movement toward liberty.

The more limited claims made on behalf of capitalist growth must also be investigated. One is that the removal by the government of economic shackles would promote the fairly rapid growth of a stable, increasingly bourgeois, black middle class, properly housed, well educated, and responsibly employed as a buffer caste against black urban militants and the rural poor.

The model upon which this strategy is based undoubtedly is the relatively successful capitalist co-optation of middle-class blacks in the United States in the wake of the urban riots of 1965–1968. Previously the leaders of the American black community mostly lived in the black ghettos. Especially since 1969 there has been an accelerated movement by them to better-class black suburbs (what Alexandra in Johannesburg may be by 1985) and later to white residential areas. In the period following the civil disorders in

American cities, there developed a much greater differentiation in the black community. During the 1970s there were still high levels of unemployment, higher in fact than in the period of the civil disorders, but concentrated heavily in the lower-income black communities, with middle-class blacks not so much getting better opportunities for increased integration but being able to move into suburbs with better housing and somewhat better schools. Later middle-class black children moved into white private schools and still later into white public schools. By the end of the 1970s it was estimated that about one-third of the black community had made it into the American middle class.[16] Although they still pay lip-service to the plight of their fellow blacks in the ghetto, most are effectively divorced from the marginal, unemployed urban poor. From 1968 until the 1980 uprising in Miami, American cities saw few racial disturbances. The leadership of the 1965–1968 disturbances and other potential leadership had been effectively bought off.

Can the same recipe work in South Africa? The first fact to be noted about the South African black middle class is that it is extremely small. The 1970 population census revealed that there were only some 97,000 blacks in the top occupational categories of professionals and administrative workers (and about three-quarters of that number were teachers and nurses). In the next category, clerical and related workers, there were about 96,000 people. All of these together constituted a mere 3.4 percent of the black economically active population. If other middle-class blacks not members of these occupational categories were added, the proportion of blacks that could be regarded as middle class would still be barely 4 percent.[17] (Although the total numbers in these categories have increased during the 1970s, the percentages have not significantly changed.)

The removal of the existing shackles by the implementation of the Wiehahn and Riekert proposals will not alone bring about a dramatic improvement. In a recent study Robert Davies used minimum and maximum estimates of the number of nonmanual jobs that could be created for blacks in circumstances of an annual growth rate of 5 percent. He found that even with the new jobs created, no more than 8.7 percent of the economically active African population would occupy "supervisory" or "mental" positions by 1990.[18] It would seem that even the so-called insiders of the black urban areas, as distinct from those restricted to the rural areas, will remain overwhelmingly working class in the foreseeable future.

One must also briefly examine another claim of the free marketeers: that by allowing maximum play of market forces, the equitable redistribution of wealth between rich and poor, and white and black can be achieved. Here one should note some empirical studies undertaken in the United States where the belief in "people's capitalism" has taken strongest root. Herman Miller effectively dispelled the common myth that incomes were becoming more evenly distributed in the United States.[19] Dividing the population into fifths, Miller showed that the poorest fifth of families received only 4 percent of the income in 1929, rising to 5 percent in 1944 and remaining at that level until 1965. Between 1929 and 1965, the share of the fourth fifth went up from about 8 percent to 12 percent, the middle fifth from 14 percent to 18 percent, and the second fifth from about 19 percent to 24 percent. The income of the highest fifth dropped from about 54 percent in 1929 to 41 percent in 1965.

Thus in the period 1930 to 1965, when the United States experienced a far higher growth than since 1965, there was remarkably little redistribution of income. And even in this small redistribution an important factor was government intervention in the form of the New Deal and subsequent social security and welfare measures. This picture hardly supports the claim of the free marketeers that a high growth rate in itself brings about great improvement toward a more equitable distribution of incomes. The most significant change that did take place in the period 1930 to 1965 involved a redistribution of income among families in the top and middle brackets. A similar redistribution occurred in South Africa where the personal income of the English-speaking white group dropped from 44.5 percent of the total in 1946 to 31.5 percent in 1976. In this period the personal income ratio of Afrikaners to English narrowed from a ratio of 40 to 60 toward parity. However, the ratio of Afrikaner to English per-capita income in 1976 was still 100 to 141.[20] In this redistribution the role of exclusive Afrikaner political power since 1948 was a major, although by no means the sole, factor.

Miller also showed that the earnings differential between whites and nonwhites in periods of relatively high growth remains remarkably stable in the absence of any state intervention or some other extraeconomical considerations. In 1939 the average nonwhite man's wage in the United States was only 41 percent of the average white man's. As the result of war-induced shortages of unskilled labor and government regulations designed generally to raise the incomes of lower-paid workers, this figure rose to 61 percent by 1950. But the improvement stopped there, and by 1960 the figure was still the same.[21] Analyses of the subsequent narrowing of the gap emphasize the factor of increased black political power since the first half of the 1960s and the role of federal government intervention.

In South Africa there has been a dramatic narrowing of the racial wage gap since 1970; in mining it shrank from nearly 20 to 1 in 1970 to 7 to 1 in 1979 and in manufacturing from 5.6 to 1 to 4.2 to 1. But one wonders how much the gap would have narrowed had it not been for factors such as the disruption of the supply of labor to the gold mines from countries beyond our borders, the Durban strikes, and international pressure.[22] Certainly these political factors had as much to do with the trend toward equalization, if not more, than economic factors. This confirms the American trend.

Through a combination of the redistributive effects of growth and a state intervention to meet black aspirations and assist the poor, South Africa during the past three decades has witnessed a not-inconsiderable redistribution of income between whites and blacks. According to one study the black population's share of the personal income of the South African population rose from 19.6 percent in 1946 to 26 percent in 1976. In the same period that of the whites dropped from 74 percent to 63 percent. In another study two forecasts were made about the pattern of future redistribution.[23] Forecast A considered it feasible that at a projected growth rate of 4.75 percent between 1980 and 1990 and 4.7 percent between 1990 and 2000, the share of the whites of the total disposable income would decline from 63.5 percent in 1980 to 52.5 percent in the year 2000, while the black (African) share would increase from 25.5 percent in 1980 to 32.4 percent in 2000. Forecast B assumed a redistribution at a somewhat faster rate than in the past, mainly as a result of sociopolitical pressures and attempts by the state as well as the private sector to contain these pressures. Forecast B thus envisages a drop of the white share from 63.5 percent in 1980 to 42.8 percent in 2000 and a rise of the black (African) share from 25.5 percent to 40 percent.

Some other forecasts based on the same assumptions were also made. Under the more conservative forecast A, the relative income gap between white and nonwhite incomes would change very little: from about 9.3 to 1 in 1980 to 8.8 to 1 by the end of the century. Under forecast B this gap would be 6 to 1 by the year 2000. But in spite of this relative improvement, the absolute income gap—the difference between white and nonwhite incomes in terms of rand—would increase from R4,100 per year to between R5,500 (forecast B) and R7,200 (forecast A) per year.

Few would deny that a high growth rate provides more opportunities for a redistribution of wealth between white and black through creating the need for more black skilled manpower and providing the state the means for redistribution.[24] Certainly a high growth rate is desirable to contain unemployment. According to the recent Economic Development Program, unemployment will be in the region of 11.5 percent if the economy grows at an average rate of 5 percent per year and as high as 22 percent if the economy grows at an average of 3.5 percent per year.[25]

Yet the kind of redistributive achievement effected by growth by itself will certainly not remove South Africa's political and social problems, much less set South Africans free, as promised by the free marketeers. As Merton Dagut, deputy general manager of Nedbank, observed toward the end of 1980; "All our old problems of inflation, shortage of key skills, inadequate social infrastructure, the juxtaposition of the haves and the have-nots, or urban crowding and rural poverty have not and will not just go away just because the growth rate is high."[26]

An unqualified acceptance of the demand that the government must restrict its interventions in the economy and put an end to welfarism will greatly exacerbate these political problems. A curbing of the expansion of the public sector and the maze of bureaucratic controls is to be welcomed because it contributes to a higher growth rate. However, faced with this kind of disparity in income between white and black, which will persist, the state will have to continue to play a major role in easing the plight of the poor and attempt to stabilize society through welfare measures.

Recent evidence indicates that the state is gradually extending its welfare services to all sectors of the population. There is now a far greater concern than before with social security for blacks as a stabilizing mechanism. This will take the form of more adequate pensions, better housing, and the improvement of the quality of life in the townships. Little has yet materialized, but the trend is unmistakable: a state where planning for welfare promotion assumes a central position. This is the issue with which liberals must grapple today. Do they welcome this movement, however hesitant and inadequate it is, toward more social democracy for blacks, as well as whites, or do they sympathize with the demands of the classical liberals that South Africa should proceed on the basis of a free market economy and that an end should be made to the centrally planned welfare state, which, according to Jan Lombard, "has developed into a malignant growth," absorbing one-third to one-fourth of the national income of South Africa?[27] Presumably the assumption is that a high growth rate will enable the poor to buy social services at free market prices. What will happen to those who cannot afford it is not spelled out. There is evidence that the state in response to black political pressure is increasing spending on black social services. In its *Prospects for 1981* the Stellenbosch Bureau for Economic Research notes, "Increased pressure to invest in social infrastructure, such as low cost housing and educational and training facilities, must be expected. It is therefore estimated that fixed investment by the public authorities will increase by about 2 percent in 1981."[28]

The evidence about redistribution also raises important questions for socially responsible people in the disinvestment lobby in South Africa and abroad. Those who base their call for disinvestment on the grounds that South Africa practices statutory racial discrimination against the majority of the population need to take these figures into account; they are quite irrelevant. However, there are also those in the disinvestment lobby who try to build up an economic argument for disinvestment. They argue that South Africa has experienced nearly a hundred years of economic growth and that this has not, until ten years ago, significantly altered the racial division of wealth and that the racial income disparities have again begun to widen since the end of the 1970s. But there can be little doubt that the last three decades of this century will see a significant redistribution of wealth in favor of the blacks. It seems to me a dubious exercise for anyone abroad to set himself up as a judge as to whether this redistribution is sufficient. Ultimately this is an issue on which only the blacks in South Africa have a right to speak.

Conclusion

In conclusion one must return to one of the questions posed at the beginning of this chapter. Under what historical conditions do societies characterized by racial discrimination and oppression embark upon an extension of political rights across previous racial barriers? The model upon which some people base their thoughts about the incorporation of the African "insiders" in South Africa is that of the co-optation of the American blacks in the wake of the urban riots of 1965–1968 in the United States. This model also influences the attitudes of Americans toward South Africa. But the model derives from a false analogy. The American blacks constitute a 10 percent minority, and they were concentrated in what was then the more underdeveloped part of the country. Although it turned out to be a remarkably traumatic affair, it was not politically impossible for the upper and middle classes in the United States to achieve a fuller incorporation of the American blacks and to do so without sacrificing the civil liberties provided in the U.S. Constitution.

A better analogy may be that of Brazil where whites formed only 38 percent of the population in 1870 and today effectively rule Brazil without enforcing statutory racial discrimination. If one leaves aside all the cultural factors making for racial integration in Brazil, with its Catholic-Iberian heritage, this integration was essentially brought about by the fact that the free colored class (the equivalent of South Africa's "insiders") so much increased in size and power in the nineteenth and twentieth century that it became impossible to enforce discriminatory laws against all nonwhites. Many mixed bloods were allowed to "pass" into the white category, while the mulatto class, which comprises 30 to 40 percent of the population, forms a buffer between the largely affluent whites and most destitute blacks.[29] Compare this with the South African situation, with a black middle class of about 8 percent of the African population in 1990. With the Immorality Act and Group Areas Act firmly intact, the prospects for South Africa's evolving along the Brazilian lines in the next decade do not look good, although this may well be the political and social pattern of the 1990s and beyond. The acute problems of race and class in economic development constitute one of the important reasons why Brazil has not been able to maintain a democratic society with entrenched civil rights.

What of Rhodesia as an analogy? Whites in Rhodesia had a much weaker demographic and economic base from which to fight the black popular struggle for political rights and a redistribution of wealth. In South

Africa the traditional hegemony is not being seriously challenged as it was in Alabama, for instance, before Alabama embarked on the dismantling of its racial segregation. But every thinking person in South Africa knows that the black base will grow steadily in the future. Time is surely on the side of the Africans who would like to capture the state, as the Afrikaners did, and use it to narrow the racial income gap, instead of relying on the effects of a high growth rate.

What happens when a long-term threat hangs over a society where most business leaders still tend to manage the immediate crisis, while the politicians keep their eyes on the next election? They obviously try to splinter the threat or reduce it to such proportions as can be handled over the short term. Thus South Africa is experiencing the new strategy of the ruling class to effect a separation between the more-privileged urban insiders and the rural outsiders.

A cardinal assumption of this strategy is that the more privileged urban insiders increasingly will come to see their interests as separable from the excluded rural Africans and migrant laborers. This may turn out to be a serious miscalculation, however. Rhodesia showed that a policy of gradualist economic and social liberalization was unable to accommodate the rising aspirations of the urban insiders. In general, discontented insiders did not pursue the struggle in the urban areas where security controls were strictest. They turned to the rural areas and the mobilization of the rural blacks to achieve their goals. In the ultimate defeat of Rhodesia's ruling class, a decisive role was played by educated and semieducated urban blacks who politicized and radicalized their kinsmen in the rural areas.

In these circumstances the argument is now being put forward in South Africa, and also in English academic and business circles, that a government that derives its authority from a white popular constituency can do no more than merely tamper with the structure whose overall oligarchic nature suits its constituency very well. Some, like Professor Arnheim in his recent book, *South Africa after Vorster,* argue that no purpose is served even by tampering because either the structural causes of conflict will remain or such tampering may lead to rising black expectations, which ultimately will get out of hand. In essence this particular argument comes down to the belief that politically South Africa is faced with only one stark choice: white oppression or black oppression.[30]

There are several fallacies in this argument, which derive from the abstract and unhistorical terms in which the alternatives are presented. First, whether black expectations can be contained or not depends on the power base from which reforms are instituted. A comparative analysis of the strength of the security apparatus and the resolve of the ruling class in societies that faced revolution (France in 1789, Russia in 1917, and Iran in 1979) shows that South Africa does not have a power base that will weakly cave in to black demands.

This power base should also be viewed in relative terms, however. It is formidable if all the potential resources of the South African economy and society as a whole are considered. It is much weaker if only the resources of the white sector are taken into account. In the short term this white sector has the resources to crush any black rebellion. But this sector is no longer strong enough to retain undiluted white rule through coercive measures and at the same time maintain a high growth rate, attract foreign investment, and prevent growing numbers of blacks from becoming totally alienated from the system of rule. White supremacy has benefits but, as the 1970s showed, it also has steadily rising costs. The business sector knows only too well the high cost of greatly diminished business confidence and retarded economic growth that the 1976–1977 upheavals brought in their wake. And these upheavals were restricted mainly to the black townships.

If white South Africa wants to counter the security threats confronting the country and to maintain a high growth rate, it will increasingly have to draw on the total resources of the society. In strengthening the defense force South Africa will have to rely increasingly on blacks if it wants to utilize the declining proportion of whites to optimum capacity in the economy. And even then there will be a growing shortage of whites to fill the skilled jobs in the economy.

The blacks in the military and skilled ranks of the economy will bring the African population into a position of growing strategic strength. If the significance of this is properly realized, it will become clear that South Africa does not have any choice between maintaining undiluted white rule and accommodating black aspirations. Through a number of processes South Africa is already committed to the cause of the incorporation of blacks into its social and economic system.

By the end of the century there will be three times more black matriculants[31] than white matriculants and four times more if Indian and colored matriculants are included. Moreover, this leaves out of consideration the numbers that will receive advanced industrial training. It needs no argument to show that traditional employment patterns cannot absorb such numbers. At the same time the prospect of a rapidly growing group of unemployed students and educated youth is unacceptable from a security point of view, particularly if the pattern of events in Rhodesia is taken into account. To ensure that work opportunities commensurate with their level of education are found and to afford them the opportunity of being included in our community as real citizens is the challenge that business and government face in the decade to come. To fail would mean that through our educational and industrial training policies we are sowing the seeds of revolution.

These educational and training policies cannot be reversed. Further, there is no doubt that the hesitant steps that the P.W. Botha government is now taking are simply the precursors of other steps that will have to be taken by his or succeeding administrations to meet the demands of political stability and economic growth and to avert the disaster of a long and widespread racial war.

What is not known is whether the political and civil rights that currently remain will survive these attempts to incorporate blacks, establish greater security in the homelands, and contain a rising level of black resistance. Economic growth and the free market by themselves will not bring political freedom. Black political aspirations can be met only by political decisions to accommodate them. The price of the failure to grasp the nettle of political reform in rapidly developing countries has often been the denial of civil rights to all and an increase of the potential for violence. And as the dictatorship of Chile has shown, the free market can coexist with political oppression, however high the cost in human values.

In a leading article accompanying a most perceptive essay on South Africa by Simon Jenkins, the *Economist* warned that the strategy of incorporating blacks only partially (that is, only the urban insiders and even them only economically) will be threatened by a rising level of internal violence. More violence will force the government into increased defense expenditure and white mobilization, which in turn will erode the economic base that is so vital to the strategy of incorporation. But the greatest danger, in the words of the *Economist,* is "that it will turn South Africa into the sort of dictatorship all too popular in modern Africa; in which no human freedoms are respected and in which the colour of the rulers no longer matters to the ruled."[32] South Africa can avoid the danger of such a dictatorship, but it will need great political courage from government and business, both looking beyond their respective short-term interests. Neither government nor business should be under any illusion as to what will happen if they leave it to the free market by itself and posterity to solve the present political problems of South Africa.

Through a number of irreversible processes, South Africa has embarked on the road of reform and the partial incorporation of blacks into its society. What must still be decided is whether government and business will meet the challenges ahead by extending or sacrificing existing freedoms and rights.

It seems that the present could be a magic moment in another sense. It may be the magic moment when opinion formers in South Africa have a last chance to dispel the chimeras and panaceas underlying much of the thinking about reform and change. Much of the wishfulness of the thinking about separate development was brutally exposed, and rightly so, in the 1970s. Now is the time to look at the claim that growth and the free market by themselves will bring political freedom and rights for all South Africans. American opinion formers and policymakers, with their historic experience of capitalism and civil rights, can play a constructive role in this debate if they so wish. In any case, American attitudes towards South Africa, and those of the West generally, will be crucially affected by the outcome of the debate.

Notes

1. *South African Digest,* August 24, 1979, p. 1, August 31, 1979, p. 4.
2. Stanley B. Greenberg, *Race and State in Capitalist Development* (New Haven: Yale University Press, 1980).
3. Antonio Gramsci, cited by ibid., p. 400.
4. Stanley B. Greenberg, "The Political Economy of Change: Problems of Hegemony in Contemporary South Africa," in *South Africa: Dilemmas of Evolutionary Change,* ed. F. van Zyl Slabbert and Jeff Opland (Grahamstown: Institute of Social and Economic Research, 1980), p. 106.
5. This is discussed more fully in Hermann Giliomee, *South Africa's Relationship with the West,* Occasional Paper 80/4 (Stellenbosch: Unit for Futures Research, October 1980).
6. On Carter see "Carter and Africa: Atlantic or Azania," *Africa Confidential* 18 (1977):1-3; on Mondale see W. Scott Thompson and Brett Silvers, "South Africa in Soviet Strategy," in *South Africa into the 1980s,* eds. Richard E. Bissel and Chester A. Crocker (Boulder, Colo.: Westview Press, 1979), p. 154.
7. The Commission of Inquiry into Labour Legislation (the Wiehahn commission) was appointed by the state president on June 21, 1977. It was asked to inquire into, report upon, and make recommendations in connection with the existing legislation administered by the Departments of Labour and of Mines, with specific reference to modernizing the existing system for the regulation of labor relations and the prevention and settlement of disputes eliminating bottlenecks and problems within the entire sphere of labor and laying a sound foundation for labor relations in the future. South Africa Republic White Paper on Part I of the Commission of Inquiry into Labour Legislation (1979), p. 5. The Commission of Inquiry into Legislation Affecting the Utilization of Manpower (the Riekert commission) was appointed on August 18, 1977. The commission confined itself mainly to the acts administered by the Departments of Plural Relations and Development, of Education and Training, and of Planning and the Environment.
8. On the flight of capital after the 1976 upheavals, see Brian Hackland, "The Economic and Political Context of the Growth of the Progressive Federal Party in South Africa, 1959-1978," citing *Financial Times,* June 21, 1978, January 10, 1979, *Journal of Southern African Studies* 7 (1980):8. On U.S. disinvestment see Robert Manning, "South Africa Tries

to Regain Confidence of Foreign Firms," *Christian Science Monitor,* December 18, 1980.

9. On foreign pressure as a factor in the deliberations of the Wiehahn commission see "Introduction to Special Issues: Focus on Wiehahn," *South Africa Labour Bulletin* 5 (1979):7–10.

10. R. Davies, "Capital Restructuring and the Modification of the Racial Division of Labor in South Africa," *Journal of Southern African Studies* 5 (1979).

11. Fleur de Villiers, *Johannesburg Sunday Times,* March 30, 1980, p. 21.

12. Fleur de Villiers, "The Law Gives Way to the Profits," *Johannesburg Sunday Times,* May 6, 1979, p. 21.

13. M.C. O'Dowd, "The Stages of Economic Growth and the Future of South Africa," in *Change, Reform and Economic Growth in South Africa,* eds. Lawrence Schlemmer and Eddie Webster (Johannesburg: Raven Press, 1978), pp. 28–50.

14. Statement quoted by Stephen Orpen, "What Pretoria Must Do to Save the Boom," *Johannesburg Sunday Times,* December 14, 1980. See also Milton Friedman, *Capitalism and Freedom* (Chicago: University of Chicago Press, 1962), pp. 13–15, and Friedrich A. Hayek, *The Road to Serfdom* (Chicago: University of Chicago Press, 1944), pp. 14–17, 36.

15. The relationship between private enterprise and democracy is analyzed in a major study by Charles Lindblom, *Politics and Markets: The World's Political Economic Systems* (New York: Basic Books, 1977), pp. 45–51, 161–233. See also the brief statements by Robert Heilbronner and Eldon Kenworthy, *New York Review of Books,* November 20, 1980, p. 53.

16. See "Black-White Wage Gap Grows in US," *Johannesburg Star,* June 21, 1979.

17. John Kane-Berman, "The Search for a Black Middle Class," *Energos,* no. 1 (1980).

18. Davies, "Capital Restructuring and the Modification of the Racial Division of Labour in South Africa" (unpublished paper, 1980).

19. Herman P. Millar, "Is the Income Gap Closing?" in *Perspectives on the Economic Problem,* eds. Arthur MacEwan and Thomas E. Weisskopf (Englewood Cliffs: N.J.: Prentice-Hall, 1970), p. 243.

20. Heribert Adam and Hermann Giliomee, *Ethnic Power Mobilized: Can South Africa Change?* (New Haven: Yale University Press, 1979).

21. Millar, "Is the Income Gap Closing?" p. 244.

22. For an analysis of these phenomena, see Francis Wilson, "Current Labour Issues in South Africa," in *The Apartheid Regime: Political Power and Racial Domination,* eds. Robert M. Price and Carl G. Rosberg (Berkeley: Institute of International Studies, 1980), pp. 152–173. A recent exhaustive study is Merle Lipton, "Men of Two Worlds: Migrant Labor in South Africa," *Optima* 29 (November 1980):72–201.

23. For the first study see tables 4–6 in Adam and Giliomee, *Rise and Crisis,* pp. 172–174. The study with the two forecasts is found in "Total Disposable Income and Disposable Income Per Capita According to Population Group—A Review," *Unit for Futures Research Bulletin* (July 1980).

24. For the view that the redistributive claims of capitalism are coming true, see Ken Owen, "Welfare Schemes Are Great for the Social Workers' Industry," *Johannesburg Sunday Times,* September 7, 1980.

25. See the debate about this issue in Slabbert and Opland, *South Africa: Dilemmas,* pp. 86–154.

26. Merton Dagut, "Bumpy, Exciting, Upward Ride Ahead," *Cape Times,* December 3, 1980.

27. J.A. Lombard, *Freedom, Welfare and Order* (Pretoria: Benbo, 1978), p. 183.

28. Bureau for Economic Research, Stellenbosch, Stellenbosch University, 1981, *Prospects for 1981,* p. 24.

29. On this see Carl N. Degler, *Neither Black nor White: Slavery and Race Relations in Brazil and the United States* (New York: Macmillan, 1971), and David Brion Davis, *The Problem of Slavery in Western Culture* (Ithaca: Cornell University Press, 1966).

30. This is the theme of M.T.W. Arnheim, *South Africa after Vorster* (Cape Town: Howard Timmins, 1979).

31. Statement by Professor Andries Oosthuizen, director of the Institute of Urban Studies at the Rand Afrikaans University, January 14, 1981, in *Beeld,* January 15, 1981.

32. Simon Jenkins, "South Africa's Great Evasion," *Economist,* June 21, 1980, p. 13.

12 Confronting the Common Danger: South Africa and the United States in the Reagan Era

Robert I. Rotberg

There is an enduring quality and a growing maturity in relations between South Africa and the United States. The chapters in this book have described in some detail the interest groups that affect and effect the making of policy in the United States regarding South Africa and the attitudes with which each of these constituencies approaches the several dilemmas posed by the internal political structure of South Africa.

Although no one could claim that in ordinary times South Africa is of major concern to most Americans, the arguments presented in this book should persuade decision makers everywhere and South Africans, both official and unofficial, that there are interest groups in America whose opinions cannot be ignored. In time of crisis it is clear that those groups can mobilize legislators and other Americans to focus their attentions on the discrimination that South Africa's ruling white minority inflicts upon the numerically much larger part of its population.

A decade ago this would not have been so. The conflict within South Africa was not then unknown—far from it—but the decolonization of the rest of Africa and the tragedy of the Vietnam war were of primary concern for Americans. Rhodesia was an important issue for those who followed the complex events of Africa. South Africa was then both less powerful and less isolated (Portugal still governed colonies in Africa and the white minority controlled Rhodesia). Moreover, as part of an overall strategy President Nixon's administration had begun to view the concerns of Africa primarily from globalist or neo-cold war objectives. The Nixon administration consciously decided not to interfere with the existing colonialist status quo lest any resulting destabilization, and progress toward majority rule, prove profitable for the Soviet Union.

The very existence of inequality in southern Africa, however, proved irresistible. Despite the cautious approach of the Nixon and Ford governments, by the mid-1970s Soviet backing for guerrilla movements opposed to Portuguese colonial rule in Angola and Mozambique was decisive. Soviet support of the South West Africa People's Organization (SWAPO) in its struggle to wrest Namibia from South Africa was growing. The Soviets were also beginning to establish a major position in the war against the white government of Rhodesia. For decades there had been tight links between the Soviet Union and the guerrilla forces of the African National Congress (ANC) of South Africa.

An official American inability to understand the special quality of the nationalist battle against the Portuguese in Angola and the postcolonial conflict within Angola between the different contending nationalist parties led to a series of miscalculations in American policy, Cuban and South African interventions, and a major Soviet strategic advance in a part of Africa where the Soviet Union had had little standing. When President Carter entered office, there was a natural swing in policy determination and a new emphasis upon regional considerations. The notion that a globalist strategy could best be pursued by covert assistance to proxy parties and armies was derided. A new orthodoxy arose that called for the support of genuine African autonomy in the newly decolonized states, an awareness of the historically central role of African liberation movements, and a dramatically new concentration upon a peaceful but deliberately speeded-up solution to the Rhodesian, Namibian, and South African problems. The Carter administration attempted through assiduous diplomacy (much of it in consort with its Western allies and Nigeria and the independent nations of southern Africa) and judiciously applied threats and rewards, to move the South African government to a realistic recognition of its own national self-interest. The American posture was officially chilly; there was a rupturing of some long-standing official forms of interaction, a suspending of some past obligations, and a withholding of a number of customary economic, political, nuclear, and military incentives.

The United States publicly urged South Africa to move toward full political participation. It refrained from specifying precisely what forms this participation might take, how it might be accomplished, or the time period in which it might be achieved. Indeed with regard to the long-standing white denial of black political and social rights within South Africa, the American approach was to abstain from prescribing how South Africa should reform. Instead the Americans said over and over that a successful restructuring of South Africa, and the kinds of shifts in internal policy that would avoid violence and a revolutionary-like conflagration would come about only as a result of long-term negotiations in good faith between the white power wielders and authentic representatives of the disenfranchised. Moreover, official Americans in the Carter years were motivated only in part by their sense of injustice and their president's feelings of moral rectitude. The other prime consideration—in the late 1970s the overwhelming motive—was a firm belief that only by ending the practice of apartheid in South Africa could the threat of Soviet intervention in southern Africa be removed permanently. In the absence of inequality in South Africa, black Africans would have no need for or interest in Soviet backing.

During the Carter years the government of South Africa began, but not necessarily as a result of American or Western encouragement, to alter its rhetoric, its outlook, and, after the accession of Prime Minister Pieter W. Botha to the prime ministership in 1978, some of the basic superstructure of apartheid. As the administration of President Reagan took office in 1981 and a general election in South Africa was scheduled for April 1981, this rearrangement was still in process. It appeared that it might be underway for years to come.

But if the Carter administration was inconclusive, it could claim a much clearer impact on South African thinking over Namibia. Denying until 1977 that Namibia was rightfully a responsibility of the United Nations, Western pressure and discussion focused South Africa on the realistic options for Namibia, persuaded South Africa to abort its attempt to manufacture an internal settlement, and began an interminable round of negotiations between the West and South Africa, and South Africa and the United Nations, which led, in admittedly difficult stages, to a series of specific agreements over how an internationally supervised election might be organized in Namibia and how South African control might be phased out and an independent government established. As the outcome of the unhappy conference at Geneva in 1981 made clear, however, South Africa was still not ready to transfer power in Namibia. South Africa feared the victory of SWAPO; and it still hoped that with the assistance of the Reagan administration, because of a worsening of relations between the Soviet Union and the United States, or perhaps merely because of the instability of the world in the 1980s, it could arrange a validated shift of government to the Democratic Turnhalle Alliance, its multiracial ally in Namibia, despite continued guerrilla activity and U.N. support for SWAPO.

The perspective of the Reagan administration is expected to be determinedly globalist, with an emphasis on how regional dramas may or should effect America's much more important struggle for world hegemony against the Soviet Union. Yet this return to globalism cannot mark a simple return to the Nixon-Ford posture toward southern South Africa. Even if the U.S.-Soviet competition can be put in a context striking in its familiarity, southern Africa has vastly changed. Zimbabwe, Angola, and Mozambique are independent. Angola and Mozambique, both officially Marxist, the former still harboring 20,000 Cuban soldiers, the latter having forged official economic ties with the Soviet bloc, are nevertheless moving noticeably toward some more centrist, African-based form of economic organization. Zimbabwe, despite the heady rhetoric of the revolution that ended only early in 1980, has a remarkably responsible and incentive-oriented government, which welcomes foreign investment and is determined to maximize its own opportunities for development and long-term growth. It has not embraced the Soviets and has refused to give facilities to ANC guerrillas in their unequal battle against South Africa.

The return to globalism must also take into account significant shifts both in the nature of South Africa (and the way in which its internal problems are being addressed) and also in the way in which Americans perceive and are conscious of South Africa. A decade ago separate development was little more than a name. Neither South Africa nor the rest of the world had taken seriously the notion that Bantustans/homelands/black states could or should gain autonomy or that a modernizing South Africa would ever contemplate (and hope to have others regard doing so with favor) disinheriting its entire black population by assigning their political aspirations solely to ten rural units carved haphazardly out of the much larger body of the white-dominated but still (in 1981) overwhelmingly black-populated South Africa.

The government of South Africa still intends to infuse legitimacy into the homelands and thus to legitimize its denial to blacks of political rights and citizenship in South Africa. But its unilateral grant of independence to three of the homelands has met with little favor in the rest of the world and no recognition. Nor has it persuaded blacks to abandon their agitation for the end of apartheid in South Africa. On the contrary, politically conscious Africans are more cynical and anxious than before; they view separate development as an elaborate subterfuge that has brought no benefits, not even to those Africans who reside in what have become vastly overcrowded, largely poor, and unproductive rural slums. They accuse South Africa of exporting unemployment to the homelands. Young urban Africans overwhelmingly are contemptuous of the homelands and of the leaders of the homelands—whatever the good intentions of those leaders. This distrust was deepened in 1980 when, despite the adverse report of an international commission, a fourth homeland decided to seek local independence without having obtained important concessions on land, citizenship rights, permanent financial aid, and employment guarantees from South Africa.

The West is much more aware of the issues involved in South Africa's confrontation than ever before. A post-Vietnam generation of students has agitated, American corporations have altered their approach to South Africa, and the media have become much more sophisticated in their coverage of South Africa than in the 1960s or 1970s. That concern has been fueled by a decade in which there were well-publicized deaths in South African police detention of African militants, in which a major spate of rioting left 600 dead and at least 2,000 wounded, in which about 100,000 Africans and coloureds boycotted schools to protest inequality, in which Africans began to contest and to win industrial disputes, in which the ANC sabotaged an oil-producing facility and perpetrated other threatening breaches of security, and in which there was much more defiance than ever before of white authority by distinctly nonradical, nationalist-minded Africans and coloureds of respectable mien and appearance.

Recently American policymakers and Americans generally were compelled to note the government's shutting down of two black-oriented newspapers and the banning of a number of prominent African journalists. At the same time South Africa raided an ANC center in neighboring Mozambique, took a hard line on Namibia, and (with an election in the offing) made none of the much-vaunted modifications in apartheid that had been foreshadowed by the prime minister's public pronouncements in 1979 and 1980.

In fact it was more than coincidence that South Africa embarked upon fundamental reappraisal of its political direction with regard to African advancement and the internalization of the Namibian question in the month when Ronald Reagan became president of the United States. Would his administration, the South Africans wondered, support the thrust of policy that despite the turbulent 1970s enabled South Africa to survive and prosper in a hostile and antagonistic world? Would it at least provide a psychological buffer between the antiracist second and third worlds and South Africa? Would it do more? Would it interpose itself economically, even politically? Could the hostility toward South African apartheid of American blacks, churches, students, and others safely be ignored by even a Republican president with a significant conservative mandate? Could American policies toward South Africa be formulated meaningfully without the concurrence of such groups and, of equal importance, without the acquiescence of our quondam allies in the third world, especially our key suppliers of oil?

Obviously the Reagan victory emboldened the leaders of South Africa. Obviously, too, in 1981 they calculated that a Reagan administration would both be preoccupied and be more concerned strategically with anticommunism in Europe and globally than with the so far only marginally rewarding campaign for change in South Africa. South African policymakers also were aware that conservative Republicans are historically more sympathetic to continued white rule in the third world, that the record of democracy in black Africa was not unblemished, and that South Africa had a reasonable chance of persuading a Reagan administration that its intentions were ultimately for the best. More directly, South Africa saw a renewed opportunity to gain credit for its long and loudly trumpeted insistence that it and it alone was the final bulwark against the spread of Soviet domination into the wealthy southland of Africa. South Africa could prevent the spread of communism. White-run South Africa was and would remain an ally of the West, guarding the South Atlantic and the oil-bearing route from east to west around the Cape of Good Hope. Moreover, only from a white-run South Africa could Europe and the United States be sure of an uninterrupted flow of strategic minerals. As 1981 began, South Africa was confident that those and analogous arguments would neutralize the emotional, ideological anti–South African attitudes that had been so dominant during the presidency of Jimmy Carter.

South African and many Western policymakers assume, because of the dramatic change of power in the United States coinciding with a reawakening in the West to the common danger, that a secure South Africa will now be of paramount importance. Indeed South Africans expect those of influence in the West openly to condone the perpetuation of apartheid because the menace of Soviet communism (in the bitter battle between good and evil in the world) is the greater of the two dangers. There has always been a concern, minimized by strategic thinkers in the Carter era, that the subversion of South Africa by blacks could or would lead inevitably to Marxist control of South Africa and therefore ineluctably to the denial to the West of minerals and of a vital shoreline.

That these propositions are not self-evident should be obvious, but that they are strongly held in both the United States and South Africa, as well as Europe, cannot be gainsaid. The Reagan administration believes in the general tenor of such conclusions; globalism is partial to them. Many of the groups whose views are examined in this book are, however, regionalist in the sense that Chester Crocker's chapter has described. They, and the former Carter administration, pay close attention in their analyses to South Africa as a problem that can be resolved only by South Africans. They believe that the solution arrived at by all South Africans will have profound implications for southern Africa, if not necessarily for the peace of the world. Globalists tend to have a utilitarian regard for South Africa. What role, they ask, can South Africa play in the titanic struggle for the world?

There is merit in both positions. South Africa's resources and coastline are important to the West. Its pivotal position in southern Africa cannot be overlooked. It cannot be wished away simply because of its discriminatory local policies. But a detached analysis of the main strategic issues ought to demonstrate that South Africa is essential to the West only given a number of crucial assumptions. The first, and the most debatable, is that a white-run South Africa is inherently a guarantor of stability. There is the powerful contrary view that there can be no security for the West until South Africa successfully makes the transition from minority rule to some form of equitable sharing of authority. Until blacks have a stake in the stability of their own society, South African whites can never be secure. And if they cannot, an alliance between white South Africa and the West imperils the West.

Prime Minister Botha himself urged South African whites to "adapt or die."[1] He warned them of the revolution at the door. But neither he nor a range of foreign political analysts believed that adaptation necessarily meant an immediate transfer of all power from whites to blacks. Short of revolution—an inherently unlikely scenario—there were a number of gradual ways of giving blacks a stake in the stability of their own society.[2] The Botha government may introduce some of those possibilities. But whether they include indirect representation in a quasi-parliament, the sharing of authority in some kind of multistate confederal system, greater autonomy at the regional or municipal level, or alterations in the very fabric of South African society that could provide Africans with truly tangible increments of power, Africans will test what is offered by its origin (whether the alterations are handed down or are arrived at by negotiation) and by its likely efficacy (whether the proposed changes are cosmetic or appropriately evolutionary). The strictness of the test will grow more rather than less severe with every delay in the implementation of Botha's adaptive strategy, with the inevitable further alienation of young blacks and with the continued potential for more and more rather than less and less violence in the work place, in the schools, and in the always-tense African cities. Those who are persuaded that whites will or can maintain the status quo in terms of the distribution of power or will or can unilaterally determine the pace of change misread the very recent history of South Africa and are ignorant of the contemporary condition of the confrontation within the country. Even the military leaders of South Africa, as aware as they are of the prowess of their defense force and security police, are concerned that the politicians move rapidly and vigorously to give Africans an unambiguous position in the future societal distribution of power.

In early 1981 African minimum demands were clear. Six months before Bishop Desmond Tutu, secretary of the South African Council of Churches and a persistent but measured black critic of the government, spoke of the dangerous crisis in race relations. But, optimistically, he indicated that Botha only had to act in four ways to resolve the conflict and lead South Africa in an orderly and evolutionary way toward political power sharing. Bishop Tutu said that the government must commit itself to a common citizenship for all South Africans in an undivided South Africa, irrespective of color; abolish the pass laws, which restrict black mobility; cease sending urban Africans involuntarily to barren, rural dumping grounds; and establish a single educational system for all. He said nothing, surprisingly, about a common franchise or about power sharing.

Politicized Africans do appreciate that only through a growing stake in some form of plural democracy can they evolve toward majority rule without cataclysmic bloodshed and years of repression and without upsetting or destroying the structure of the rich society, which they wish to inherit. Whether the followers of the jailed heroes of the ANC, or the adherents of the black consciousness movement begun by Steve Biko, or even the Zulu-speaking members of Chief Gatsha Buthelezi's Inkatha movement will be patient while the whites decide how quickly they will choose to adapt is the unanswerable question.

A stable South Africa is valuable to the West, not least because such stability is crucial to the development of the entire southern African region. Soviet adventurism is dependent upon instability; the new nations of southern Africa are as anxious as white-ruled South Africa to maximize stability in their own self-interest. None wishes to diminish its own developmental potential, to increase the area's tension, to inhibit Western interest and investment, or to provide excuses for Soviet intervention. If the lessons of contemporary Zimbabwe, and even Mozambique and Angola, are applicable to South Africa, it is not certain that a black-ruled South Africa would be a willing client of Soviet Marxism. In any short run, the attitudes toward the West of any black-dominated South Africa would depend upon how such a government had come to power and by whom or by what its authority was mortgaged. But only under extreme, and very unlikely, circumstances does it make sense to assume that a Marxist black government would be desirous or capable of hindering the traffic of supertankers around the Cape of Good Hope. Such tankers generally travel forty miles offshore, rarely needing to call at South Africa's ports and could be halted only as part of a broader scenario of war. If the scenario is of a South Africa allied to the Soviets in a third world war, the crucial attacks on Europe's oil supplies would be in the Persian Gulf, many miles closer to the Soviet Union, and within a close strike capability of Soviet aircraft. In sum, the importance of the Cape sea route is a poor and much-removed argument for the strategic significance of South Africa to the West.

The fact that South Africa provides minerals on which Europe, Japan, and the United States depend industrially and strategically is a stronger argument. It begs the question of whether the shift from white to black rule in South Africa would necessarily impede that supply. It presumes that whatever the long-term adaptability of the West, any abrupt interruption of crucial minerals would be economically and therefore strategically damaging. It further presumes (and many newly influential Americans subscribe religiously to this view) that every other consideration becomes irrelevant once white-run South Africa's preeminent position as supplier of scarce resources is appreciated. The West, they say, should do nothing to undermine its smooth access to those resources. Taking a worst-case view, they also point with appropriate horror to the strategic denial that could occur if South African minerals were to become Soviet controlled. As a sole-source cartel, the Soviets could strangle the industrial might of the West and at the very least reduce the bargaining capacity of the West.

In addition to gold, diamonds, and coal, South Africa mines and has abundant reserves of twenty-two minerals. Of significance to the West, it is the world's first, second, or third most important supplier of nine critical minerals and the dominant supplier of platinum, gold, vanadium, andalusites, and antimony. It ranks second in the world among exporters of manganese and chrome. South Africa has about 81 percent of the world's known reserves of chrome, 75 percent of manganese, 71 percent of platinum, 49 percent of vanadium, and 17 percent of fluorspar. South Africa has the richest mineral resources in the non-Soviet world; on the globe its abundance can be matched only by the Soviet Union.

In 1977 Japan imported 90 percent of its mineral requirements, the countries of the European Economic Community imported 75 percent, and the United States as much as 15 percent. Despite the relative self-sufficiency of the United States, in 1977 it imported 86 percent of its asbestos, 91 percent of its antimony, and 99 percent of its manganese. South Africa provided the United States directly with 43 percent of its antimony, 30 percent of its chrome, 25 percent of its diamonds, 21 percent of its chromite and 35 percent of its ferrochrome, 36 percent of all of its ferromanganese, 48 percent of its platinum, and 57 percent of its vanadium. (Additionally many American imports of these metals from other nations with no indigenous resources originate ultimately in South Africa—for example, platinum refined in Britain and ferroalloys in France.) In value the mineral exports from South Africa in 1978 amounted to $1.5 billion. Europe as a whole draws upon South Africa for 52 percent of its manganese, 31 percent of its chrome and chrome alloys, and 24 percent of its platinum. Britain depends upon South Africa for large proportions of its minerals: chrome, 45 percent; manganese, 35 percent; platinum, 55 percent; antimony, 80 percent; and vanadium, 15 percent. West Germany imports 60 percent of its chrome and forty-eight other raw materials (especially manganese, asbestos, and wolframite) from South Africa.

In other words, given present industrial patterns in the developed countries of the northern hemisphere, South Africa possesses an importance as a raw material supplier crucial at least in the short run to the peak performance of several major economies. Defense-related and ferrous metals industries are the most vulnerable. A look at the supply picture of the four most critical minerals will make this notion of vulnerability more precise.

Of the identifiable world resources of chromite, 97 percent is located in South Africa and Zimbabwe. South Africa alone has 81 percent of the total reserves of the world, although the Zimbabwean ore is higher in chromium content. In 1978 South Africa was the world's second-largest supplier of chromite, contributing 2.5 million tons, or 28 percent of the total. Of that amount, about a third was in the form of chrome alloys. In 1978, for example, South Africa, the world's leading producer, exported about 525,000 tons of ferrochrome. Two-fifths went to the United States, about 160,000 tons to Europe, and about 130,000 tons to Japan. In late 1978 charge-grade ferrochrome exports were fetching about $400 a ton on the world market. In 1978 South Africa exported R89 million worth of chromite and ferrochrome.

The United States mines no chromite. It is dependent upon imports for 91 percent of its supply, the remainder being derived from stockpiles and recycling. Before the repeal of the Byrd amendment (which permitted the United States to import chromium from Rhodesia despite U.N. trade sanctions against the breakaway colony) in 1977, the United States obtained 7 percent of its chromium needs from Rhodesia and 30 percent from South Africa. Thus about 40 percent of its chromium requirements are now customarily satisfied by imports from South Africa and Zimbabwe. The Soviet Union, Turkey, and the Philippines together provide the remaining 50 percent (some of the Soviet chrome was alleged to have been originally Rhodesian in 1979). However, since at present extraction rates the known deposits of chromite in the Soviet Union, Turkey, and the Philippines will be exhausted in nine, nine, and five years, respectively, and since the refractory-grade chromite of the Philippines is more valuable for refractories than for metallurgical or chemical applications, the American reliance upon South Africa and Zimbabwean chromium is even greater than those percentages would imply, and it will grow. The importance of chromium to American industry, and of employees in chrome-related industries as a fraction of overall American employment, is also more extensive than is generally realized. Chrome is much more important to the United States and to the other developed nations of the non-Communist northern hemisphere than it ever will be as an earner of foreign currency for South Africa. Chrome, along with platinum, manganese, vanadium, and possibly uranium, provides South Africa with a unique source of economic leverage.

Ninety percent of the world's available manganese is consumed in the manufacture of steel. It is a critical hardening element; without manganese, steel stays brittle. Precision instruments are also formed of manganese. Given present methods of steelmaking, which differ only in the percentage of manganese required to produce each ton of steel, there are no known substitutes.

The Soviet Union mines more manganese than South Africa, the world's second-ranked producer with about 24 percent of the total, but Soviet steel mills are unusually heavy consumers of the metal. As a consequence, little Soviet manganese is exported to the West. Brazil, Gabon, Australia, and India also mine manganese, but South Africa is by far the largest supplier to the non-Soviet industrial nations, being responsible for 40 percent of their imports. The United States had no indigenous access to manganese and is thought to depend on South Africa for about 55 percent of its total requirements. Since South Africa holds 75 percent of world proven and probable reserves, American dependence upon South African manganese is certain to grow as long as steel production methods remain the same. In the United States about 26 percent of all manufacturing is steel related. Thus South African manganese may be even more important to the

United States than is generally appreciated. The holding of stockpiles of manganese would certainly cushion the shock of any abrupt loss of access to supplies from South Africa. But in the longer run, American reliance on imports of manganese could be reduced significantly only through the exploitation of the manganese that now sits on ocean beds in the form of nodules.

South Africa and its homelands are the world's leading producers of platinum, palladium, rhodium, and rare related metals, supplying 47 percent of the world total and 87 percent of the non-Soviet bloc total. Of platinum alone, in 1976 South Africa mined 68 percent of the total; of palladium, 30 percent. Canada and the Soviet Union are the other large producers of both metals, but there they are mined as by-products of nickel. South Africa is the world's sole primary producer of both metals. About 71 percent of the proven reserves of the world are within its borders and the borders of its subordinate homelands.

The six metals of the platinum group usually can be employed interchangeably by the chemical, petroleum, and electronics industries of the northern hemisphere. Outside the group, however, substitutes are either unavailable or inferior in performance. Platinum is unusually ductile and malleable, does not oxidize in air, and has the quality of changing the nature of the substances with which it comes into contact without altering its own properties. It does not flake and can be used to make optical glass. It restricts friction and is used in screens through which synthetic fibers are drawn. Because of its high melting point, it is employed to line furnaces and aircraft engines. As a catalyst, it upgrades the octanes of gasoline. It is as the main constituent in antipollution devices—the catalytic converters of American-made automobiles—that platinum becomes essential to ordinary consumers. Without platinum (unless rhenium can be substituted) these automobiles would have to be designed differently, at great expense. Platinum is also used extensively for fashioning jewelry in Japan but not in the United States.

Palladium is used especially for the coating of telephone contact points because of its resistance to friction. Rhodium has nearly all of the characteristics of platinum and palladium but is much rarer and costs far more. Rhenium, which is not found in South Africa, has a very high melting point (nearly twice that of platinum) and is used in electrical contacts and high-temperature thermocouples.

The United States depends upon foreign sources of platinum, palladium, rhodium, and rhenium for about 80 percent of its needs. South Africa alone supplies about 33 percent directly. Another 23 percent comes from a refinery in Britain with strong South African connections. In the event of a South African decision to withhold supplies, American and European industry would be limited in their options, especially since the alternative Canadian and Soviet supplies, being by-products of nickel extraction, cannot rapidly expand.

In 1978 South Africa and the Soviet Union each produced about 3 million of the 6.4 million troy ounces of platinum-group metals mined in the world.

South Africa is the world's largest producer of vanadium, with an annual output of about 54 million pounds, or 40 percent of the world total and about 52 percent of total Western capacity. South Africa's reserves of nearly 8 million metric tons of vanadium pentoxide are also the world's largest and about half of proven global supplies. The Soviet Union is self-sufficient in vanadium and exports to Eastern Europe. In the West, the other main producers are the United States (35 million pounds annually) and Finland (11.5 million pounds annually). Namibia, which is a declining factor in the world supply situation, and Chile also mine vanadium.

Vanadium is an important alloying element in the manufacture of specialty steels; 90 percent of all vanadium is consumed in this way. The remainder is employed in the fabrication of titanium-based alloys and the production of catalysts for use by chemical industries. Traditionally steel mills used vanadium to produce conventional full-alloy steels and, along with tungsten and molybdenum, in tool steel to form complex carbides that impart hardness, strength, and wear characteristics. Since the 1960s, vanadium (in the form of solid vanadium nitride) has been a crucial component of high-strength, low-alloy steels used for the construction of buildings, bridges, pressure storage tanks, and, notably, oil and gas pipelines. Increasingly vanadium is also used for automobile steel in order to meet new U.S. weight-economy and damage-vulnerability standards. Columbium, molybdenum, titanium, tungsten, and tantalum sometimes can be substituted for vanadium, depending upon specific end uses, but columbium (a by-product of tin mining in Nigeria, Brazil, and Canada) and tantalum are usually in short supply.

In the United States, vanadium oxide is produced by a number of companies as a by-product of uranium mined on the Colorado plateau. It is also derived from vanadium-bearing ferrophosphorous slags, along with phosphorous production, in Idaho; from spent catalysts; and from the vanadium-rich ash that results from the combustion of high-sulfur petroleum. The main source of American-produced vanadium as a single entity, however, is a Union Carbide vanadiferous clay-extraction process in Arkansas. The major American sources of supply have comparatively short life spans.

In Finland, vanadium oxide is extracted as a single product as well as a coproduct with titania from the titaniferous magnetite near the Arctic Circle. Australia, Canada, India, China, and Eastern Europe have titaniferous magnetites that could yield large quantities of vanadium if they ever become economically viable sources of iron. Vanadium is also recoverable from the desulfurization of Venezuelan oil and Canadian tar sands. In the short term, certainly, the importance of South African vanadium to American steel producers will grow from its present 56 percent of total imports as the ability of indigenous sources to supply American needs (now 63 percent satisfied) declines.[3]

Although the West is dependent (Europe and Japan far more than the United States) upon the supply of manganese and platinum from South Africa and ferrochrome from South Africa and Zimbabwe, and—somewhat less massively—vanadium from South Africa, that dependence may be lessened in at least the medium-term and long-term futures by a series of likely economic developments:

1. Mining of the ocean beds promises to alter the supply picture dramatically.
2. Non–South African Africa has been little prospected. New sources of many minerals may soon be discovered.
3. The West has hardly begun to practice resource recovery from scrap, emissions, or abandoned mines and slag heaps.
4. New methods being perfected promise to diminish the need for today's amounts of, say, ferrochrome in the fabrication of stainless steel.
5. The need for manganese in steel can already be lessened experimentally without loss of quality.
6. Stockpiles could be increased to provide a multiyear cushion. The United States already has such a cushion for some minerals; Japan has anticipated supply shrinkage, too; Europe has little such capacity.

Complacency need not be advocated. Nevertheless even in the improbable event that a South Africa, however controlled, would be unable to mine and ship its minerals or would refuse to sell them to the West, those who prophesize industrial catastrophe overplay the danger. They do so, moreover, with little regard for Western foresight, adaptability, and innovation.

If short-term considerations govern American relations with South Africa, then it is safe to predict that its importance as a mineral supplier will be overshadowed by Nigeria, the supplier of 16 percent of the petroleum resources of the United States. Nigeria worked closely with the Carter administration. There is a new government in Nigeria as well as the United States, but its posture gives no comfort to those who want to see a growing American–South African entente. Nigerians, as well as the leaders of Zimbabwe, Mozambique, Angola, Zambia, and Tanzania, suspect that a Reagan administration will be "easy" on South Africa. They intend to use whatever leverage they have—mostly in the form of oil—to stiffen the American resolve over Namibia. Any overt support for South Africa will be

opposed, at first diplomatically and then—to the extent that Africa is capable—economically. As oil and gas suppliers, some of the countries of
Africa will have influence.

None, however, wishes confrontation between black Africa and the
United States. If South Africa decides to flaunt the United Nations by
authorizing an internal settlement in Namibia and the West stands idly by,
Africa will be compelled to react. If there is renewed violence and then
repression in South Africa, and the West backs white-ruled South Africa, or
if the United States publicly welcomes the kinds of modest changes in South
Africa derided by its black leaders, then Nigeria and others may attempt to
employ their resource muscle.

Short of an unlikely American embrace of South Africa, the Reagan
administration has made it clear that although it will not bully South
Africa, it expects white-ruled South Africa to embark upon an evolutionary
process capable within a few years of transforming South Africa into a less-
tense and secure multiracial society. There will be a willingness to accept the
good faith of the South African government—to support as much as to
exert pressure for change. And there is certain to be movement in and by
South Africa: renewed negotiations with the West over Namibia; a dismantling of some of the more egregious legal underpinnings of apartheid; a
relaxation of laws that prohibit multiracial sport, dancing, and drinking; an
attempt to set up a national consultative machinery involving black homeland leaders and the white government; the devolution of more authority to
elected black local governments; further emphasis on black professional
and industrial advancement; the unionization of the black mining sector;
some form of dual citizenship, short of a color-blind national citizenship; a
granting of more authority to the president's council together with a form
of election of Asians and coloureds to the council are all possibilities.

Yet the fact that the South African government, despite its mandate at
the polls, will not immediately signal an intent to meet Bishop Tutu's four
criteria or engage in discussions about change with representative Africans
may vitiate the internal importance of any alterations to the framework of
minority rule. Even absent African outpourings of violence, the Reagan
administration will be hard pressed to regard the moves of the Botha government as sufficient unless they elicit legitimate African enthusiasm. However much a Reagan administration may want on strategic grounds to welcome sensible initiatives on the part of South Africa, the government there
may not do enough or may do what it does so churlishly that the Reagan
administration will be unable to respond. Then too, the Reagan government
may come to appreciate that a reforming South Africa is in the American
global interest. Overshadowing minerals, overshadowing the Cape sea
route, overshadowing nagging tactical worries that South Africa may move
too fast (like Pahlevi Iran), the Reagan government could well see that it

and it alone has an unparalleled, unrepeatable opportunity to eliminate the threat of Marxism in southern Africa by pressing (even for purposes of international credit, publicly) for significant increments of negotiated change—or, to turn that concept around, for negotiations capable of leading to change. A complacent administration either in South Africa or the United States will betray both its own global and its regional self-interest and the self-interest of its electorate.

Notes

1. See Robert I. Rotberg, "South Africa under Botha: How Deep a Change?" *Foreign Policy* 38 (Spring 1980):132.

2. See the essays of Robert I. Rotberg and John Barratt, eds., *Conflict and Compromise in South Africa* (Lexington, Mass.: Lexington Books, D.C. Heath and Company, 1980).

3. Robert I. Rotberg, *Suffer the Future: Policy Choices in Southern Africa* (Cambridge, Mass.: Harvard University Press, 1980), pp. 101–114.

Index

About the Contributors

Philip L. Christenson was at the time that he wrote the chapter for this book associate director of the United States-South Africa Leader Exchange Program (USSALEP). Prior to assuming that post he was deputy manager for sub-Saharan African affairs, U.S. Department of Commerce. In January 1981 he became a professional staff member of the Committee on Foreign Relations, the U.S. Senate.

Chester A. Crocker was associate professor of international relations at the Georgetown University School of Foreign Service and director of African studies at the Center for Strategic and International Studies at that university when he wrote the chapter for this book. Currently he is U.S. Assistant Secretary of State for Africa affairs. Among his recent publications is *South Africa into the 1980s,* of which he was coeditor, and "South Africa: Strategy for Change," which appeared in *Foreign Affairs.*

Paul Deats is a minister in the United Methodist Church and is Walter G. Muelder Professor of Social Ethics and chairperson of the Division of Theological and Religious Studies, Boston University School of Theology and Graduate School. For a decade he has been one of two faculty members on the Trustees' Advisory Committee on Investments at Boston University. He spent a 1962 sabbatical in West African universities.

Hermann Giliomee teaches South African history at the University of Stellenbosch. He is coauthor of *Ethnic Power Mobilized: Can South Africa Change?* (1979), coeditor of *The Shaping of South African Society, 1652–1820* (1979), and author of a study of British occupation of the Cape Colony, *Die Kaaptydens die Eerste Bewind* (1974). He is working with André du Toit on a study of Afrikaner political thought since 1778.

James G. Lubetkin is director of college relations at Oberlin College and was for seven years chairman of its investment advisory committee. He has long been involved in South African issues and was the director of the Ford Foundation conferences in 1978 and 1979 on the role of U.S. corporations in South Africa and how that role relates to American colleges and universities.

Desaix Myers III is deputy director of the Investor Responsibility Research Center in Washington, D.C. He is author of *U.S. Business in South Africa:*

227

The Economic, Political, and Moral Issues (1980), *The Labor Practices of U.S. Corporations in South Africa* (1977), and *The Nuclear Power Debate* (1977).

Robert I. Rotberg is professor of political science and history, Massachusetts Institute of Technology; coeditor of the *Journal of Interdisciplinary History;* trustee of the World Peace Foundation; and author of a number of books on the politics and history of Africa and the Caribbean. His four latest books are *Suffer the Future: Policy Choices in Southern Africa* (1980); *Conflict and Compromise in South Africa,* coedited with John Barratt (Lexington Books, 1980); *Black Heart: Gore-Browne and the Politics of Multiracial Zambia* (1978); and *The Black Homelands of South Africa* (1977).

Lawrence F. Stevens, a graduate of Harvard University (1965), received the Master's degree from the Harvard University Graduate School of Education in 1969, and has been a member of the Harvard administration since 1966, where he is director of the South Africa Fellowship Program and secretary of the Advisory Committee on Shareholder Responsibility.

Sanford J. Ungar, a graduate of Harvard University and the London School of Economics, is a journalist with experience in Europe and Africa. His articles on African issues have appeared in *The Atlantic Monthly, Foreign Policy, The New Republic, Saturday Review, The Washington Post,* and *The New York Times.* Formerly managing editor of *Foreign Policy,* he is now host of the daily newsmagazine "All Things Considered" on National Public Radio.

Philip V. White, assistant professor of political science and Afro-American studies at Yale University when he wrote this chapter, became deputy director of research at the Joint Center for Political Studies in Washington, D.C., in January 1981.

About the Editors

John Barratt has been director of the South African Institute of International Affairs since 1967. Previously he was a South African foreign service officer, spending seven years at the United Nations. He is a member of the executive committee of the United States/South Africa Leader Exchange Program. He has written and edited extensively on South Africa and its foreign relations, including the earlier volume of which this book is a sequel, *Conflict and Compromise in South Africa,* coedited with Robert I. Rotberg (Lexington Books, 1980).

Alfred O. Hero, Jr., director of the World Peace Foundation in Boston, Massachusetts, has written extensively on the role of public opinion in U.S. foreign policymaking and on U.S.-Canadian relations. His books include, *Natural Resources in U.S.-Canadian Relations,* of which he was coeditor (three volumes, 1980–1981); *Canada and the United States: Transnational and Transgovernmental Relations,* which he coedited (1975); *American Religious Groups View Foreign Policy* (1973); *The Reuther-Meany Foreign Policy Dispute,* which he coedited (1970); and *The Southerner and World Affairs* (1965).